A SHORT HISTORY OF
THE FUTURE

Why didn't you do something about it?
You could have done.

Prince Charles, expressing his concern about
what his grandchildren might say about
climate change, in a BBC interview in 2005

A SHORT HISTORY OF THE FUTURE

SURVIVING THE 2030 SPIKE

Colin Mason

London • Sterling, VA

First published by Earthscan in the UK and USA in 2006
Reprinted 2006, 2007

First edition published as *The 2030 Spike: Countdown to Global Catastrophe* by
Earthscan in the UK and USA in 2003

Copyright © 2006, Colin Mason

ISBN: 978-1-84407-346-7   paperback

Typesetting by FiSH Books
Printed and bound in the UK by Cromwell Press, Trowbridge
Cover design by Nick Shah

For a full list of publications please contact:

Earthscan
8–12 Camden High Street
London, NW1 0JH, UK
Tel: +44 (0)20 7387 8558
Fax: +44 (0)20 7387 8998
Email: earthinfo@earthscan.co.uk
Web: www.earthscan.co.uk

22883 Quicksilver Drive, Sterling, VA 20166-2012, USA

Earthscan is an imprint of James and James (Science Publishers) Ltd and
publishes in association with the International Institute for Environment and
Development

A catalogue record for this book is available from the British Library

Library of Congress Cataloging-in-Publication Data

Mason, Colin J.
    A short history of the future: surviving the 2030 Spike/by Colin J. Mason.
        p. cm.
    Includes bibliographical references and index.
    ISBN-13: 978-1-84407-346-7 (pbk.)
    ISBN-10: 1-84407-346-7 (pbk.)
    1. Twenty-first century–Forecasts. 2. Two thousand thirty, A.D. I.
Title.
    CB161.M3843 2006
    303.49–dc22

                                                    2006002507

The paper used for this book is FSC-certified and
totally chlorine-free. FSC (the Forest Stewardship
Council) is an international network to promote
responsible management of the world's forests.

CONTENTS

ABOUT THE AUTHOR

Colin Mason, a former foreign correspondent, broadcaster and SEATO adviser to the Thai Government, was a senator in the Australian Federal Parliament for nine years, as deputy leader of the Australian Democrats. He served on the Senate Standing Committee for Science and the Environment, a Select Committee on the effects of Agent Orange on Australian servicemen, and the first delegation of the Australian Parliament to China, and initiated the private member's bill that led to the salvation of the pristine Franklin River in Tasmania. He has published 12 books including the international bestselling novel *Hostage* and, most recently, *A Short History of Asia*, now in its second edition and currently a bestseller in its field around the world.

Comment or discussion on any of the issues raised in this book are welcomed by the author at www.2030spike.com.

PREFACE

Yes, it is possible, even necessary, to have a history of the future – the last President of China, Jiang Zemin, remarked: 'History is a mirror for the future'. Hence, if we want to find out how to build an optimal future, we first need an accurate knowledge of what exists now, and what kind of shadows these things cast ahead. That is the way this book works.

It is also an update and considerable development of my earlier book, *The 2030 Spike*. Although it contains much of the same material, a great deal has happened in the last four years – the major issues of the world are developing very fast. What was written in 2002 can hardly do for 2006, so some fairly extensive updating and additions have been necessary. The 2030 Spike? This is the name I gave to the challenging and massive confluence of at least six influences, natural and manmade, which can either be controlled by the intelligent efforts of people, or which, if we elect to do nothing, will visit on the world a degree of catastrophe far beyond our present experience. On the best available evidence these six 'drivers' are set to spike no later than the 2030 decade, so there is not much time.

However, you don't have to be a pessimist. Although in the years since *The 2030 Spike* was written most of these drivers have advanced ominously, and the need to understand and deal with them has become even more urgent, there is considerable scope for optimism. There are exciting and radical new developments in the energy field, which is a major problem area. The world's first hydrogen-powered aircraft flew in June 2005. The means to control malaria should be developed within four years. Many more people are better informed over major issues and are becoming more aggressive in forcing their leaders to do necessary things – for instance, by diverting just half what we spend on weapons to proven sustainable alternative energy we could defuse both of our most threatening future problems – energy availability and climate change. Understanding this massive fact and seeing that those US$12trillion are made available is an imperative for everyone on the planet. More people now know that the best way to control business is through the combined spending power of large numbers of people, and this is good. Mass consumer organizations on a global scale are not far off, and will become a major influence in determining the fate of the world. Former 'basket case' countries are now transforming themselves, and have contributed largely to reduced poverty and disadvantage on a world scale. China is a major and classic example. Regional wars have become somewhat less destructive.

On the other hand, there is still too much poverty, too much disease, too many weapons, not enough world law, too much conservatism and denial, not enough concern for the natural world. I hope what you are about to read will tell you some of what you need to know, and help you to make up your mind on what you might do.

C. M.
Sydney,
March, 2006

PART ONE

IS THERE A CRISIS?

Chapter 1

The Drivers

On the edge of the sea, a modern village. Low set houses, built strong to withstand the severe storms of the near future, each flowing out into its own open space, grouped around a large, circular compound. Inside this are the school/youth leisure centre – for they are the same – the entertainment/community complex, theatre, tennis courts, swimming pool, whatever. There is a lot of live theatre, music, art and sport – almost everyone here has an active talent. All this can be, and has to be, approached on foot, for no wheeled traffic is allowed inside the village perimeter.

This place is largely autonomous for energy, water and food. If you looked down from above, you'd see all the roofs are blue – 'blue denim' solar collectors – with more than a few small wind generators spinning silently. Most people grow their own food, but the village shares its own orchards and community vegetable gardens. Water recycling is so efficient only that transpired to the air by growing plants is lost – this economy is necessary in a drier world.

Housing is quite varied and individual, but the majority choose the communal grouping – private self-contained accommodation within a community of perhaps 30 adults and children sharing facilities like a library, music room, hobby centre. Here, stress and tension are minimal – people get support from those they know and choose to live near, children have easy and regular contact with their peer group.

The landscape is dominated by one huge feature, a slender tower rising over half a mile into the air, surrounded by a greenhouse which drives hot air past generators inside the tower. This, the solar chimney, provides the baseload electric power for this village and the 20 others that make up this spacious, dispersed town. From the ground you can't see the other villages for the shelter belts of trees between them, but they are all linked, and to the metropolis, by high-speed magnetic levitation trains running in a regular, automated shuttle. Looking out along the single elevated line on its slender pylons, you see beneath what looks like a shining highway at ground level – the solar panels that power these trains.

This village – call it Satu – is largely self-sufficient, but it prospers by operating on a co-operative basis its specialized industry, in this case making thoughtboards for the world computers now helping to transform the developing world with new ideas and appropriate technology. The neighbouring village, Dua, specializes in a world-popular computer game called Ideas.

You can use money or not, as you wish, here. It is possible to live and be content without it. But those who want to work harder, be smarter, can get money and use it for luxuries – maybe their own electric car, rather than a pooled one, works of art, foreign travel. The money circulates efficiently, because it loses value just a little each day you hold it.

Work on the International Space Station has been deferred indefinitely while the problems of this planet are solved. There are still armed forces and weapons, but they are being progressively reduced and incorporated into a world police. Nuclear weapons have been reduced to about 800, with a set programme to eliminate them all within another 10 years. The technology, the knowhow, for all this exist. The people in these villages feel secure, they have everything they need, they have a firm hold on the earth. They are tranquil and happy.

The midday sun struggles to penetrate a dense brown smog that has enveloped the city since early morning. But this is nothing new, it happens every day. However, the city is strangling in more ways than this. Rubbish is uncollected on the streets, which are choked continuously with motor traffic emitting the severe pollution from petrol substitutes. And these streets are dangerous – the absence of community support and breakdown in law and order have given free scope to large numbers of desperate unemployed youths, criminal gangs and deranged individuals the state no longer cares for. Children must stay inside their apartments – traffic problems and the huge cost of running a car make it almost impossible to reach any facility for them other than the school, which is drab and conventional. They have little chance to play with other children, they become silent and withdrawn. Virtual reality games are popular – they are so much more attractive than real life.

Food on the whole is monotonous and of poor quality – the economic rationalist imperative to make everything as cheaply as possible makes sure of that. Almost all the food is manufactured, with doubtful additives. Most people are unhealthy, big pharm thrives as never before. The government, which has long since stopped trying to struggle with these problems, maintains its authority by continuously frightening people about 'terror'. There are some very wealthy people. They live in gated suburbs, surrounded by high walls and razor wire, protected by armed guards, in constant fear they, or their children, will be kidnapped. Almost everyone in this city is unhappy, insecure and frightened.

Yes, there is a crisis – the two contrasting and admittedly extreme word pictures above hint at its nature, and our responsibilities to choose. In the decade from 2030 six major forces – the 'drivers' – are set to combine dangerously, a spike on the graph paper of life that will influence our world for good or ill as never before. Combating its worst effects will need urgent action, informed by the clearest possible understanding of where we are now and where we might go. The history of the future will be profoundly affected by the way we deal with these drivers over the next 20 years. Our options for reacting to them are, accordingly, a major theme in this book.

The right choices will lead us to a saner, healthier and safer society – the not too distant future could be one of unparalleled peace, prosperity and general well-being. The knowledge and resources for this are in place, or can be seen not too far away. We have the best educated generation ever; wealth and potential wealth, although badly distributed, are at their highest and increasing, the automation of industry and agriculture promises almost universally high living standards and an end to the tyranny of heavy and tedious work. The world's population may stabilize – but only if the poverty afflicting most humans can be alleviated.

Speaking in London in 2001, former American president, Bill Clinton, called for 'a truly global consciousness' to spread the benefits of the 21st century around the world.[1] 'We have the means to make the 21st century the most peaceful and prosperous in human history. The question is whether we have the will.' That hope is unlikely to be realized by 2030, no matter what we do. But, if effective social and economic reform can be started now, we could see a peaceful and productive transition to a new society shaped by, and successfully adapted to, the oncoming adverse influences – the 2030 drivers. Beyond that is a reasonable prospect of a world order better than the planet has ever seen.

Over the last couple of years there have been some major breakthroughs in the energy field. If these achieve their promise there are indeed prospects beyond the end of oil – energy will be scarcer, more expensive, for several decades at least, but it will be available. Poverty and avoidable disease are being tackled effectively in a number of places – notably China. There is growing public awareness of the dangers of climate change, and some governments are bowing to these. In spite of the negative influence of much major business, new conservational technologies are developing.

But if the wrong choices are made – like taking up the nuclear option, ignoring the reality of climate change, refusing to acknowledge the links between 'terrorism' and poverty, or simple denial that there must be change – the near future could be bad enough to kill tens of millions of people in a variety of terrible disasters, even plunge us into a global dark age, and damage the very foundations of life in ways that would take centuries to repair. The harbingers of these disasters are already with us; as I write these words an ugly and costly war is still threatening security in the Middle East, 10 million people are facing starvation in Africa, natural disasters like hurricanes and drought are killing more and more people, while the warnings of severe water shortages and ecological damage are becoming more urgent. So there is a clear need to choose, to establish the courses of action that would contribute to one outcome or the other. Those informed choices will have to be made quickly, and enforced by public opinion and by spending power.

For instance: The International Energy Agency (IEA)[2] has forecast that more than $1 trillion ($ refers to US$ throughout this book) will be spent on non-hydro renewable energy technologies by 2030 to triple their share of world power generation to 6 per cent. Not good enough – not nearly good enough. Almost all climate experts now say that there needs to be at least a 60 per cent replacement of carbon-based energy to prevent greenhouse gases reaching dangerous levels. Could we do it? Yes. Using that IEA costing as a base, it emerges that by spending $12 trillion over the next 25 years – half what we spend on armaments – the necessary infrastructure could be built. The money and the means are there – it's as simple as that. If we do it, we are controlling our future. If we don't, we're in bad trouble.

There is compelling evidence for the 2030 spike – the combined effect of at least six adverse drivers. The most reliable estimates set readily available oil resources at under a trillion barrels – probably considerably under – and world consumption at 30 billion barrels a year, indicating exhaustion in, at most, 32 years. Predicted increases in oil use would reduce this time substantially. If this is not cushioned by urgent development of alternatives, this will have major and unexpected consequences, not least a catastrophic drop in world food supplies for a population that will grow above 8 billion by that time.

Continued nuclear proliferation, policy changes for the use of atomic weapons by the US and Russia, confrontation in the Middle

East, and political pressures from the drivers, make a nuclear war of unpredictable intensity only too possible within 20 years. The consequences of this would seriously aggravate greenhouse effects, due to become significant by 2030. The 'war against terror', the growing tension between Islam and 'the West', the doctrine that nuclear weapons can safely be used in a 'limited' way – all these will tend to aggravate the effect of the drivers. There needs to be a clear understanding of these likely consequences with, unfortunately, little evidence that governments are taking them into account now.

The International Water Management Institute predicts that a billion people will face an absolute water shortage by 2025; the United Nations warns of war over use of the world's rivers by 2032. Problems of soil degradation, desert spread and salination, already considerable, will be out of control by 2030 in much of the world.[3] Unless these threats are recognized and effectively countered, we risk famine and deaths counted in the millions. Recent research into climate trends warn that severe global warming associated with carbon release from the Amazon rainforests, recently afflicted with the worst drought for 40 years, and methane from hydrates in the Arctic is possible by 2030, with perhaps catastrophic effects by 2050.[4] Even global warming and sea level rises on a much lesser scale would adversely affect agricultural land in developing countries.

Failure to redress the poverty most humans live in, and an almost total lack of political control over globalization – which is irresponsible in the pure sense of the word – are likely to increase economic disproportion and the conflict it causes. Populations will increase most rapidly in the poorest countries, with the West containing no more than 15 per cent of the world's people by 2030. The world is anarchic, it urgently needs global law – but the largest and most powerful nations are backing away from it.

Most people are aware of some of the facts surrounding some of these issues. However, because the drivers gain force by the simple fact of their interaction, their coincidence presents unique dangers. This major cumulative effect of the drivers, if they are permitted to peak, will be within the lifetime of most of us –

certainly within that of our children. Can we avert it, or at least soften its impact? This is feasible but only as a result of fundamental changes in technology and society, beginning now. Unfortunately, there is too little evidence that these dangers have been recognized. So, who will make the necessary decisions? Judging by the available demonstrable facts, governments, political hierarchies, think-tanks, dictators and military juntas are mostly saying and doing the wrong things – according to Bill Morrison, retired agricultural scientist and a pioneer of permaculture, in the *Sydney Sun-Herald* in August 2005: 'We've got suicidal idiots in charge'. Those new holders of power, the multinationals, could play a crucial role, simply because they are global and so big. But to be useful, including to themselves, their perception of the dangers of the near future must become clearer, their accountability guaranteed, their influence more responsible. And they must stop confusing the issues with slick public relations exercises, behind which not enough of significance is being done.

For the first time in history, the means are emerging for individuals to collectively influence the necessary decisions, using two potent tools – the internet and spending power. It is possible to discern the beginnings of international networks that could put decisive pressure on offending corporations simply by the way consumers spend their money – there have already been a number of successful exercises along these lines. But such pressure needs to be well informed by a reliable assessment of the state of the world and an agenda of reasonable priorities for action.

What follows, then, is an attempt to distil from the formidable range of information available, a broad picture of the world as it is, and courses of action that might logically be deduced from this and which might shape the future we all want. This has taken a lot of time and effort, because the public record is indeed a minefield, full of misinformation, spin, lies, call it what you will, often coming from dishonest think tanks financed by big business. And to quote Woody Allen: 'Don't underestimate the power of distraction to keep our minds off the truth of our situation.' Elements of distraction exist in our world as never before – traffic, television, 'terrorism', telephones, computer games...

We all suffer from information overload, which is, in itself, a distraction. The sheer volume of available information tends not only to obscure the important issues, but also to dissuade people from coping with the problem of understanding its relevance to their lives. Hence this book is planned as a single volume of reasonable size, accessible to people with no prior knowledge of the subject, covering the major facts and trends. This objective, and its necessary limitations, must be my only apology to those who feel their specialist area has been dealt with too briefly, too superficially or even omitted – and I am sure there will be many of those.

If we want change, we must find out what reasonable conditions it requires. If an interest group, be it students, workers, Balinese or capitalists, see themselves as threatened by change, they will fight it. Much of the lack of progress in solving obvious and urgent world problems can be traced back to a lack of recognition of this fact. So important and self evident is this, that I believe it ranks as one of two axioms upon which much of the argument of this book is based. We might state Axiom One as:

> *Useful change is likely to come only if it can provide as, equal, obvious and general a benefit as possible.*

Regrettably, much of the recent debate about the future has been confrontational and extreme. Two of the better known examples, books published in the 1970s, have without doubt influenced decision-makers of today. *The Limits to Growth*[5] was typical of the 'doomsayers' – those who warned of an imminent crisis because of population pressures, pollution and the exhaustion of natural resources. While many of its premises are still valid, its modelling of world problems has been criticized, and some of its conclusions – such as the exhaustion of mineral resources like aluminium, lead, zinc and silver, and 'a sudden and serious shortage of arable land' by 2000 – have not been justified by events.

The Next 200 Years[6] took almost exactly the opposite point of view, aiming, in its own words, 'to present a plausible scenario for a "growth" world that leads not to disaster but to prosperity and plenty'. Here again, many of the conclusions have subsequently been shown to be flawed, especially in regard to the availability of energy, which, as we shall see, is one of the most important and imminent areas of crisis now facing the world. Prediction of the future is notoriously risky, and it is not the purpose of these comments to criticize the writers of these two books and many others like them. The essential point is that the world needs plain facts and balanced, rather than adversarial, points of view, as tools to shape the future.

At this stage, consider a single issue – 'planned obsolescence'. If indeed our sins include 'building up a vast array of totally unwarrantable wants',[7] planned obsolescence certainly compounds them. It has created, among other things, the 'throwaway society', which most well intentioned people deplore. Most manufacturers seem to believe all this is necessary, so 'productivity' can be maintained and they and their workers can stay in business. They may also console themselves with the idea that if everything is left to 'market forces', to the laws of supply and demand, all will be well. The consequences are familiar enough – short-lived devices, with service and spare part costs so high that it is easier and cheaper to throw the thing away and buy another one, gadgets of illusory appeal, but not much use, too much stuff for the rich and not enough necessities for the poor. In this way, the goal of short-term profit is served, but at what cost to the general good and the longer-term sustainability of our economy?

The system, then, seems at fault. How about a different system, still competitive, still private enterprise, in which manufacturers contract with customers to lease them a washing machine, a refrigerator, a car that works well for as long a period as they require? The picture immediately changes. As we shall see in Chapter 11, the beginnings of this transition already exist, and may well become valuable, even essential, to the new society.

Such considerations bring us to another area. The 'idealist' approach – that people should be good, honest, reliable, compassionate and thoughtful towards others – is undeniably worthy, but regrettably unrealistic so far as the majority of humans are concerned. Most people seem to be motivated by other things –

their own self-interest, a desire for security, a fear of the radical and unknown. As a result, all proposals for change should recognize this formidable factor of human nature, which we can rate as Axiom Two:

> *If proposed solutions don't take the lowest common denominators of human nature realistically into account, they will not work.*

One of the mainsprings of human effort is self-interest – it cannot be argued away or ignored. In the words of pioneer economist Adam Smith: 'It is not from the benevolence of the butcher, the brewer, or the baker that we expect our dinner, but from their regard for their own interest'.[8]

This book is not in the business of doomsaying. Its purpose is to recognize and define the threats of the near future so that effective action can be mustered against them. In many cases the solutions are logical and obvious, deriving naturally from the facts. Hence every chapter ventures ideas for possible solutions. If these do no more than inspire thought they will have fulfilled their purpose.

But no one person can credibly put forward his or her ideas alone as a model for useful change. Compiling this book has been a search, a reaching out to the ideas of hundreds of other minds in its subject areas. This 'borrowing' of the thoughts of others from books, the internet and other media has been so extensive, influencing virtually every paragraph, that to try to acknowledge them completely would result in a list of notes almost as large as the book itself. Hence I take the opportunity here to record my debt to all those who have not been acknowledged, and thank them collectively. The list of notes exists mainly to amplify points that may be of special interest, or to indicate sources, especially of direct quotes. The chapters are fairly independent – if a particular chapter doesn't much interest you, go on to what does.

The crisis areas listed earlier – the potential contributors to the 2030 spike – have an obvious priority, and the next six chapters deal with them one by one. At the end of these chapters, and in others where appropriate, there is a summary of objectives –

optimal future history. I believe that if we could even approach these requirements we could successfully cope with the challenge of the drivers – even benefit from them. That is the theme of Part Four – The New Society. Can we evolve this changed and better world in the light of the two axioms? Why not? We do have the power to curb the worst aspects of human nature – we do it all the time; we train our children to do it. We call that power civilization.

CHAPTER 2

RUNNING OUT OF FUEL: THE COMING ENERGY CRUNCH

Ice that burns like a candle, the use of light to make hydrogen from water, huge advances in battery technology, cheaper and better means of harvesting the energy of the sun, the tides and the winds – all these are rising above the horizon in the energy field. And not before time. Unless major efforts are made to develop these new technologies at the necessary economy of scale, the coming fuel drought will cripple world trade and economies. But this, serious though it is, is only one aspect of the problem. The mechanization of agriculture and dependence on petrochemical fertilizers and pesticides largely created the green revolution – it has been said that modern agriculture uses land to convert petroleum into food. As much as 17 per cent of US energy use is for growing, processing and transporting food. Some scientists are predicting that, denied oil, world agriculture will be able to provide food for many less people[1] – on one estimate, only 2 billion, with current corn yields in the US, now 130 bushels an acre, falling to around 30 bushels.[2] The implications of this in a 2030 world of 8 billion people are obvious – billions could go even hungrier, millions starve to death. And, as the catastrophes of the new millennium so far have shown us, sadly, most of these dead will be children.

Intensifying world competition for fuel is only too likely to create an ongoing series of oil wars, such as the bitter and longlasting conflict in Iraq. John Pilger alleged 'weapons of mass destruction' had little to do with the American attack on that country. 'America wants a more compliant thug to run the world's second greatest source of oil.' A number of recent American policy documents tend to support this view, warning that the US is running out of oil, with a painful end to cheap oil already in sight, and suggesting armed force to secure oil supplies – even 'painting over the real US motives for war with a nobly high minded veneer' to mobilize public support for war.[3] Ironically, US political philosopher Leo Strauss' ideas for reinforcing national identity by promoting 'powerful and inspiring myths' – which don't necessarily need to be true – seem to have contributed to both Islamic Jihad extremism and American neo-conservatism. Four years after the invasion of Iraq, the earlier-stated mythic motive for war – weapons of mass destruction – has been revealed as baseless, while Iraq remains in chaos and its oilfields under effective US and British control.

The influence of this driver is difficult to overestimate. Its potential to combine with some of the others, among them accelerated 'terrorism' and poverty, is very serious. It is possible that war or substantial insurrection in the Middle East could cut off the world's major oil supplies abruptly. If the Saudi Arabian oil installations were damaged or sabotaged, as the Iraqi ones have been repeatedly, there would be intense crises, involving severe food shortages and mass unemployment , in most parts of the world.

The outriders of these advancing social and economic problems are already with us, but so also are possible solutions. There will be nothing easy or quick about these, but they are available – government 'carrot-and-stick' tax measures to encourage alternatives at the necessary economy of scale; community acceptance of radically changed lifestyles; a much more labour intensive post oil agriculture; and energy conservation among them. These should spearhead a crash programme to develop adequate alternative infrastructures within the 20 to 30 years left to us.

The remaining oil will be needed to fuel the manufacture of this necessary new infrastructure. Action taken only when the oil shows signs of running out – and that could be within a decade – will be too late. After decades of talk and hope about alternative sources of energy like wind and solar, they still amount to barely 2 per cent of world energy supply. If development is not pressed a great deal more vigorously, and our remaining oil conserved, we can expect trouble from now on. Rising fuel prices will impact first and most severely on developing countries – they provoked major rioting in Indonesia in 2001, and more unrest in 2005. As home heating costs rise, people will migrate out of cold winter regions, with social and economic consequences for Europe, America and Japan. Predicted ocean current changes could interlock with the energy crisis, making northern Europe and Britain much colder – more on this in Chapter 4. Anxiety to reduce its dependence on oil drove the Japanese government in 2005 to revive a dangerous and unreliable technology, the fast breeder nuclear reactor, in spite of major community protests.

At present the 'old' hydrocarbons, oil, gas and coal, still provide 80 per cent of the world's energy, generating most of its electricity and powering every major form of transport, including more than two-thirds of a billion cars. Crude oil accounts for 36 per cent; coal, 23 per cent and natural gas 21 per cent. The amount of light and medium crude oil still available is under 1 trillion barrels,[4] about two-thirds of which is in a politically unstable region, the Middle East, with much of the rest in the former Soviet Union.

The world is now consuming around 30 billion barrels of crude oil a year, more than 7 billion of which are used in the US. Simple arithmetic indicates exhaustion around 2035 if that rate is maintained. However, consumption will almost certainly increase to 43 billion barrels a year by 2020, according to an International Energy Agency estimate.[5] This would advance the exhaustion time to 2028. Even unexpectedly large new finds of oil, and much more fuel efficient vehicles, would extend that time by no more than ten years.

Conventional wisdom says we will always find a lot more. Not so likely. Modern geophysics, associated with satellite observations, can make informed guesses at the amount of readily available oil still undiscovered, and it is quite small. For instance, initial estimates put Caspian Sea reserves at between 8 and 50 billion barrels, later ones at a maximum of 33 billion – enough to meet present world demand for little more than a year. Proven reserves there were estimated in 2005 at 10 billion barrels – world demand for four months. This 'may well be the largest discovery in the world for 20 years'.[6]

After studying data from the world's 18,000 oilfields, analyst Colin Campbell concluded, in November 2000, that oil would start to run out in 2005 and that a 40 per cent shortfall was likely by 2025. In 2005, Campbell reiterated his assertion that oil would peak over the next few years, causing regular supply difficulties and much higher fuel costs, and that 'this would set the stage for the second great depression'. Other experts placed the date of declining supplies at 2008, but almost all estimated it before 2020. Richard Hardman, vice president with responsibility for exploration at the American Amerada Hess Corporation, said: 'I think there will be a real crunch this time. High-tech global X rays now allow the industry to determine how much oil is left – and it's not much. This time the wolf is really at the door.'[7]

The concept of 'peak oil' is very important. As oilfields pass their peak production, output declines. Now global oil production is at or closely approaching its peak, after which output is expected to decline at about 3 per cent a year, while demand will rise at about the same rate. The peak in world gas production is more distant, but there will be declines in production within 20 years.

There are large amounts of oil which would be energy expensive, costly and polluting to recover and refine, such as 'sour' sulphur high crudes, oil shales and tars. Some is actually solid at ambient temperatures. Much of it would require more energy to extract than it would yield. Shale oil extraction requires open cut mining, crushing and heating rock to 500°C, then water intensive and polluting extraction not of oil, but of a kerogen, which has to be further distilled to yield petroleum – a total process which is expensive in terms of both money and energy and which Greenpeace says causes massive emissions of greenhouse gases.

A 1980 experiment in the US produced oil which cost $40 a barrel. Conventional oil yields 30 times the energy it takes to extract, shale and 'oil' sands one to one-and-a-half times.

What about the other sources of energy? Nuclear power – steady at around 6 per cent – and hydroelectricity – perhaps 5 per cent – are small by comparison with the hydrocarbons. Even smaller are the 'alternates' – solar, wind, tidal, geothermal, currently no more than 2 per cent in total. Wood is burned as fuel, frequently in the form of charcoal, by the majority of humans, and together with other 'natural combustibles' like animal dung, provides 10 to 12 per cent of world energy,[8] and hence is the most important source of fuel after the hydrocarbons. The growing shortage of fuel wood is the greatest immediate energy problem for perhaps the largest number of people, and indicates a need for planning and special planting to maintain this resource, and a major effort to provide efficient wood burning stoves to the developing world to replace the present, wasteful and unhealthy open hearths.[9] Chinese villagers have reduced their use of fuel wood by building methane pits – more than a million have been installed since 1997, and 300,000 more are planned. Fed by plant material and pig manure, these gas producers are providing cooking fuel and light for millions of people.[10]

The world still has slightly over 1 trillion tons of coal – enough for more than 200 years at present consumption rates – but using more presents serious problems. Burning more coal would aggravate climate change and increase pollution so severely that food production would be affected in regions inhabited by hundreds of millions of people, as in China, where approximately 2 billion tons are now being burned each year, mostly to generate electricity. Current lines of research include obtaining pure carbon from coal, eliminating pollutants, conversion of coal to a liquid fuel, and producing hydrogen from coal. However, whether a reasonably clean fuel can be economically derived from coal remains in serious doubt.

Construction of the International Thermonuclear Experimental Reactor at Cadarache, in France has been likened to 'building a star on earth.' Thermonuclear fusion, harnessing the power to the hydrogen bomb, the power of the sun, has been touted for decades as the fuel of the future, and, to date, more than $60 billion has been spent on trying to develop it. However, the research stage of the major international fusion project, ITER,[11] is still proceeding after decades of enormously costly experiments which sought to develop a 'magnetic bottle' capable of containing plasma at the necessary temperature of 100 million degrees Centigrade. 'Breakeven' point, at which more energy is produced than is actually consumed in the process, has not been reached, and the reaction has been sustained only momentarily. Development of the 1998 version of the design, estimated at nine years, is expected to commence soon. In 2005 a decision was taken to build the reactor in France, at a cost of 10 million euros. It is hoped that the reactor, seen as 'a near-term experiment', will prove feasible, but it is not designed to produce useful amounts of power. Greenpeace criticized ITER as 'a dangerous toy', claiming that the same money could build 10,000 megawatts (generally abbreviated to MW – one million watts hours) of wind power – enough for 7.5 million people. It seems safe to predict that there will be no significant fusion power by 2030.

Methane hydrate is the result of water and natural gas combining at low temperatures under high pressure. It is located under the polar icecaps and on deep ocean floors. Mining this resource is likely to be expensive, damaging to the environment and dangerous, since explosions can result when the methane is dissociated from the water. The methane, highly concentrated within lattice-like cages of water molecules, expands 160 times when liberated. Because it is 20 times more potent than carbon dioxide as a greenhouse gas, major releases of methane to the environment could seriously contribute to global warming. Nevertheless, this vast reserve, conservatively estimated at 200 thousand trillion cubic feet – at least four times current natural gas reserves – will be a high priority for research and development. Its use as a fuel would release about half as much carbon dioxide to the air as burning coal or oil.

The Methane Hydrate Research and Development Act was passed by the US Congress in 2000, and as a result a major research programme was begun 'to allow commercial production of methane from hydrate deposits by 2015. The magnitude of this previously unconsidered global storehouse of methane is truly staggering.'[13] In 2005, the US voted a further $165 million to this project. A joint Japanese–Canadian research programme has also started to establish safe and practicable ways of mining methane hydrate. In 2002, at its Mallik research wells on the Mackenzie Delta, in Canada's northwest, hot water was pumped down to produce gas from hydrates which was then burned on a flare tower. However, commercial production, while considered feasible, is not likely for several decades, with tentative price estimates of $4 to $6 per thousand cubic feet.

If new areas of sustainable energy production could be created in the poorest nations of the world, so giving them a source of income, several major objectives would be served. The use of hydrogen as a fuel is one suggestion. The developing countries in the tropics that have deserts – among the poorest of the poor – could be economically transformed by new energy industries based on hydrogen. In *The Skeptical Environmentalist*, Bjørn Lomborg has calculated that with present solar cell technology, an area 469 kilometres square – 2.6 per cent of the Sahara Desert – would provide enough power to meet all world energy requirements.[14] Solar technologies, which are a permanently renewable energy source, have the potential to generate electricity to split water or ammonia. The resultant hydrogen could be carried by pipeline and existing tanker fleets to the metropolitan powers, which would benefit from greatly reduced urban air pollution, since the 'exhaust' from using hydrogen in fuel cells consists only of water.

A pipedream? Not really. One technology has been extensively developed in Israel and elsewhere. This involves using solar power to generate electricity to split water into its constituents – hydrogen and oxygen. But a newer, more exciting prospect offers the generation of hydrogen from water simply by exposure to light, with no use of any outside power source and no pollution. This technology goes by the jaw-cracking name of photoelectrochemical production. Hydrogen Solar, a British company, is developing what it calls the Tandem Cell ™, which uses nano-crystalline materials. The company claims that a domestic double garage roof covered with Tandem Cells would produce enough hydrogen to run a car 11,000 miles a year on a completely sustainable basis. Using low-cost materials, it is expected that the technology will provide hydrogen fuel at about a third the current price of petrol. Construction of a 100 square metre demonstration facility was announced in 2005, in cooperation with a major energy company, the BOC Group. Other active research areas include engineering bacteria to produce hydrogen and production of hydrogen from sunflower oil.

Desert land, at present regarded as having little value, and constant, strong sunlight are potent raw materials for some of these technologies. Such a world programme would offer an investment opportunity for money now devoted to weaponry, would provide work for many of the unemployed of the developing world, and would generate income for governments of the producing nations in the form of royalties. Spin-offs would include: a cheap source of electricity for the domestic needs of the producing nation; a reduction in the demand for firewood; better control of advancing deserts; and a rising consumer market in the developing world.

Already trucks, buses and cars in Iceland's capital, Reykjavik, are running on hydrogen, and plans are well advanced to convert its large fleet of fishing boats. Iceland's ambition to end all dependence on fossil fuels by 2050[15] will make it the first country to move to a pollution free hydrogen economy. In the words of Professor Bragi Amason, the original proponent of the idea: 'I think we are living a vision of the world to come'.[16] This nation of fewer than 300,000 people has the natural resources ideally suited to the transition. Demand is met by only 10 per cent of Iceland's hydroelectric potential, hence there is abundant surplus power available. Four international companies with considerable resources signed an agreement with Iceland early in 1999 to carry out the nationwide experiment.[17] It has been known for 160 years that reconstituting oxygen and hydrogen to water in a cell with a platinum catalyst will produce electricity. Fuel cells have long been used in specialist ways where cost is not a prime consideration, for example, in spacecraft. However, one obstacle to their widespread use is the cost of the cells, mainly due to the use of platinum, a rare and costly metal. The first two Mercedes Benz fuel cell buses, now running in Reykjavik, cost over $1.5 million each. In 2005, a major breakthrough seemed possible with the production of nano particles of nickel. It is now considered likely that the vastly less expensive nanonickel can replace platinum as the fuel cell catalyst, so making fuel cells as much as 70 per cent cheaper.

One of the more important and controversial decisions for the future is whether or not to return to the nuclear option, and there is already considerable pressure to do so, including a major public relations campaign in 2004 and 2005, promoting fission power as clean, cheap and safe, and consequently 'green'. In 2002, the Finnish Parliament voted 107 to 92 to build western Europe's first new reactor in more than 10 years to meet their energy demand, in spite of vigorous protests from environmental groups. Construction began in 2005, and the reactor is due for completion in 2009. According to the *New Scientist*, the British government has 'secret plans to push through a major programme of new nuclear power stations'.[18] This kind of pressure could involve not only nuclear power stations, but nuclear shipping, possibly even nuclear aircraft. The problems with nuclear technology are too well known to spell out here, other than merely to note the high risk of serious accidents like Chernobyl, very expensive power in real terms, and the unsolved problem of disposing of nuclear waste.

There are more than 400 power generating nuclear reactors in 30 countries, which have accumulated hundreds of thousands of tons of spent fuel and other dangerous waste. This amount is being increased by around 10,000 tons a year. All this material is radioactive to some extent. High level waste is very hazardous – plutonium 239, for instance, generally resulting from nuclear power production, has a half life of 24,000 years – this means that in that time it is half as dangerous as it is now. These huge time spans reaching into the future exacerbate the waste problem. Much of it is being held in tanks, ponds and other storage designed to be used for only a few decades. Some of this storage has already deteriorated to an alarming extent. Even low-level waste can explode dangerously – in 1972 the US Atomic Energy Commission reported that low-level waste dumped into unlined trenches had spontaneously created a layer of concentrated plutonium, which could have resulted in an explosive nuclear chain reaction. A major nuclear disaster in Kyshtym, in Russia in 1957, is considered to have resulted from such an explosion in nuclear waste, and nearby Lake Karachay is so polluted Russian scientists have warned that to stand on its shores for even a few hours would risk dangerous radiation sickness. There is a very high rate of cancer, sterility and deformed children in this region.

Germany plans to phase out its reactors over the next two decades, and eight older ones are due for decommissioning in the United Kingdom, but three are being built in China, two in Japan, and two in South Korea. Both India and Japan are committed to fast neutron breeders, which can produce more plutonium than the fuel they actually consume, but which have a record of high cost and unreliability, and a potential for supercritical accidents at a catastrophic level.

The true cost of nuclear power must factor in huge amounts – as much as $1 trillion worldwide – for subsidies and cleaning up and decommissioning obsolete facilities – for instance, for the closed down Superphenix fast breeder and the Marcoule reprocessing plants in France, about $5 billion each. Such costs have typically been deferred by delaying total decommissioning until far in the future – in the case of British facilities, 130 years. It will cost almost $100 billion to clean up 20 nuclear sites in Britain. These vast amounts, the unknown cost of permanently disposing of nuclear waste, and very considerable government subsidies, in the US $150 billion over the past 60 years, are generally not factored into the industry's estimates of the real cost of the power produced, or they are under-estimated. Hence claims that nuclear power is cheap need to be looked at rather carefully.

Cheap and safe is the claim. So how safe are the new generation of fission power reactors? The new designs, still in the research stage, use over 300,000 billiard-ball sized 'pebbles' made of uranium and graphite which fuel the reactor, greatly reducing the risk of 'meltdown'. However, unless all of these are perfectly shaped they will jam – such a jamming caused the West German government to close down its programme in 1986 as too dangerous. Graphite is inflammable – it has been involved in a number of reactor accidents in the past, so there is a fire risk. Because of a requirement to be open to natural convectional air cooling some pebble bed reactor designs have no containment vessel, giving easier access to sabotage or terrorists. And the reactors produce a larger amount of somewhat less potent, but still dangerous, nuclear waste. The technology appeals to investors because these reactors are cheaper to build.

But perhaps the most alarming manifestation of the new drive for nuclear power is the Russian government's programme to build small nuclear power plants on barges, which can be towed to remote locations or sold to developing world countries. These reactors, the first of which will be available in 2008, will use highly enriched uranium, which could readily be applied to making bombs. Their vulnerability to sabotage, rogue state or terrorist activity is potentially disastrous.

What then, are the sustainable alternatives, and how can they be developed? Biomass is one of the more promising sources of permanently renewable fuels. It has been used in many parts of the world for some decades – Brazil, for instance, produces ethanol from sugarcane, and many of its road vehicles are designed to use it. In the US around 7 per cent of the corn crop is used to produce almost 2 billion gallons of ethanol, heavily subsidized, a year. However, ethanol production from food crops has been criticized, both on humanitarian grounds and because its production often demands more energy than it yields.

Vegetable oils can be readily converted into diesel fuel. Such a fuel made from rapeseed (canola) has been in use in Europe for some time. A German plant even produces 4000 litres of diesel fuel a day from waste water from restaurants and food factories, reclaiming the oil and grease in a centrifuge, and delivering clean water to the environment. Trees are an important source of biomass – the United States Department of Energy is working with a hardy, high yielding hybrid poplar that will grow 60 feet (20 metres) high in 6 years. The most promising biomass plant may well turn out to be seaweed, specifically *Macrocystis*, a giant kelp which grows very quickly on the coasts of most of the world's continents in temperate waters under 20°C. Using nothing more than the nutrients in seawater and the sun's energy, this giant kelp is the fastest growing plant on Earth.

Every day, solar energy amounting to around 200,000 times present global electricity generating capacity falls on the planet. This has long induced speculation and research into means of harvesting it. Probably the most dramatic concept is the solar chimney – a vast concrete tower as high as a kilometre in which an updraught of heated air drives a succession of generators. At the base of the huge cylinder is a 'greenhouse' – a massive solar collector made of glass sheets which directs superheated air into the chimney.[19] Heat banks inside the greenhouse allow operation for 24 hours a day, so in some areas such a greenhouse might also be used for agriculture. Solar towers are proposed for Rajasthan, in India, China and rural Victoria, in Australia.

At a cost of around $600 million, the Mildura tower in Victoria is in the final stages of technical development. The technology has gained flexibility, and is said to be adaptable to power stations ranging from 50 to 200MW. The original kilometre-high tower will now be somewhat smaller. It will produce power 24 hours a day. The glass 'skirt' around it will have a diameter of several kilometres. Although the height of these proposed towers will make them the world's tallest buildings, their sponsors are confident the technology and materials are available to build them, and that they will be justified by low maintenance costs and a long operating life – as much as 100 years.

New, simpler and high output technology is developing in solar thermal systems in which mirrors focus sunlight on pipes for steam electricity generation. An initial Australian system, using a mirror array 300 metres long, is under construction to preheat water for a coal-fired power station, but according to Solar Heat and Power Pty future projects will generate power directly without the use of fossil fuel – a demonstration plant is under construction in southern Portugal. The chairman of the company, Dr David Mills, says these systems become most cost effective in the 500–1000MW range, similar to moderate-sized nuclear plants, and added: 'The technology can be expanded to meet any conceivable power demand. Expansion can be faster than the nuclear option because of inherent environmental safety. The global solar electric resource is huge at 600 terawatts – current human use is 13 TW.'

A TV screen converts electrons – electricity – into photons – light. This process operates in reverse in photovoltaic cells. Most people own one of these, powering a pocket calculator or a watch. This technology has advanced considerably in recent years, and its usage is increasing, especially in remote localities far from transmission lines, which were previously dependent on diesel generators. The power-producing element in one type of cell is applied like paint to a surface, and can be coated onto roof tiles. These 'amorphous' solar cells are now being used for generators in the megawatt range. Several manufacturers are working on thin, lightweight flexible materials that deliver power from the sun, among them Spheral Solar and Iowa Thin Film Technologies, who are producing such materials for army tents and cladding for solar powered airships. An American firm called HelioVolt is developing solar technology it says can be built into roofing materials and which could reduce the cost of solar panels by more than 50 per cent. Very small nanocrystals called Quantam Dots may be used for much more efficient solar panels. Solar power is especially important because it can be installed where it is to be used, that is, on rooftops, so eliminating the huge costs of transmission lines, and line loss of power when it has to be reticulated over long distances. For these reasons and for those of business profitability consumers pay far higher retail prices for power than its production cost. This means that in many areas solar power is already competitive in real terms with power coming in from the grid.

Where towns are located on or near rivers, hydroelectricity is an important practical resource. The most striking, and also the largest engineering project in the world, is the $25 billion Three

Gorges Dam on China's Yangsi River, which will generate 18,200 MW of electricity. It is by far the largest power generator in existence, equal to the burning of 50 million tons of coal a year. It will also make the river navigable 1800 kilometres from the coast, conserve water in a vast lake, and control flooding on the Yangsi Plain that has caused millions of deaths over the millennia. It is due for completion in 2009.[20] However, such large schemes can have adverse environmental effects and involve high energy losses along lengthy transmission lines. There is a case for small, local plants, as simple as combined impellor generator units which float on the surface of a river, driven by the current.

In order for alternates to provide a stable and reliable supply of energy, the various forms will probably have to be used in combination – utilizing water, wave, tidal, wind and solar power as appropriate, and, where possible, feeding them into a common grid. These are the main forms of alternate energy, and all are being developed, although not yet at anything like sufficient levels to meet the 2030 energy shortfalls. Wind generators are clearly only economically viable in places where the wind blows strongly and fairly constantly, although in favourable locations they are now very close to being competitive in price with fossil fuels – about 3.5 US cents a kilowatt hour. Modern wind generators, which can be as large as 5MW with a blade span of 120 metres, can use direct induction to generate power. This eliminates complex gearing systems, and makes the machines simpler, cheaper and quieter.

However, even at this level of efficiency, they must still be regarded as complementary to other sources of power, such as hydroelectricity, other than in those few places where the wind blows constantly. It is salutary to remember that while the amount of wind-generated power is increasing rapidly – to 47,000MW worldwide in 2005,[21] it still amounts to little over half of 1 per cent of world energy use. In 2001, Germany announced plans to build 4000 wind generators in the North Sea – part of a programme intended to eventually provide half the nation's electricity and to phase out nuclear power. In 2002, the British government announced plans to produce 10 per cent of the nation's electricity by renewable means by 2010 – mostly through wind generators, one of which, planned for Lowestoft, will be 150 metres high.

The movements of the sea – tides and waves – and also the temperature difference between the depths and the ocean surface, are being used to generate electricity. A Canadian power plant at Annapolis, in the Bay of Fundy, generates 20MW. It is a pilot for a huge project which would generate 5000MW– roughly equivalent to five nuclear power stations or the burning of 15 million tons of coal a year. South Korea is building the world's biggest tidal power generator on a 300-metre-wide channel between the sea and Shihwa Lake. Due for completion in 2008, it will generate 254MW – the total requirement for 500,000 people in the adjacent city of Ansan. Geothermal energy, using hot springs or steam plumes of volcanic origin, is in use in many countries, including the US, Japan, New Zealand and Iceland, to generate electricity and to heat buildings. In many parts of the world there are areas of hot subsurface rock, and several countries are researching ways to use this heat for energy generation.

Conservation, at all levels, must be a major factor in current strategies, and this is how the average householder and business can influence events. Given even the most effective and dedicated efforts, it is unlikely that alternates will be able to replace oil completely in the short term. The most important and promising aspect of energy research is therefore conservation, intimately associated with evolving low energy devices, such as LED (light-emitting diode) lighting and 'passive' solar technology, which involves the best possible design of buildings to utilize the sun's energy. Passive techniques are generally simple, requiring few moving parts other than small capacity electric fans. There are a number of techniques which can be employed, for example, siting part or all of a building underground, providing massive masonry 'heat banks', or running pipe loops a few feet under the ground, where temperatures are almost constant, to provide air to a building to help warm or cool it. Other means are as simple as designing buildings so that they are warmed by the winter sun but sheltered from the summer sun. However, sophisticated technology now emerging could exert an enormous conservational influence if it is applied reasonably. For example, LED lamps, providing an acceptable white light that is considered superior to that of fluorescent tubes, are now available, use 80 per cent less power than a conventional light bulb and have a life of at least 10 years. Philips is planning a major conversion to this technology, with light bulbs that look just like conventional incandescent bulbs, and another, called Chameleon, which can sense the colour of objects around it, then change its own colour to match. It has been estimated that if every lamp in the US could be converted to LED or other low use technology, no new power stations would be needed for 20 years.[22]

Major changes in lifestyle, especially in forms of habitat, consumption and transport, could do much to counter, even overcome, the energy crisis. These changes are scarcely likely to be achieved by governments alone, although governments have it in their power to apply tax incentives and penalties sufficient to deter the use of hydrocarbons, especially oil, and, in terms of Axiom One, make it profitable for multinational and national energy companies to cooperate in the development of alternatives. Granted this, these businesses are likely to respond to determined and informed public opinion. As with so much of the necessary new society, change must come from an intelligent appreciation of the facts by individual humans, and maximum pressure from the grassroots. This will be especially important as major pressure increases, as it will, for much larger use of nuclear power as 'the obvious answer' to a growing world hunger for energy.

And speaking of this, how about what I am calling the Coal Burners' Club – otherwise the Asia-Pacific Partnership for Clean Development and Climate – entered into by the six nations who are indeed the world's biggest coal users? The US, Australia, China, India, Japan and South Korea in 2005 signed an 'understanding' as an alternative to the Kyoto Protocol. The proposals are vague indeed, with no target dates and no firm commitments, but basically the idea seems to be to burn much more coal – the dirtiest fuel – and install more nuclear power – the most dangerous – and somehow clean them up. The message is that we can continue 'development' pretty much as now, and that 'technology' will solve all the problems.

But can it, and in time?

One idea is somehow to capture the greenhouse gas carbon dioxide and 'sequester' it – a magic word that really means getting the stuff away underground somewhere. Is this a good idea? – a 'bubble' of CO_2 that emerged from Lake Nyos in the Cameroons in 1986 killed 2000 people. Next, no-one knows how to do it in significant quantities, where to put such huge amounts or what it will cost.

However, it is estimated that to retrofit the world's existing coal-fired plants with equipment to capture the gas would cost around $40 a ton – a total for six billion tons a year from powerhouses of a staggering $240billion. You could build a lot of windfarms for that. On top of this would be another enormous bill for 'sequestering' it. *Scientific American* (14 February 2005) estimates total CO_2 emissions at 25 billion tons a year and present costs of sequestering at $40 to $100 a ton. And even these prodigious costs do not take into account the additional emissions which will result from plans to build 560 new coal-fired plants in China and 213 in India, which do not appear to include gas scrubbers. Beyond this, sequestration would be very energy expensive.

Clean coal? Over the last 30 years billions have been spent trying for this, with very limited success – powdered coal, gas-making – all these have been tried with slight results in terms of the problem. Most coal-burning power stations waste 70 per cent of the energy in the coal, with best new technology only getting this down to 60 per cent. Integrated gasification combined cycle? Two existing plants operate at under 40 per cent efficiency.

However, if we made the charitable assumption that miracles could be achieved, on the most optimistic lead time estimates their effect could only become manifest at a sufficient scale by perhaps 2070, 2080 – much too late to avert the 2030 crisis. And on present showing they would still involve massive pollution, more rapid climate change and astronomical costs.

Unless the sponsors of this programme can do better than this, it can scarcely be taken seriously.

OPTIMAL FUTURE HISTORY

- Fossil fuel and nuclear powerhouses replaced with established renewable technology like solar towers, wind farms, large-scale solar thermal, small-scale hydroelectrics, all on a massive scale – the sooner the better. We must do it while we still have oil left to fuel making the necessary infrastructure, and before climate change gets out of hand.

- People live, work and play in ways that are conservational and sustainable, with houses that use less power and can provide at least some of their own, in habitat forms that do not require the constant use of cars.

- Government imposes major penalties and incentives to switch transport forms to fuel cells and electric drive, plus a sustainable hydrogen fuelling infrastructure, as fast as possible. This could be financed by an immediate doubling in taxes on oil-based fuels, and a progressive supertax on all vehicles with petrol engines over two litres.

- Mandatory provision for all new buildings, and all new appliances, to use minimal energy, and for all buildings to generate at least half of their electricity through on-site sustainable means, like wind or solar.

- Government subsidies on the retail price of low energy use light bulbs, as has been the case in New Zealand.

CHAPTER 3

POPULATION AND POVERTY

A significant area of US policy expounded at an international forum in 2004 is a major contributor to the death of eight times more people, every day, than were killed in the World Trade Center in New York. Yes, read that again. Consider it.

The 110 nations represented at this UN sponsored meeting endorsed a campaign to raise an additional $50billion to combat world hunger, declaring: 'The greatest scandal is not that hunger exists, but that it persists, even when we have the means to eliminate it. It is time to take action.' The declaration proposed a global tax on financial transactions, a tax on the sale of heavy armaments, and a credit card scheme that would direct a small amount of transaction charges to a hunger fund.

However, the US opposed these ideas, its delegation leader, Agriculture Secretary Ann Veneman, saying 'Economic growth is the long-term solution to hunger and poverty ... there is too much emphasis on schemes such as global taxes to raise external resources. Global taxes are inherently undemocratic. Implement-ation is impossible.'

Granted that economic growth is really desirable, how is it possible for the sick and starving to start viable businesses from nothing? And there are plenty of the sick and starving. More than 9 million people, three-quarters of them children under 5, are killed by hunger every year, 25,000 every day.[1] This compares with 12.5 million 10 years ago, 15 million 20 years ago. Almost a billion are classified as 'desperately hungry'.[2] There are over a billion people with incomes lower than $1 a day – just how many, no-one seems to know, with estimates from respectable sources ranging from 1.2 to 1.8 billion. Three billion people – half the global population – live on $2 a day, and get less protein daily than the average domestic cat in the Western world. Around 800 million are severely malnourished, while 600 million are overweight.

The raw statistics in this area are deceptive because apparent improvements largely reflect better living conditions in China. According to Per Pinstrup-Andersen, former director general of the International Food Policy Research Institute in Washington, DC, the situation elsewhere has deteriorated overall, with the number of 'insecure and chronically malnourished people' increasing by 40 million during the 1990s.[3]

Billions of individuals suffer from a variety of endemic diseases, mostly due to infected water supplies and similar inadequate infrastructure. At least half of the population of the world has never used a telephone. One estimate states that 1.5 billion people are unemployed in the sense that they do not have paid work.[4] All these statistics relate particularly to the great majority of the human race who live in the developing world, especially those living outside the cities.

The world's population is projected to grow from 6 to 8.2 billion by 2030, with almost all of this growth taking place in the developing nations. As many as half of the world's people will be living in areas which will not be able to sustain them, substantially due to dwindling water resources.[5] Rapidly growing global population and its attendant problems remain a threat to the world for several reasons. In his final interview retiring president of the World Bank James Wolfensohn forecast a 'tsunami', a great wave of instability, threatening world peace and causing great suffering around the globe, if the problems of world poverty and equity were not urgently addressed. Why, in the face of such an informed warning, do these problems continue? Can they be controlled before 2030? Here again, the means and resources are available, if we choose to use them. There is a close and well documented association of high birth rates with poverty and illiteracy, yet the US has turned its back on this problem, cancelling its contribution to the UN Population Fund in 2002 under pressure from the pseudo-Christian right. Surely real Christians have no wish to see millions of children brought into the world who will die horribly before they are five?

Where everyone is well educated and adequately fed and housed, the rate of growth is generally a little above, or even below, replacement level. The average world population growth is 1.2 per cent a year; in India it is 1.5 per cent, but in the US it is 0.9 per cent, and in Britain a low 0.2 per cent. The populations of Italy and Japan are actually falling. Between 1950 and 2000, the population of 'the West' grew by two-thirds to 1.25 billion; in Asia, Africa and South America it grew more than two and a half times to 4.75 billion. Effectively, the population of the West dwindled over that period from a little under a half to less than a quarter of the world's total population. On present trends, in which future population growth will almost all be in the developing world, the 'more developed' nations are likely to represent only 15 per cent of world population by 2030. The best estimate here is 7 billion in the developing world, 1.2 billion in the developed world.

There are certainly implications here for the West – is it on the way to opting out of the human race? Research in a number of countries has noted that birth rates at or below replacement level seem to be due to the financial cost of having children in economies where women are expected to work. Such birth rates are causing concern in Singapore, Japan and Italy.

The need to improve the lives of the world's poor is obvious on compassionate grounds alone. No less important are the catastrophic demographic, economic, environmental and social consequences if the remedies are delayed. The world's population increased from 5 to 6 billion in only 12 years to 1999. Since then, there has been some slowing in the rate of population increase, but this is mainly due to the one child policy in China – although this is becoming increasingly unpopular and difficult to police – low birth rates in Western countries, and rising death rates from diseases like malaria, AIDS, tuberculosis and stomach infections in infants, which kill millions every year.

Demographic history makes very plain the perils of attempting to predict future outcomes from current trends. There is no guarantee that the world's population is on its way to stabilizing, quite apart from the fact that lower growth rates are largely due to unacceptable reasons. Population equilibrium is most unlikely by 2030, when 8.2 billion people on the planet seems to be the likeliest outcome. That means that for every three people on the Earth now there will be four in 2030. And what will happen in the crucial decades beyond 2030? In 1998, United Nations' demographers set out three scenarios for future population growth. In the worst scenario, in which poverty in developing countries continues to increase, the world would have a catastrophic 15 billion people before the end of the century, associated with an appalling rate of infant mortality.

Most humans still live in villages – there are more than 2 million in India and China alone. In theory these villages are self sufficient but, in reality, they are becoming increasingly impoverished. Huge numbers now also live in city slums. The needs of these people, for many decades at least, will be quite different from those of people in the Western world, and may seem simple to the point of being primitive. Nevertheless, these needs are real and pressing, and are frequently and disastrously misunderstood, even ignored, by decision-makers administering foreign aid.

A conventional view of history places the end of the colonial era about halfway through the 20th century, when most of the former Asian, African and American colonies became independent states. This is, however, only partly true. During the ensuing half century, economic dominance of much of the developing world by the West continued, as the ability of new nations to govern themselves effectively diminished. 'Government' by military juntas became the rule rather than the exception. In many cases such oppressors have been supported by Western powers for muddled political and economic reasons. These military regimes have seriously impeded even well intentioned efforts by Western countries to assist developing countries. Financial grants have too often ended up in the Swiss bank accounts of authoritarian 'leaders' and their hangers-on. Other 'aid' has been dissipated on inappropriate infrastructure, such as golf courses and city office buildings, and on weapons systems mainly designed to allow regimes to oppress their own people.

Speaking of mass deaths, how do you feel about a financial instrument that is killing thousands of children every day? This is just one cost of the crippling burden of developing world debt – variously estimated at between $1.5 and 2 trillion – which is preventing proper health care, education and poverty alleviation programmes in developing countries. In addition to aid and grants, Western countries and financial institutions have also offered loans to developing nations – many of them 'odious' debts. These consist of money paid over to support tyrannical regimes, or in some cases, debts inherited from the colonial era. Over the last three decades the relentless progress of compound interest has worsened this growing problem of debt, leaving many poorer countries obliged to meet interest payments greater than their spending on education or health services. For instance, 40 per cent of Ecuador's annual budget in 1999 was used to pay interest on a $16 billion debt. Two-thirds of its people live in poverty, even though Ecuador has major oil and other mineral reserves and is well endowed with fertile land. Some movement was made late in 1999, with an International Monetary Fund and World Bank decision to write off $60 billion, with special attention being given to the most disadvantaged countries. For instance, 85 per cent of Nicaragua's debt was cancelled. However, these concessions came with strings attached, and had little immediate effect on the payments required of the debtor countries, who were obliged to accept IMF directions on how to run their economies. These constraints typically involved even harsher restrictions on budgets for health and education, and the elimination of food subsidies. Similar restrictions accompanied a much publicized write-off of $40 billion in 2005. This represents barely 2.5 per cent of total developing world debt.

A major campaign by a non-governmental global charity, Jubilee 2000 – aimed at the elimination of developing-world debt –

organized a petition of 17 million signatures which was presented to a meeting of the G8, the world's richest nations, in Cologne in 1999. However, to offer some perspective, the following year almost a billion dollars were spent organizing the G8 summit on the Japanese island of Okinawa, including construction of a replica of then US President Clinton's Arkansas home, at a cost of three-quarters of a million dollars, for his use during the conference.

Meanwhile, the obligation to pay the interest on the remaining debts, many of which are plainly unmeetable, is responsible for hundreds of thousands of avoidable deaths in developing countries, mostly of children, and contrasts badly with the growing affluence of some areas of the West. According to the Worldwatch Institute, the complete cancellation of debt in African countries would save the lives of millions of children each year and provide access to basic education for approximately 90 million young women.[6] The effects of AIDS, internal conflicts in six African countries and crop failures due to drought had brought additional urgency to this issue by 2005, when the United Nations declared a humanitarian disaster affecting at least 10 million people who were facing acute food shortages.

A gloomy enough picture, but it does point up the issue of how aid funds should be channelled to the people in developing countries and how they can best be spent. There is evidence that aid supplied by non-governmental organizations – charities such as Oxfam Community Aid Abroad – is the most effective in terms of getting maximum results per dollar spent and in directing aid to the people who really need it. Aid money gets better results when advisers from the donor country are actually on the ground, and can discuss practical needs with the people, rather than with the governing officials of the recipient country.

I lived for a time in northeast Thailand in a region where a new hydroelectric scheme, the Nampong Dam, was built, largely financed by foreign aid. The only suitable place for the dam was a shallow basin surrounded by low hills. This flat area also happened to be one of the few areas of good arable soil in that region. When it was flooded, hundreds of families who had farmed there for generations were forced off their land. With the small amounts of money they had been given as compensation they could not afford to buy other land – nothing else as good was available anyway. When the scheme began to operate it did so at only a limited capacity. It provided power for a few towns and a small minority of wealthy people. In that area the hundreds of villages and their people could not afford to pay for connecting lines or electrical appliances. Most villages did not even have a road. This was inappropriate technology.

Appropriate technology can only be assessed by looking at the conditions of the lives of the people concerned. Most village headmen and councils in northeast Thailand knew what would have been appropriate, but they were seldom asked. Huge infrastructure projects are 'easier' – a stroke of a pen in London, Washington or Paris can allocate money in one large dollop to achieve a highly visible end, the consequences of which have frequently not been thought through. In most village areas around the world, appropriate technology is more likely to take the following forms, in order of priority:

- The means to supply safe, non-infected drinking water – deep tube wells or impervious roofing to collect rainwater in tanks. According to one estimate, contaminated water kills 2 million people a year.[7]
- Water pumps driven by sustainable means, such as windmills, solar panels and hydraulic motors, or at least by fuel economical engines, perhaps diesel. Billions of people in the developing world have to spend hours of backbreaking and monotonous labour raising water into irrigation channels. An intriguing development here for village use is the promotion by a South African company of a childrens' roundabout connected to a pump capable of raising 1400 litres of water an hour from a depth of 40 metres as the children play.
- Simple agricultural implements made of good steel, preferably stainless, that are easy to use and maintain. In most places the economy and ecology are dependent on the use of draught animals, which automatically fertilize the

soil. Appropriate technology would be designed to mesh with this situation, not seek to replace it with motor vehicles, artificial fertilizers and patented genetically modified seeds.

- Efficient stoves to replace fuel hungry open hearths. Solar cooking appliances would not only be convenient, but would also help to arrest the destruction of trees and the attendant loss of soil fertility, and at the same time reduce deaths from indoor smoke pollution. Such simple cookers, using parabolic metal mirrors, are in regular use in India.
- A road and bridges connecting the village to the outside world; carts with rubber pneumatic tyres and sealed low friction wheel bearings.
- Permanent roofing to remove the constant repetitive work of thatching and to catch rainwater.
- Grafted higher producing fruit trees, better breeding stock for poultry, and higher producing livestock generally.
- A travelling medical clinic specialized in birth control mechanisms, control of endemic disease, and pain alleviation, with staff having sufficient diagnostic skills to decide which cases should be referred to hospitals.
- A school, using modern methods to achieve literacy and numeracy, and teaching practical engineering and science relevant to the appropriate technology for that region.

If possible, artifacts should be low tech, low cost, and able to be made and repaired locally with local materials. A good example of this is the prosthetic Jaipur foot, developed in India. A thousand of these were sent to Afghanistan in 2002 to benefit people who had had their feet blown off by one of the West's major exports to the developing world – landmines.[8] Appropriate technology then, involves studying what is already there, and building on it progressively. This should allow a modest industrial base to evolve naturally, providing added value to local products for export – goods such as prepared and packaged foods, woven goods, wooden furniture and other handicrafts.

There are research and aid agencies which understand the problems of the developing countries, which are collectively

achieving 'sustainable agriculture' techniques that have dramatically increased food crop yields for millions of poor farmers.
One Madagascan venture that has greatly increased rice yields
through quite simple changes to crop management[9] has since
been extended to China, Indonesia and Cambodia.

The International Centre for Research in Agroforestry is
tackling the serious problem of a loss of soil fertility in equatorial
Africa – not with increasing fertilizer use, which the farmers
cannot afford anyway, but by natural and sustainable means.
Farmers have been introduced to a selection of leguminous plants
that add nitrogen to the soil, and to cover crops which can be
ploughed in. Mexican sunflower, which is already being used
extensively, has in some cases trebled maize crops sown
subsequently. Another of the centre's rapidly expanding concepts
is 'living fences' of suitable growing shrubs and trees, to enclose
fields where crops of higher value than maize, such as vegetables,
are grown to protect them from animals. Much higher yields of
food crops can be achieved when several varieties are planted
together, rather than operating a monoculture. Millions of farmers
have abandoned ploughing, using zero tillage methods instead. A
major survey in 2001 of 208 sustainable agriculture projects in 52
countries, indicated that some small farms were achieving
increasing yields of 50 to 100 per cent, without using artificial
fertilizers or pesticides.[10]

Among the more elegant applications of postmodern appropriate technologies is a huge 'seawater greenhouse' on an arid
island off Abu Dhabi. This project has successfully tested a low
energy technology that irrigates the desert and grows vegetables
in a giant 'dew making machine that produces fresh water and
cool air from sun and seawater'.[11] Described as 'a truly original
idea which has the potential to impact on the lives of millions of
people living in coastal water-starved areas around the world',[12]
the seawater greenhouse will surely take its place in the new
society. It serves as evidence that raising the poor from their misery
and poverty by frugal and renewable means is feasible and
affordable, and also as a reminder that any idea of influencing
developing countries into becoming clones of the consumerist

West should be forgotten immediately. Even granted major concessions of affluence by the West, the natural resources and environment of the planet could not support the pollution created and energy and resources demanded, which has been estimated at five times present use. That estimate alone indicates how different the new society must be if it is to be truly global.

OPTIMAL FUTURE HISTORY

- The developing nations need to have money put into them, not taken out. This demands immediate cancellation of debts which are longstanding and plainly oppressive – this would mean most developing-world debt and large infusions of money as grants, not loans.

- Mass production methods developed to provide new appropriate technology, and experts appointed to explain its use. This could be achieved by establishing a new world agency for appropriate agriculture and technology, with financial backing in the order of $100 billion a year.

- Provision of basic schooling throughout the world, mainly through the internet, available at the village level, especially to young women and children forced to labour in inefficient agricultural systems.

- Recognition that deaths, illness and blindness from preventable causes are inexcusable in world terms, and provision of enough money to control them. It is communally disgraceful – although greatly to his individual credit – that Bill Gates, last year provided more than three-quarters of the research funds to fight malaria, which kills more than two million people every year.

Chapter 4

Climate: How Long to Tipping Point?

We must take climate change – and indeed the apocalyptic 'tipping point' concept – very seriously. The evidence is fast growing that it will be highly dangerous if the current disinclination to do much about it continues.

The year 2005 was the hottest, driest and stormiest on record in many places, setting a new record damage cost of more than $200 billion as a result of extreme weather. Hurricane Katrina in the US accounted for well over $100 billion of this. The previous record year for disaster damage was 2004.

Paradoxically, a little ice age severely affecting western Europe, especially the UK, seems likely quite soon. Temperatures would drop as much as 8°C, London would be snowbound for many months, huge areas of cropland would no longer produce food. This would result from disruption of the Atlantic Conveyor system of sea currents, which includes the Gulf Stream. This disastrous event could occur abruptly, within a decade, and last for decades, if not centuries. It could co-exist with global warming in other areas, indeed mainstream scientists consider that warming would be a major factor influencing the shutdown. Larger amounts of fresh water in the North Atlantic have disrupted the conveyor several times before, and this is starting to happen again now. Fresh water is increased in the sea as ice melts and higher rainfall is increasing river flows.

These are some of the conclusions of a briefing paper delivered to the World Economic Forum in Davos in 2003 by the Woods Hole Oceanographic Institution in the US. In 2005, Ruth Curry of that institution and Cecilie Mauritzen of the Norwegian Meteorological Institute, reported repeated major pulses of fresh water from the Arctic to the North Atlantic over each of the last four decades. Late in 2005 British researchers at the National Oceanographic Centre in Southampton released the results of a study showing that the conveyor had indeed weakened by 30 per cent since 1992. When the earth began to warm after the last ice age 12,300 years ago the conveyor was disrupted, resulting in an abrupt temperature fall of about 5°C. This renewed cold phase, known as the Younger Dryas, lasted for 1300 years.

Glaciologists at a Royal Society meeting in London late in 2005 reversed earlier opinions that Antarctica was not contributing to climate change. Two big glaciers, Pine Island and Thwaites, are sliding into the sea much faster – these two glaciers alone could raise sea levels by more than a metre. Since they deposit more than 100 cubic kilometres of ice into the ocean each year, they will almost certainly contribute to the sea level rises already causing concern as Arctic ice melts. A vast area of permafrost in Siberia – a million hectares – is melting for the first time since the last ice age. This is likely to release huge amounts of methane, a greenhouse gas 20 times as potent as CO_2, and could result in an irreversible 'tipping point' for the world's climate. More CO_2 in the air is making the sea more acid and this is likely to result in a 'potentially gigantic' disturbance of fish populations, according to Carol Turley, head of science at Plymouth Marine Laboratory in Plymouth, England. And according to Janos Bogardi, director of environment and human society studies at the UN University in Bonn, there are likely to be as many as 50 million 'environmental refugees' by the end of this decade.

Climate change ranks as a principal driver for these and many other reasons, including one not always given due prominence – its potential to severely reduce world food supplies, especially in poor and heavily populated areas. Food, water and energy resources are now at the stage where, by 2030, even quite small changes in climate could cause major famine. Health is also an issue. The World Health Organization in 2005 predicted that by 2030 global warming could cause 300,000 deaths and 10 million illnesses in the developing world over and above very high present disease rates. There were already signs of this in that year, when mosquito-borne dengue fever reached epidemic proportions in south Asia, infecting 120,000 people and killing 1000. Researchers made the point that it is the developed world that is driving global warming, but it is the undeveloped world that will suffer most.

Hotter, wilder, less predictable weather is indeed the early prospect, and is likely to increase progressively over the next 30 years. There is now almost complete consensus among scientists that it will happen, and that human activities, especially burning coal and oil, that increase the amount of greenhouse gases in the air are the trigger.

These points were made by the Intergovernmental Panel on Climate Change in a major assessment of the problem.[1] That report predicted average global temperature increases between 1.4°C and 5.8°C during this century, the most rapid warming the world has experienced in 10,000 years. The worst case scenario of a rise of 5.8°C would result if efforts to resolve the problem continue to be as ineffectual as they have been over the past decade. The panel's fourth major report is due in 2007.

However, other scientists consider that on the evidence of recent research a rise of as much as 15°C is possible, with huge and unforeseeable consequences. This prediction is based on two factors. The first is the possibility that the Amazon rainforest, now believed to be operating as a major carbon sink, could in circumstances such as protracted drought or major forest fires, return huge amounts of carbon to the atmosphere, creating a temperature rise of as much as 8°C. The Amazon forest was at the time of writing severely affected by its worst drought in 40 years, with satellites recording more than 150 fires. Cattle ranchers, loggers and soy bean farmers are cutting down more than 25,000 square kilometres of the Amazon every year, a rate that would destroy the entire forest in 50 years. The cattle herd has increased since 1990 by 20 million to 60 million, and is the largest in the world. Soy farms have doubled to 20 million hectares. The Peruvian glaciers, which provide 50 per cent of the water to the upper Amazon, are fast shrinking and may disappear totally within 40 years, with potentially devastating consequences for the forest.

The effect at the poles of an 8°C temperature rise could be a major release of methane from the methane hydrate (clathrate) on the shallow seabed of the Arctic, currently frozen in place. Past ice core and sediment records indicate that something like this might happen in as little as 50 years. A phase of rapid and intense global warming 55 million years ago may have been caused by a methane release.[2] In late 2002, Arctic sea ice was at its lowest since records were first taken in the 1950s, and was perhaps the lowest for several centuries, due to a warm summer and unusual air circulation patterns, and by 2005 it became so low it was predicted that the fabled and much-sought north-west passage through the Arctic seas would soon be open to shipping.

Climatologists, like economists, have many and divergent opinions about their subject. Most claim the world will continue getting hotter and that this will be catastrophic. A few still consider that this is not yet proven – that warmer temperatures, the retreat of glaciers, and the melting of polar ice over the past three decades might be a passing fluctuation. The concept of global warming is a fairly simple one: that increasing emissions of 'greenhouse gases', mainly carbon dioxide, nitrous oxide and methane, are thickening the insulating blanket that prevents heat – specifically infrared radiation – escaping from the planet. Increased carbon dioxide emissions result from industry, especially the burning of fossil fuels for transport and generating electric power. Emissions of nitrous oxide, a very potent greenhouse gas, are increasing with the greater use of nitrogenous fertilizers. Over 20 per cent of greenhouse emissions come from the US, which has under 5 per cent of the world's population. However, on a per capita basis, Australia is the worst offender, emitting 25 per cent more carbon dioxide per capita than the US, and twice that of Europe.[4] Exxon Mobil, the world's biggest oil conglomerate, is actually increasing its greenhouse emissions. Twenty per cent more gas was 'flared' – burned off – in 2003 than in 2002, and this is, of course, both pollutant and wasteful.

The major likely consequence of global warming is higher temperatures everywhere, but the change will be greater at the poles than in equatorial and temperate regions. Mainstream theorists believe there will be gradual global warming, perhaps above 5°C, over the next century. While this may not sound much, dire consequences have been predicted with any rise above 2°C, including more frequent and severe hurricanes, typhoons, cyclones and flood rains in some areas, drought in others. Weather conditions extreme enough to destroy buildings could become more prevalent. There are strong indications that this process is already with us. Damage from natural catastrophes was estimated at over $200 billion for 2005, the most costly total ever.[5]

Much warmer conditions – temperatures up to 10°C higher – are predicted for the polar regions. It is this difference between that figure and the smaller increases in the tropics that will drive violent weather fluctuations. It will also result in greater melting of the Arctic and Antarctic ice, potentially increasing sea levels by as much as 8 feet (2.5 metres). There is already evidence of increased summer melting in the Arctic icecap, up approximately 40 per cent in half a century. If this continues it could trigger the massive releases of methane mentioned earlier. Most of the world's 33 island nations would be affected by flooding, especially some smaller countries on low lying coral based islands in the Pacific. In 2005, a decision was taken to permanently evacuate the 980 people living on the Carteret atolls in Papua New Guinea because sea level rises and more violent weather had rendered the islands uninhabitable. The islands are expected to be completely submerged by 2015. The 40,000 people of Tuvalu will soon be flooded out. A serious loss of arable land in one large nation, Bangladesh, where 140 million people live on the low lying delta of the Ganges River, is also predicted. Major problems could also result in the Netherlands, Belgium and Egypt.

There are already reports that early thawing in the Arctic region of Canada is adversely affecting the lifestyle and hunting patterns among the 25,000 Inuit – formerly known as Eskimo – people there.[6] A three-year study, released late in 1999, estimated that an unchecked increase in greenhouse gas emissions, to 750 parts per million of carbon dioxide in the air – around double the current levels of 380ppm – would kill most of the world's forests, including the rainforest of the Amazon.[7] This would trigger an immense additional release of carbon dioxide into the atmosphere, with uncontrollable knock-on effects.

Limiting the increase to 550ppm might save the forests, but would not avert sea level rises. Anything beyond 400ppm is considered dangerous. However, if the polar ice caps started to break up – the fragile West Antarctic shelf appears to be the most vulnerable – sea level rises as high as 20 feet (6 metres) could happen relatively quickly, probably within a century. According to one estimate even a 3 feet (1 metre) rise could adversely affect one billion people and a third of the world's cropland.[8] Most of the world's big cities are near the coast and the low lying fertile valleys or deltas of the great rivers are densely populated. The Netherlands has already estimated that it must spend at least $5 billion in the 21st century to protect reclaimed land from rising sea levels. New York, Miami, London, Tokyo, Venice and Bangkok would be among the cities severely affected.

Warmer conditions are expected to affect plant life in quite complex ways. Major changes in plant distribution would be likely. Some places would become more fertile, others less so. There is a considerable difference of opinion on just how this might happen, but there is some consensus that the industrialized nations may become more food productive, the developing world less productive. Although much semi desert could become useful land, productive and forested land in tropical areas could be affected by severe drought. Global warming increases the amount of water vapour in the air, and water vapour is itself a potent greenhouse gas.

On balance, a disturbing bill of consequences, even more so in view of global warming's likely influence in combination with the other 2030 drivers. Will it really happen? Can it be avoided? The answer to the first question is probably yes, and to the second, probably no. Refusal by the US and Australia to sign the 1997 Kyoto Protocol on climate change and the massive and increasing use of coal-fired power stations in China and India make continued high rates of carbon dioxide emissions almost inevitable. In any case, it is now generally acknowledged that the Kyoto target of reducing greenhouse gases 5 per cent by 2012 from 1990 levels is grossly inadequate – as much as 50 per cent would be necessary to check global warming. While US President George W Bush announced some measures to combat climate change in 2002, these seem unlikely to reduce actual carbon dioxide emissions, which critics claim may rise as much as 14 per cent by 2010. At the 2002 meeting of the Kyoto signatories in Delhi, developing countries criticized the developed world's performance on greenhouse gas reduction and called on it to reduce emissions before they were expected to do so.

In 1999 research evidence resulting from the study of fossil leaves indicated that a massive extinction of plants at the end of the Triassic period more than 200 million years ago was associated with a phase of global warming.[9] The fossil studies indicate a temperature rise of as much as 4°C associated with a near trebling of carbon dioxide levels.

Late in 1999 the Intergovernmental Panel on Climate Change seriously questioned the value of forests as 'carbon sinks'. These findings have considerable implications for a new worldwide industry which arose from decisions in the Kyoto Protocol. The proposal was to give nations and businesses 'carbon credits' for new tree planting; credits which could be bought and sold. The rationale has it that industries prepared to pay for forest planting anywhere on the planet should be permitted to cause greater carbon emissions. However, it is now considered that such planting would result only in short-term advantages, since the carbon in them would be returned to the atmosphere when the trees died and decayed – a cycle of around 40 years is suggested. Vegetation in any case emits huge amounts of methane – a previously unsuspected factor only revealed in 2006 following research at the Max Planck Institute for Nuclear Physics in Germany. The clean, green credentials of hydro-electric power are in question for similar reasons – considerable amounts of methane created by rotting material at the bottom of large dams are released to the atmosphere when the water goes through the generating turbines.

There are proposals[10] to reduce carbon dioxide in the atmosphere by 'ocean nourishment' with nitrogen fixed from the air. The theory is that nitrogen pumped into the sea would increase the growth of phytoplankton, which would, in turn, extract carbon dioxide from the air. The resultant 'carbon credits' could be sold. Although this idea appears attractive to businesses and governments, there are others who oppose ocean nourishment, believing that it would pose unacceptable risks to natural systems in the ocean.[11] They cite several computer models that indicate that ocean nourishment is not the answer to global warming.

To try to put the issue into a clearer focus, there are a few facts that should be taken into account:

- Recent weather fluctuations have been more noticeable because the planet enjoyed a 'benign' phase of unusually good weather from around 1890 to 1970 – the most stable and warmest period for almost 1000 years.
- There has always been a belt of 'greenhouse gases'. Without them we would either freeze to death, or perhaps just manage to survive in greatly reduced numbers. It is the volume of 'greenhouse gases', not their existence, that is the issue.
- A significant quantity of the emissions come from natural sources, including the metabolic processes of ruminant animals or, to put this less politically correctly, the belching and farting of cows and sheep. There is evidence this could be substantially reduced by feeding the animals a modified diet, which could be natural – herbs like thyme and mint have been suggested.[12] A stomach bacteria in kangaroos causes them to emit hydrogen, not methane, and there are hopes that this can be transferred to cud chewing animals.

Whatever conferences are held, whatever decisions are taken, carbon dioxide emissions will almost certainly increase at least until 2030. This is partly because developing nations, especially the world's two largest, China and India, want more of what the West has. They are industrializing, burning huge amounts of coal, crowding their cities with motor vehicles, doing what they can to satisfy the rising expectations of their populations. While it must be noted that China has made vigorous, and to an extent successful, attempts to address this problem, the overall world situation is not encouraging.

This is, of course, regrettable, but it is difficult to foresee any change for some time to come. It is worth noting that asking the developing nations to adapt their industries without major help from the rest of the world runs counter to both of our axioms. To allow the situation to conform to the axioms a great deal of money must be spent, and some very elaborate rethinking and technology shaping must occur. This will take a considerable amount of time, which increasingly we do not have, but it must necessarily be part of a broad world plan.

Global warming is sometimes confused with damage to the ozone layer, and this is understandable. Indeed, very recent research shows there is probably an association. However, the first concerns the blocking of infrared radiation returned from the Earth into space, the second is about the amount of ultraviolet (UV) radiation coming in. Ozone, created by the effects of the UV component of sunlight on oxygen, provides a protective blanket about 20 miles above the Earth's surface against this searing radiation. This – as those white skinned people who expose their bodies on beaches in the summer know only too well – can soon turn you pink. Much worse, it can cause dangerous skin cancers, including deadly melanoma. The thinner the ozone layer, the stronger the radiation, and the greater these risks become. Higher UV levels can also affect phytoplankton, which are at the bottom of the marine food chain, and may also damage other marine life. Reduction of phytoplankton numbers is particularly serious, since they take up massive amounts of carbon. Yields from plants like soybeans, peas and beans are reduced if they are exposed to excessive UV radiation.

During the last quarter of the 20th century a hole appeared in the ozone layer above the Antarctic. Almost every year it became larger. Then a similar effect threatened to occur in the northern hemisphere. In temperate zone areas, first in Australia, then elsewhere, the effects were soon evident. It became dangerous to stay out in the midday sun, even for short periods. The incidence of skin cancer and melanoma increased. Manmade chemicals caused this effect: the offenders are chlorofluorocarbons (CFCs), which are used as a propellant gas in aerosol spray cans, in refrigeration and air conditioning equipment, in dry cleaning and the manufacture of foam plastics; halons, which are used for fire fighting; and the pesticide methyl bromide. These gases, once released into the air, can persist there for as long as 120 years. When they eventually reach the ozone atoms they attack and destroy them.

The remedy here is obvious: stop using these gases. This has already been achieved in many parts of the world, but in other cases, particularly in developing countries, the cost of converting the industries involved is too great. Both axioms come into play again here, and must be taken into account. If the loss of the ozone layer is not halted, most people in the world will eventually suffer. Indeed in the 13 years after the world's governments agreed to phase out ozone-destroying substances – that is to 1999 – production of them actually increased, due almost entirely to higher levels in China.[13] While a major worldwide co-operative effort has brought them under control since then, the ozone layers at both poles remained alarmingly fragile in 2005. It is thought that aspects of climate change, such as high-level clouds, are also involved, and this has prompted an £11 million study by the European Union. Hence the ozone layer problem will not be solved by 2030 – scientists warn the effects are likely to remain severe for at least half a century.

Even though global warming is a major concern at present, the possibility of human action triggering another ice age is also worth bearing in mind. If there were even a 'limited' nuclear war, would a disastrous 'little ice age', like that which caused famine and hardship between the 14th and 19th centuries, onset? This speculation arises from a study postulating a 'nuclear' winter[14] caused by planet-wide dust and smoke clouds resulting from atomic war. That study, predicting massive famines and millions of deaths, nevertheless considered that an ice age would not result because the immense reserves of heat stored in the oceans would act as a sufficient buffer.

However, the point is far from definite. There are many variable factors, including the duration of the war, the volume of weapons used, and natural climatic conditions at the time. If there were an extended 'nuclear winter' – perhaps two years – dust clouds obscuring the sun might lower temperatures enough to increase the ice sheets, resulting in a raised 'albedo' for our planet. Albedo is the ratio of light and heat a planet reflects back into space compared to the levels received from the sun. If the Earth's albedo increases due to greater ice and snow cover, more of the sun's heat will be reflected back into space rather than being retained, causing temperatures on Earth to drop even further.

Climatologists point out that a colder world would be much more dangerous and more difficult to adjust to. We happen to be going through a warm weather phase, but for most of the last 2 million years the world was much colder than it is now, and, at times, very much colder. Through this Quaternary Period there have been at least 50 significant climate fluctuations. These changes have been cyclic: intermittent periods of warmth and cold – cold sometimes so intense that as much as a third of the Earth was covered with ice. Humankind survived the last ice age, which ended around 10,000 years ago, by the skin of its teeth, and in very small numbers.

Will there be another such ice age? The climatologists say yes, but it is almost impossible to say when it will be. There is no conclusive body of knowledge about how these glacial periods are triggered. One area of speculation is that they are caused by variations in the Earth's axis and in the Earth's orbit around the sun. The tilt of the Earth, now 23.5°, is gradually reducing, favouring the growth of ice sheets. There are respectable estimates of a cycle of around 20,000 years, with the four previous inter-glacials averaging about 10,000 years in duration. The present interglacial began around 10,000 years ago, and was at its warmest from roughly 4000BC to 2000BC – a time of virtually ideal conditions for emerging human societies based on agriculture. On this evidence, a world becoming colder during Millennium 3 is feasible. Whether the current phase of global warming is simply an overlay on this general trend remains to be seen.

However, it is thought that a wide range of events, especially those involving sea temperature and currents, might help to induce the next ice age. Higher polar temperatures will lead to increased Arctic ice melting which could affect the warm northern currents. Evidence of this increasing ice melting is provided among others by Norwegian polar research scientists Tore Furevik and Ola Johannessen[15] who reported in July 2000 that north polar ice melting was much more rapid than had been previously predicted, and that the ice may disappear entirely during the summer months in as little as 50 years.

Relatively small events could have much larger repercussions. There are theories concerning the albedo effect – snowfields reflect at least 70 per cent of sunlight, while dense tropical forest reflects as little as 10 per cent. Studies of satellite photographs of Siberia and North America[16] have indicated that large scale clearing of forest could be a significant climate factor.

But if there is another ice age surely it will develop so gradually that we will be able to accommodate ourselves to it? This idea has such important implications that it must be tested – and there is evidence that it may not be valid. During the last half century improved technology has made it possible for the first time to obtain 'cores' – drill samples – providing accurate inform-ation about climate patterns going back several million years. A major finding of this research has been, in Professor Andrew Goudie's words,[17] 'that the onset of climatic changes could be more sudden and rapid than had previously been thought'. Pollen samples taken from the seabed indicate that glacials have onset in the past in as little as 70 years. Studies of a peat bog in Alsace by Belgian botanist Genevieve Woillard have shown dramatic and rapid vegetation changes during the final three centuries of an interglacial about 115,000 years ago, with a climax of rapid cooling over just a few decades. She considers a similar event could be imminent.

The passage of our solar system through a galactic dust cloud, dust from a major series of volcanic eruptions, or very large areas of manmade clouding – pollution – could trigger a glaciation. The Toba super eruption in Sumatra 73,500 years ago, which put approximately 20 times more dust into the air than Krakatoa in 1883, is thought to have caused a protracted reduction of sunlight – possibly for as long as five years – that triggered a glacial at about that time. A $25 million research programme – the Indian Ocean Experiment[18] – has identified a huge cloud of pollution covering virtually all of Asia. Almost all the harmful pollutants are part of this brown haze – mineral dust, soot, nitrates, sulphates and carbon monoxide gas – and derive from the burning of fossil fuels. The cloud is at its worst for three or four months a year, and usually peaks in January. According to the leader of the research team, Professor Paul Grutzen, the cloud blocks out 15 per cent of sunlight, reducing sea evaporation, and hence rainfall. Drought, already severe in many parts of Asia, could be aggravated by it, leading to mass starvation because of reduced food production. NASA observation of the cloud in 2004 indicated that it was affecting areas as far away as China, south-east Asia, and the Middle East. This vast pall of pollutants, two miles thick, is now suspected of being a major influence on global climate. It is one of a number of brown clouds – there are others originating in China and the eastern US. One observer remarked that he noticed that Chinese schoolchildren colouring in the sky reached for the grey pencil.

Can climate change onset quickly? This is a matter of serious importance. A report by 11 climate scientists in 2001[19] described past occasions on which climate changes were rapid. A major instance was the Earth's initial recovery from the last ice age 12,000 years ago, followed by a sudden drop of 5°C, which persisted for more than 1000 years. It was ended by an abrupt rise in temperatures over a period of a decade.

The world's situation is such that, under present conditions of land use, we have just enough arable land to feed everyone, with future problems likely even if there is no early onset of an ice age. But what if there were? A large proportion of our major croplands, especially for food grains, are in high latitudes and would be destroyed by the advance of the ice. There are vastly more humans now in the world than during the last ice age. Billions would starve to death, many millions more would die in desperate wars for possession of those areas of the world where food could still be grown. One writer on the subject in 1974 estimated deaths from starvation as high as 2 billion, almost half of the world's population at the time.[20] These deaths would predominantly be in what are now the wealthiest and most developed parts of the world. More likely in the short term are climate 'blips' within the larger cycle of ice ages. Greenland, around the end of Millennium 1, was indeed green – it had pastures that accommodated grazing animals. The onset of colder weather in Europe saw these disappear, and the Norse migrants living in Greenland were forced to move to warmer places. The weather was unusually cold in Europe and the US between 1617 and 1650. Stalagmite records in New Zealand suggest the 17th century was also colder than usual there. These conditions were part of the 'little ice age' from about 1400 to 1850, which caused crop failures and famines in many parts of the world. Glaciers in Europe reached their greatest extent in 1670, but historically best remembered is the 'great winter' of 1708/1709. Even the fast flowing Rhone River in southern France froze over, vines and olive orchards were destroyed, wolves became a major danger, and the price of bread quadrupled. Another such climate blip could affect world food supplies even more disastrously in our current situation. Sooner or later an ice age of unknown severity will occur. Whether or not we prepare for it will determine to what extent our civilization – inevitably much reduced – will survive 20,000 cold years.

Meanwhile, the damaging and much more immediate prospect of global warming requires protective action being taken that goes far beyond what is now in existence or even planned.

Perhaps the only hope would be an effective global authority with considerable powers designed to avert the consequences of global warming as much as possible, especially the 'knock-on' effects from forest death and methane release from the Arctic. Such an authority might be in a position to undertake realistic efforts to reduce greenhouse gas emissions and to create carbon 'sinks' in the oceans and forests, if research shows these to be feasible. However, since there seems little prospect of international cooperation to control greenhouse gas before 2030, a practical fallback position must be established.

OPTIMAL FUTURE HISTORY

Since climate change is probably inevitable, inception of emergency measures to keep the effects short of disaster, including:

- Every possible effort to keep greenhouse emissions as low as possible. This involves every person – low energy lightbulbs to replace incandescent as soon as possible, walk or bicycle rather than drive, fly only when this is necessary, replace your dinosaur with a hybrid or electric car, introduce passive solar elements into your house, get appliances off standby mode. This is one area where the individual householder can really make their influence felt. Remember the weather is likely to get much worse – design your new house or business to withstand this.
- Major pressure by any means, including trade boycotts, to get heavy industrial polluters to improve their act.
- Exertion of further major pressure, via the ballot box and continuous lobbying, on members of governments to work for effective international efforts to minimize the effects of climate change.
- Sea temperature and methane hydrate monitoring to assess the risk of major methane releases to the atmosphere.
- Technical and financial help to nations likely to be flooded, and decisions on where their people are to be shifted to.
- Government-financed reinsurance to buffer much higher costs from natural calamities.
- Careful, continuous monitoring of food crop yields, and the creation of 'warehouses' able to provide large amounts of food to populations hit by natural disasters.

CHAPTER 5

IS THERE ENOUGH FOOD AND WATER?

One often reads or hears the comforting generalization that there is plenty of food in the world – the real problem is that many people can't afford it. While this remains true at present we are rapidly approaching the stage where it might not be so. As the foregoing chapters have indicated, the oil drought, population growth and climate change will severely impact on food production – just one instance of the combined effect of several drivers. At the time of writing, water shortages and soil degradation are causing famine conditions in much of Africa that are putting millions of people at risk of death from starvation; tens of millions more around the world can no longer persuade their exhausted soil to provide them with enough to eat. Between 1950 and 1996 the amount of grain land per person in the world dropped by almost half, according to the United Nations Population Fund's report, *State of World Population 2001*.[1] This report estimated that 40 per cent more grain would be needed as early as 2020. How it is to be provided remains an unanswered question. A 2003 World Bank statement said: 'With an extra two billion people to feed over the next quarter-century, food production will have to double on less land and water.' But by 2004, grainland per person in the world had fallen by more than half since 1950, to about a tenth of a hectare, and the total had fallen to 670 million hectares from a peak of 730 million in 1981. USAID estimates the number of chronically malnourished people now at 800 million.[2] Much of that undernourishment involves protein deficiency, which is the most lethal form of starvation.

Starvation and lack of hope are almost guaranteed to generate extreme anger and resentment in any human being – even worse, it may incline them towards desperate measures to find a solution. This is why the advance of the world towards more and more disastrous food and water shortages is one of the 2030 drivers – in the event, it might turn out to be the most dangerous. Granted this, it becomes both necessary and politic to make adequate provision for all the world's people, and to do so sustainably.

However, this is not happening – the pressure we are putting on the environment is becoming increasingly damaging. Human influences are now changing the world's natural systems in ways that have not happened in half a million years. Such changes could 'switch the Earth system to modes of operation that might prove irreversible and less hospitable to humans and other life'; these changes, including those to climate, might happen quickly, perhaps within a decade.[3] In *Global Environment Outlook 3* – a massive and comprehensive document aimed primarily at policy-makers – the United Nations Environment Programme forecasts a bleak prospect for 2032, stressing the disastrous effect soil degradation could have on food supplies, and predicting severe water shortages affecting more than half the people of the world.[4] This report is quite clear on one point – only a massive move towards sustainable development can avert global disaster, and this will need 'political courage and innovating financing'.[5] More than a thousand experts contributed to the report, adding considerable authority to its view that the problems identified are fundamental and serious. While some farming methods are improving, most are currently not sustainable. The Worldwatch Institute commented in its *State of the World 2002* report: 'Farms have become more technologically sophisticated ... but they have become ecologically dysfunctional and socially destructive.'[6]

The fundamental problems are the loss and degradation of the very bases of life – the sparse layer of topsoil, and increasingly scarce fresh water – on which the existence of every living thing depends. The unhappy facts are that every year more than 20 billion tons of topsoil are lost through water and wind erosion, and millions of acres of arable land are destroyed by overcropping, waterlogging and salination. Two-thirds of all the world's arable land is damaged to some extent. One-third will be dangerously depleted by 2030 if this disastrous trend continues.

The 'green revolution' of the 1960s, heavily dependent on chemical insecticides and fertilizers, had virtually run its course by the turn of the millennium. While it produced more food and made some farmers richer, 'as a solution to global hunger it was an expensive failure. In most places it has widened the gap between rich and poor, has been the cause of social upheavals in peasant cultures ... and has caused widespread ecological problems.'[7] In what is perhaps one of the most significant areas, India, overuse of chemical fertilizers and depletion of ground-water has created major problems in the two largest grain producing states, the Punjab and Haryana. According to one Indian observer, 'The cultivable lands have become sick through over-application of fertilizers, and yet the government is still encouraging farmers to apply more of them. This is a hopelessly short-term solution.'[8] Severe famines, he predicted, were likely in the future, due to the fact that 'food security in India is precariously balanced'.

Population growth, intensive farming, drought, overcropping, inappropriate irrigation methods and increasing urbanization are all contributing to this problem. In Europe, soil compaction by heavy farm machinery can cause crop yields to fall by as much as 80 per cent, and affects 70 million acres of agricultural land.[9] Cities consume huge quantities of organic matter in the form of foods, paper and other packaging products, and this generates what is generally described, quite opaquely, as waste. Billions of humans are perfectly content to dispatch this 'waste' to deep burial in landfills or into the ocean via sewage disposal outfalls. What is being disposed of is the fuel of life – virtually irreplaceable organic material which, under more natural conditions, would return to the earth and so maintain the nutrient cycle. For more than a century, these aberrations have been 'corrected' through the massive application of artificial fertilizers, which in the long term degrade the soil, cause other environmental problems, and reduce the nutritional value and flavour of food.

The deserts, which make up about 12 per cent of the Earth's land surface, are getting bigger. Millions of Africans are at risk of starvation as a result.[10] Desertification threatens more than one-third of the African continent.[11] The largest desert, the Sahara, occupies almost all of a 1000-mile wide strip across the north of Africa. More than half of that third of the world that is arid is at risk.[12] Part of the tragedy is that this endangered land is home to more than 1 billion people. Twenty-five African countries, in which 200 million people live, are in a state of crisis, which is accelerating into major drought and famine. The relentless poverty in which these people live drives them to abuse poor soils to extract as much food from them as possible, and to remove the trees – the leaves to feed starving animals and, often enough, people – and the trunks and branches for firewood. Whole villages and towns in countries like Chad have been abandoned as billions of tons of sand drift southwards. The advance of the Sahara is not uniform – it is rapid during years of drought, arrested when there is high rainfall. And there is evidence that in many places local farmers are fighting effectively to keep their soil healthy with natural methods, for example, through greater use of animal manure and the planting of leguminous crops which fix nitrogen from the air and transfer it to the soil. Aid money devoted to such sustainable methods would be well spent, paying major dividends not only for the land but also for the people living on it.

China is fighting a major battle with the deserts encroaching from its west. A 2002 study estimated that just under one-third of China's land was affected, with more than 10,000 square kilometres of arable land being lost to sand every year.[13] China is short of arable land for its population size, and the threat of actual food shortages in the future still informs many of its policies. By

2005 villages 60 miles from Beijing had been overwhelmed by sand, with major dunes only 40 miles northwest of the capital.

Millions of acres elsewhere fall victim to erosion or salination because of overcropping, unsuitable cropping or overuse of water for irrigation. In India 7 million acres have been affected, 6 million in China and 4 million in Pakistan.[14] When forest is cleared to accommodate 'productive' farming, there can be some alarming consequences. Large areas of monoculture, such as wheat fields, are most prone to both wind and water erosion. Trees are an important factor in limiting flooding when heavy rain falls. The disastrous floods that regularly kill millions of people in Bangladesh are due substantially to the destruction of forests along the upper course of the Ganges River and its tributaries. In the arid southwestern region of the US, in Canada and in Australia, rising water tables have brought salt to the surface, so that nothing can grow. Such salination occurs in many parts of the world that are lying on ancient marine sediments, and is due mainly to overclearing of trees from the land.

The lines of battle are already being drawn for the water wars of the future. Due to population pressures, one estimate puts the number of people facing water stress at 3 billion by 2025. I can recall an Israeli minister of state telling me, 25 years ago in his office in the Knesset, the Israeli Parliament, that one of his most compelling concerns was the dwindling resource of water in the Middle East. 'Future wars,' he said, 'may be about water. They might not seem to be, but they will.' In 2001 the Israeli water commissioner, Shimon Tal, warned of the country's 'deepest and most severe water crisis', forecasting a need for 2 billion cubic metres by 2020. Of this, one-quarter would need to be desalinated. Israel began building mass production desalination plants in 2002, with the aim of providing a huge 250 million cubic metres via this method by 2005. Most fresh water in the region is in the long valley that includes the Kinneret – the Biblical Sea of Galilee – and the Jordan River, which peters out in the intensely salty waters of the Dead Sea. In these places I have seen for myself some of the causes of concern. At the Allenby Bridge near the

Jordanian border, the Jordan was no more than a mere trickle, which I was told was now normal. The Dead Sea was surrounded by wide verges of blinding white – salt deposited as the lake has steadily become smaller. That long, narrow lake, the Kinneret, is also dwindling. Late in 2002 it fell to 214.37 metres below sea level, a point at which permanent damage to water quality and the ecosystem became likely. One of the biggest canal systems in the world is proposed to link the Red Sea and the Dead Sea, at a cost of $3.9billion. Because the Dead Sea is 400 metres below sea level this will create an artificial 'river' which will drive electricity generators, which, in their turn, will power desalination plants.

While the ten nations dependent on the waters of the Nile now consult over its use, this cooperation is on uneasy terms at best. Ethiopia, in the upstream sector, wants more water, but Egypt will also need vast quantities more to service the New Valley Project, an ambitious system of canals and pumping stations which aims to quadruple the nation's habitable area by turning desert into farmland. The first such new area, at Toshka, close to Lake Nasser, will require more than 5 billion cubic metres a year, around 10 per cent of Egypt's current quota of Nile water. Worldwatch estimates see the population doubling in this region by 2025, resulting in intense competition for water.[15] According to Worldwatch, 'spreading water scarcity may soon translate into world food scarcity'. Water represents 'the most unappreciated of the global challenges of our time... Water tables are falling on every continent, rivers are draining dry before they reach the sea.' Tension is increasing between India and Pakistan over use of the Indus River waters, which Pakistan depends on for the world's largest irrigated area.

The world's available fresh water is quite limited and unevenly distributed. Of the quintillions of gallons in the sea and the polar icecaps, less than 2 per cent is available as fresh water. A billion people worldwide lack clean drinking water.[16] More than a billion will be living in countries facing an absolute water shortage by 2025.[17] China is spending $60 billion on a massive canal system to move water from the south to the north of the country. Its projected 3500 kilometres of waterways will be almost twice the length of the Grand Canal in its heyday. In 2005, Chinese Deputy-construction Minister Qiu Baoxing warned that 100 of China's 660 cities were facing a water supply crisis. One actually reached it when the water supply to the 9 million people of Harbin was shut off for five days because of dangerous river pollution. Seventy per cent of the water in China's rivers is too polluted to drink, and the problem is expected to intensify 'four to five times' as the population grows from 1.3 billion to a peak of 1.6 billion in 2030.

There is a huge natural reserve of fresh water that is at present unused – the 75 per cent locked up in polar ice, covering around 11 per cent of the world's land surface. The idea of moving icebergs to regions that are short of water has been investigated many times over the years. The problems of towing such large and unwieldy objects against adverse winds and currents will be solved when the water problem becomes compelling enough. One option is to 'mine' this water by melting the ice on site, and then transporting it, perhaps in semi submersible barges.

Desalination of seawater is a viable but expensive technology – more than 2 billion gallons of fresh water a day are produced in this way at around 3500 plants, mostly in the Middle East. The technologies are energy hungry – around 5MW of electricity per million litres a day produced – but they could become more useful if and when cheap, renewable energy forms are developed. At present desalination provides about one-quarter of 1 per cent of human water needs. The world's largest such facility is planned for Sydney, Australia, because of steady depletion of water reserves, another under construction in the West Australian city of Perth is to be powered by wind generators. Meanwhile, underground reserves of water – aquifers – are being depleted worldwide. In some of China's most productive land the water table is falling 5 feet (1.6 metres) a year, and in India water is being taken from the aquifers at a rate twice that of their recharge, making a drop in India's grain production of 25 per cent likely.[18] Aquifer depletion is not only causing water shortages for the 22 million people of the world's largest city – Mexico City – but is also resulting in massive and continuing damage to the city's infrastructure.

What, then, is needed? Here again, the remedies can be defined, but they will require much hard work and money, and considerable time. Sustainable means to arrest soil degradation and improve soil that is already damaged are well known, and need only money and effort if they are to be introduced extensively. Many are low technology, involving the planting of nitrogen-producing legumes, conservation and controlled use of animal manures, community composting, the restoration of forests and reductions in the need for fuel wood. Most rainwater runs uselessly into the oceans. The countries that are likely to suffer most from water famines need help to progressively increase their water storage capacity, and the solar powered pumps proposed as part of the Billion Artifacts programme canvassed in Chapter 26. Nations with very large fresh water reserves may feel an obligation to help those who do not – although this is not generally happening at the time of writing. Canada is the world's best endowed nation in terms of fresh water. Early in 1999 its House of Commons adopted a motion to ban water exports and, significantly, to avoid international treaties that might compel Canada to export water against her will. The international trade minister, Mr Sergio Marchi, commented: 'There is clearly a feeling across the land that not only is water important today, it will be doubly so tomorrow. We need to be extremely cautious about large extractions.'

Appreciation of the problems of the environment is, fortunately, growing, and some of the answers are already known, or are being investigated. Around the world, millions of people are recycling organic material in their compost bins or using worm farms. Thousands of cities, partly because they are running out of sites for landfill, are encouraging recycling by limiting their garbage collections, even providing households with free or subsidized compost makers. More than one-third of sewage sludge is returned to the land in Europe and the US. More and more farmers all over the world are understanding that it is in their interests to plant trees, conserve water and topsoil, and convert to an agriculture suited to their environment.

Agenda 21, the blueprint for action adopted at the Earth Summit in Rio de Janeiro in 1992, set out strategies to combat desertification, including soil conservation programmes, drought relief and afforestation.[19] However, actual achievement in world terms is still inadequate except in China, where massive tree-planting has mitigated, but not yet halted, the movement of sand eastwards from the dunes of the Gobi. According to a statement by the Chinese Ministry of Forestry in 1995 an Agenda 21 afforestion programme is flourishing.[20] China, almost completely denuded of trees when the People's Republic began 55 years ago, now has 19 per cent forest cover. The almost incredible forest programme – it is claimed 550 million people planted 44 billion trees between 1982 and 2004 – is driven by a directive for every Chinese person between the ages of 11 and 60 to plant at least 3 trees a year. In 2002 China announced a $12 billion project to plant 440,000 square kilometres of forest – an area bigger than Germany – over the next 10 years.

Tree planting programmes like this are helping to balance the loss of natural forests – FAO's forest resources assessment in 2000 estimated that world tree cover had diminished by about 9 million hectares a year in the last decade of Millennium 2. This represents a reduction of 2.4 per cent in existing world forest, covering almost 4 billion hectares, around one-third of global land area. Of the timber cut and used in the world – around 3.5 billion tons a year – rather more than half is burned in developing nations as fuel. Papermaking uses around one-quarter of a billion tons a year, although the real figure in terms of trees destroyed is greater. This is because wood chipping for paper and cardboard making is wasteful, much of the wood being discarded or burned. Large areas of forest are destroyed by slash and burn cultivators in the developing world, or by developers clearing new land for agriculture. This has reduced, in particular, the huge forests of the Amazon in South America. Such big 'development' projects have often been financed by the World Bank. FAO's 2005 report was disquieting – 50 thousand square miles of forest had been cleared or logged every year since 2000. The only bright spot was China's huge tree-planting programme, the largest in the world.

There is a real threat to the rainforests, which once covered 12 per cent of the world's land, but are now not much over 5 per cent and still falling. These forests nurture more than half of the world's species – gorillas, golden crested birds of paradise, the brilliant red fruit of the zebra wood tree of the Cameroons, teak, mahogany wood, thousands of different butterflies, sources of potentially valuable pharmaceuticals among them. More than 1500 rainforest plants have potential as vegetables and fruits not yet widely used. The sap of one Amazon basin tree, *Copaifera langsdorfia*, is so similar to diesel fuel that trucks can be run on it in its pure unprocessed form.

Within these watery, beautiful tangles of vegetation, which most people would recognize as 'jungle', and which have been evolving in one way or another for almost 200 million years, are assets we can only guess at. The circle of rainforest around the world is virtually all tropical, in regions that are almost constantly wet, with rainfall of more than 80 inches (2 metres) fairly consistently distributed through the year. Tall tree trunks reach up competitively for the sunlight at the canopy 150 feet (45 metres) above. Lower down, in perpetual shade, hundreds of different vines, lianas, shrubs and ferns struggle for space and nutrients. The basins of the Amazon and Zaire Rivers have the largest remaining areas of undisturbed rainforest – more than 5 million square kilometres – although even here significant inroads are being made by human clearing and burning.

Clearing of rainforest for agriculture and cattle ranching has been based on a tragic misconception – that the soil sustaining all this lush growth must be very fertile. This happens not to be the case. The topsoil is thin, the subsoil almost devoid of nutrients because of centuries of heavy rain leaching it. Almost all the nutrients are held in the plants and trees, and under natural conditions these are regularly recycled. The dense mat of roots which covers the entire forest floor holds this fragile soil together; falling leaves and dead plants sustain it. Brazil's emerging status as the world's agricultural superpower is prompting a rate of land clearing which, if continued, would destroy the Amazon rainforest totally in 50 years. Brazil is now the world's largest exporter of beef, coffee, orange juice and sugar, and its soy and fuel alcohol industries are booming. The world's rapidly growing need for more food can only drive this expansion of agriculture faster and faster – on the other hand destruction of the forest would have dire consequences for the world's climate. While in some areas clear felled rainforest will regenerate, in most areas it will not. A 1991–1998 study in the Gunung Palung rainforest in Indonesian Borneo showed that depletion of the forests resulted in virtually no new seedlings over that period.[21] This was because vast amounts of seed are eaten by birds and animals. This study concluded that only the prolific seeding from large areas of untouched forest could ensure that enough is left for new seedlings to emerge.

The loss of trees to farming is already provoking a disastrous natural backlash. More than 10 thousand people died when a cyclone struck the coast of the Indian state of Orissa late in 1999. Coming in from the Bay of Bengal with 200 mile per hour winds, the cyclone combined with high tides and torrential rain to flood flat country as far as 10 miles from the coast. This flooding was so extensive because the mangrove forests that had previously lined the coast had been cleared to make way for ponds to raise tiger prawns commercially.[22] An appalling loss of life caused by mudslides in coastal Venezuela was the result of forests being cleared from mountainsides, and the proliferation of slum housing on flat land below these slopes. In Thailand, in 1988, a sudden flood killed 450 people and damaged millions of dollars worth of property. When it became obvious that this was due to the clearing of steep hillsides for timber and for the establishment of rubber plantations, the Thai government imposed a ban on logging such areas.

The really destructive element of logging is that landless settlers follow logging roads into rainforest areas and complete the destruction of the forests for agricultural use – although this can only be short term. As with many other issues we have looked at, this one is complicated by major social and economic factors. The main threat to the rainforest is the population explosion in the regions in which it grows. Almost all of these people are likely to be landless and poverty stricken. The pressure they must exert on their environment is likely to be irresistible unless other means of livelihood can be provided. If significant areas of rainforest are to be preserved, the issues of poverty, landlessness and major population growth, already important in themselves, must be addressed effectively. This will plainly not be done quickly or easily, but the world does have the resources to do it. In the interim period, more large protected wilderness areas will be necessary. In view of the importance of the rainforest in maintaining potential genetic material of importance, the cost of establishing and maintaining these nature reserves should be shared on a global basis.

New technologies are emerging which provide workable and sustainable solutions. A natural process developed by an Australian company, Vermitech, uses a highly mechanized and automated system to expose sewage solids to the humble earthworm, converting them into a potent, odourless, natural fertilizer that returns all the nutrients to the earth. Vermitech systems can be adapted to treat sewage from units as small as a household or a camping ground to as large as whole cities. A $2.5 million project, approved by the New South Wales government early in 2000 to convert Sydney sewage, will employ 40 million worms. A second innovation is the product Driwater, which consists of 98 per cent water and 2 per cent biodegradable gel. Driwater conserves water and delivers it accurately to the roots of plants. It has made it possible to plant millions of trees in the Sahara Desert outside Cairo, and is increasingly being used in other desert areas and on hillsides that are too steep to be watered in any other way.

Human influences on the ecosystem have resulted in a faster rate of species loss than ever before – and there is no sign of this being reversed. It has been said that 99 per cent of all species that have ever lived are extinct, that the coming and going of life forms is normal. However, according to the World Conservation Union, the current extinction rate is '1000 to 10,000 times what it would naturally be', and is apparently increasing. The Union adds that the spread of 'alien, invasive species' to habitats not natural to them, and climate change, are aggravating the situation. Rivers and islands seem to be the parts of the Earth worst affected. According to the recently retired World Bank president, James Wolfensohn, particular attention needs to be given to the 'hotspots' – the 1.6 per cent of the planet's land surface that houses 60 per cent of its biodiversity.

The United Nations *Global Environment Outlook 3* considers that almost one-quarter of all mammals will be extinct by 2030. The World Wildlife Fund says that 'at present rates of extinction as much as 20 per cent of the world's species will be gone by 2030.' The fund lists human activity as the major cause. Animals facing extinction include the blue whale, most of the primates, and the black and white giant panda, whose numbers have dropped to less than 1000. The numbers of rhinoceros in the wild have dropped from 100,000 in 1960 to less than 2600 today – although there are some signs of recovery in black rhinoceros numbers. The situation is little better for plants. A 2002 survey of 400 scientists by the American Museum of Natural History concluded that about one-eighth of plant species face extinction – a rate of loss greater than at any time in history. Worldwatch calls it the greatest mass extinction since the dinosaurs perished 65 million years ago. A recurring theme in all these statements has been concern that the larger public are still not aware of the extent of what might yet come to be called the 2030 extinction, and as a result there is too little pressure on governments to control the rate of species loss.

The compelling need for some form of effective world government is discussed in Chapter 6. The current state of the ecosystem suggests the need for a world 'green' authority, to coordinate extensive reforestation, especially in desert fringe, rainforest and irrigation areas, to preserve species diversity, and to control soil loss, desert spread and salinity.

Regional plant nurseries to provide seedling trees for planting by individuals and community groups, world standards for irrigated areas, including controlled drip irrigation and planting of deep rooted trees, genetic engineering of food crops tolerant of high salt levels, continued encouragement of domestic composting of organic and human wastes where this is practicable – all these are achievable objectives, and if implemented on a large enough scale, would do much to reverse and correct the damage to the ecosystem. But the basic need is for radical changes in human behaviour. This will only be achieved when a significantly large number of humans understand what is at stake, and what might be done. Meanwhile, the odds for catastrophe are shortening with every day that passes.

OPTIMAL FUTURE HISTORY

- Identification of world trouble spots for famine, disease, land degradation, water shortage, so these things can be fixed by defined courses of action that make sense – based on adequate finance, sound technology and the work of professional experts.
- Agreed common and enforceable world policies to protect all aspects of the environment.
- A world debate on water policy, to work towards fair distribution of the world's fresh water resources.
- Research into and communication of methods for a post-oil agriculture that is sustainable, and which gives food quality and flavour a clear priority.
- Promotion, design research and funding for appropriate developing world technology.

CHAPTER 6

ONE WORLD?

Two minority gangs of thugs, wearing military uniforms, grievously oppress the nations they affect to govern. In Sudan their instruments are the irregulars known as the *janjaweed*, who have killed 200,000 people in the province of Darfur – men, women and children, even small babies are not spared – raped women indiscriminately and burned thousands of homes, driving more than two million people into exile and penury. In Burma the *junta* refused to accept the will of the people expressed in elections, still imprisons the woman who should be prime minister, shot down in thousands people who dared to protest, forced hundreds of others into slavery to work for the military and reduced a once wealthy country to one of the poorest in the world. These tyrannies are now well entrenched – 3 years and 15 years respectively. In spite of massive international disapproval both of these 'governments' persist in evil. Attempts to effectively control events in Darfur have been blocked in the UN Security Council by China, which does not want to lose its access to Sudanese oil. Burma is able to ignore sanctions against her because one country – again China – maintains trade and economic links.

Is there a need for an effective international authority, with police powers and the muscle to maintain a coherent and just body of world law? Ask the women of Darfur, the conscripted slaves of Burma – and for that matter the starved and stunted children of North Korea, denied the very means of life to maintain a privileged, heavily regimented minority in the capital, Pyongyang, supporting the military autocracy. And these are not the only 'rogue states', there is a long list of others and more crop up every year.

But even so, the majority of countries have some form of rule of law – so why can't we have it for the world? World anarchy is one of the most dangerous of the 2030 drivers – whether or not we can control it will have a profound effect on the history of the future. As more and more nations get nuclear weapons, and as the drivers force a steady decline in overall prosperity, the precarious balance of power in the world will become less effective. Less and less will be done for the starving and afflicted, there will be no coordinated care of the oceans and the air, the 'fortress' mentality in the dwindling populations of the West will become more entrenched. All of these things are bad, so it becomes necessary to consider – and carefully – whether, when and how a body of world law can become effective.

It certainly won't happen quickly – most considered thinking about world government suggests a slow, progressive evolution, a time during which nations surrender some of their powers by careful multilateral agreement. Plainly the world's major powers, Europe, the US, China, Japan, India and Russia, could scarcely entertain any other approach. But at present some are not even doing that. Opposition to the establishment of the International Criminal Court and other international agreements indicates that most of the world's biggest powers are against new global initiatives.

Nevertheless, the steady advance of the 2030 drivers will sharpen the alternatives for the big powers – to become self sufficient, heavily armed fortresses, or to undertake serious engagement with the problems of the planet as a whole. The point then arises that if the drivers proceed unchecked, no 'fortress' nation, no matter how wealthy and well armed, will be able to protect itself against the consequences of say, a global plague like

H5N1, extreme global warming or major contamination and a 'winter' resulting from large scale nuclear conflict or extensive air pollution. Readjustment of their policies at that point would surely prove expensive, painful and perhaps unsuccessful. A general worldview is needed now.

It is tempting to envisage a global community with a common language, in which people who are citizens of the world move freely around, allied more by common interests than nationality, taking peace and prosperity for granted. In many ways the stage is set for that, the technology is rapidly becoming available. There are, after all, no essential reasons against the extension of the rule of law from the national to the international scene. A society without crime, without dissension, is scarcely possible in terms of Axiom Two, but a reasonable global rule of law should not be out of reach. But do we really want to lose regional cultures and languages? Many of those participating in a lively debate on world government on the internet and elsewhere do not – or at least not yet. A unilaterally imposed world government would almost certainly offend Axiom One. Most of those who favour world government tend more towards a federation, allowing regional governments to deal with local matters.

If a comprehensive world authority could be achieved – even approached – before 2030, the trauma of the transitional stage could be greatly reduced. Such an authority might coordinate global standards for working conditions, wages, ecology, productive capacity and the use of energy; evolve a world law, running a world police to enforce that law and to control war, 'rogue' states and terrorism; and, not least, provide a check on the unfettered and less than responsible economic power of the multinationals. Perhaps we might give it a name, a little more specific and pointed than the United Nations – Oneworld.

At the end of World War II Albert Einstein urged the victorious Allies to set up a world government to avoid a nuclear arms race. He admitted he feared the tyranny of a world government – 'any government is certain to be evil to some extent'– but this would be 'preferable to the greater evil of wars'.[1] Princeton University primatologist, Alison Jolly, believes in a future human super organism, 'a highly structured global society in which the lives of everyone on the planet will become so interdependent that they may grow and develop with a common purpose'.[2] Our task now is to do what we can to influence the outcome, she says. The design will require somse sacrifices, 'nationalism and religious fanaticism, those twin enemies of cooperation, for starters'. Sociologist Anthony Giddens remarks: 'To me the goal is developing a cosmopolitan global society, based on ecologically acceptable principles, in which wealth generation and control of inequality are reconciled. I don't see this as wholly Utopian.'[3]

Can the United Nations evolve into Oneworld? Perhaps, in time. The World Commission on Environment and Development (commonly known as the Brundtland Commission) advocated this, saying: 'The UN, as the only intergovernmental organization with universal membership, should clearly be the locus for new institutional initiatives of a global character.'[4] However, the reality is that the United Nations is restricted by deliberate withholding of funds, the veto powers of Security Council members, and a naive and impracticable system of voting in the General Assembly where each nation, regardless of its size, gets one vote. The US, which accounts for 31 per cent of global income, was $1.3 billion in arrears in its dues to the UN in 2000. While most of this has been paid since, the US persists in paying its dues ten months, or even a year, late, using this financial weapon to urge changes in the world body. Governments ignore the International Court of Justice at will – this means among other things, that crimes against humanity, as in Sudan, cannot be prosecuted effectively. The UN, nevertheless, has established agencies that have a global reach, and although these have been much criticized, often justly enough, they have assembled a vast volume of experience and expertise, and a dedicated staff who are well aware of world problems.

The difficulties of a single central issue – the eventual surrender by nation states of the right to make war, and to depend instead on world policing – are immense, and would take much time to overcome. US President George W Bush stated that 'the American way of life is not negotiable', and yet that way of life is so plainly based on inequality and an unfairly large share of the world's resources. Such a philosophy, when held in a world that also witnesses events as awful as the attack on the World Trade Center, and the ensuing 'war against terror' serves to suggest that violence such as suicide bombings and subsequent armed retaliation by nation states are likely to become a regular, rather than an occasional, part of life. But do the ordinary people of the US, Britain and Australia, want this, even after the intense propaganda conditioning their governments have subjected them to?

There are plenty of other controversial areas – whether the nation state is outdated, whether special taxes should be imposed on the developed world to effectively assist the least advantaged, whether there ought to be massive population transfers between the rich and poor regions. All these ideas have their adherents in varying degrees.

It does seem reasonable that Oneworld should evolve within a federal system, in which present day nations remain responsible for their internal affairs, provided these conform with world law. Many national boundaries, however, need adjustment in the interest of avoiding future conflict. The Afghan–Pakistan border divides the Pashtun people; there is strong justification for a Kurdish state; the conflict between the Tamils and Sinhalese in Sri Lanka may perhaps only be brought to an end by dividing the island into two states. These are only a few of many frontier anomalies, most of them the result of boundaries having been set by the colonial powers and inherited by independent successor states. Modern adjustments, which would prove difficult in any case, would only be acceptable if they complied with Axiom One. This would almost certainly only be possible through the good offices of a world authority.

Oneworld's most important function would be to maintain global peace, but it could also set standards for human rights, transparent government and reasonably equal opportunities for economic and educational advancement. This would leave local government and domestic issues to regions, which might be much smaller than the nations of today, ensuring, among other things, that individual cultures were not smothered by a global monolith, and that racial minorities were protected and allowed the right of self determination.

Oneworld would need specialized agencies, dealing among other things with science, genetic engineering and the sea. There is a clear need for a balancing global economic authority, with political and policing powers covering the entire planet. These areas are dealt with in more detail in other chapters but one example can be canvassed here – that of maritime flags of convenience. A number of small countries that have little merchant shipping of their own allow shipowners of other nations to register their fleets there – often this is done to avoid the home country's regulations on shipping safety, manning, wages and working conditions. Approximately 70 per cent of the world's merchant shipping is registered in countries other than the one where they are owned. The International Transport Workers' Federation claims that flags of convenience ships are twice as likely to sink than others, that crews are recruited in countries like the Philippines where poverty is extreme, that these crews will be blacklisted if they complain about conditions such as long working hours, poor food and ship safety. Ships and crews are said to be generally underinsured or not insured. Attempts to bring these irregularities under control have been made for many years, but there has been little progress, due to the lack of an effective world authority. If the world does resort to nuclear powered cargo and passenger ships, this questionable approach to safety could make disasters and severe ocean contamination inevitable.

It is a curious irony that there is a global economic authority which, however, is widely accused of conniving in multinational domination of the world rather than seeking to balance it. This is the World Trade Organization, the target of massive and furious opposition from all parts of the planet. Formed in 1995, it describes its objective as to 'help trade flow smoothly, freely, fairly and predictably'.[5] The World Trade Organization has 148 member nations, with almost 30 more seeking entry, allowing it to influence 97 per cent of world trade. On its own account it claims to operate on a consensus basis, but how this is achieved is cast into doubt by the fact that all negotiations are held in secret. The major point about the World Trade Organization in this context is the fact of its existence and its considerable global influence. If the nations of the world can get together over trade they should be able to work together for other global objectives, hopefully with less controversy than the World Trade Organization attracts. But given this, how do we avoid cumbersome, even tyrannical bureaucracies? This issue makes the institution of global referenda attractive. These, administered by an elected independent Consultation Commission, could set broad lines of policy, and provide effective checks and balances through mechanisms that could put controversial bureaucratic decisions to the vote if sufficiently large world citizen petitions required this.

How would an effective Oneworld work? Think back briefly to the cases at the beginning of this chapter. The crimes in Darfur and Burma would clearly be against world law. Given evidence, and there is plenty of that in both cases, a World Court would issue warrants. The World Police would then enter the country concerned and restore legality – as other police do, by force if necessary. If crimes against humanity had occurred, they would arrest those responsible. It is unlikely that this would have to happen more than once or twice. Once 'rogue' governments knew they were on notice for their crimes, they would change their ways quickly. It is only world anarchy, and the enthroning of the principle of 'nationalism' as a sacred cow, that let them get away with it now.

Nationalism has recently indeed had a bad track record. The world learned a new and unpleasant phrase late in the 20th century – ethnic cleansing. In 1994 in the African nation of Rwanda, a carefully planned pattern of mass killing of the minority Tutsi people by elements of the Hutu government resulted in the murder of 800,000 people. In Cambodia during 4 nightmare years of Khmer Rouge government from 1975, more than 1.5 million were killed in a frenzy of 'class struggle'.

In 1946, the first international tribunal designed to deal with such crimes was established – the court at Nuremberg after the Nazi holocaust against the Jews. Thus was introduced the principle of crimes against humanity, in the words of Geoffrey Robertson, 'the logic that future state agents who authorized torture or genocide against their own populations, were criminally responsible, in international law, and might be punished by any court capable of catching them'.[6] However, again in Robertson's words, 'the movement for global justice has been a struggle against sovereignty'. The human rights issue remains controversial into Millennium 3, with little agreement on what human rights might be, or how they should be enforced. When 120 nations voted in Rome in 1998 for an International Criminal Court to punish those violating 'fundamental freedoms', the world's four largest nations, China, India, the US and Indonesia, opposed it and continued to do so when it was ratified by 66 countries and established on 1 July 2002.

Not surprisingly, a large number of people and organizations are thinking about possible world government. There are numerous websites claiming that a shadowy conspiracy already exists for a sinister world dictatorship. All sorts of candidates are proposed – Jews, Chinese, black people, multinationals, churches, to name but a few. High on the list is the Bilderberg Group, a secretive collection of politicians, businessmen and princes formed 50 years ago to consider world events. This group, without doubt extremely influential, is closed to the media and is unwilling to disclose the result of its deliberations. It has been accused of planning world government, its farthest-out critics claiming it is controlled by intergalactic lizards!

The chief anxiety is that the world state could be authoritarian, and not necessarily benevolent. Since there are plenty of precedents for this in the nation states – 120 states torture people systematically – this fear is far from irrational.[7] But at least in the case of rogue nations it has sometimes been possible to escape elsewhere. There could be no escape from an oppressive world government.

Both axioms, then, suggest a gradual and cautious approach. The early stages could involve globalizing segments of existing national authority – such things as the coordination of energy resources, the development of a code of conduct for multinationals, a reduction in spending on weapons, and the transformation of war industries to the production of things we really do need, like alternative energy infrastructure. The evolution of *de facto* world 'zones' by 2030 is likely – Europe, the Americas, Russia/China/East Asia are fairly obvious early candidates. A practical working relationship between these zones, however wary, must be preferable to hostility and the threat of war.

Oneworld's initial powers would ideally be agreed by consensus, preferably after consulting the people of the participating states by electronic referenda. Of interest are the comments of IBM chairman Lou Gerster, envisioning a day 'when issues are presented to all the people of the world and we vote as a global statement of individual preference without regard for conventions like political parties or national boundaries', while executive director of the Campaign for Digital Democracy, Marc Strassman, foresees 'a global aggregation and merging of like minded individuals and groups to form global parties', which 'would eventually undermine the authority of nation states'.[8] The idea that human society may become more like an integrated organism, and that this is controversial, is conceded by artificial intelligence researcher Francis Heylighen.[9] Nevertheless, he believes that a 'global brain' will develop, and that the internet is its embryo. If we accept that developments along these lines are possible, it becomes no more than an assumption that national cultures, traditions and languages can continue in the long term.

Universal teaching of a world language could be a preparatory step to a process of peaceful transition. Such a world language exists. Esperanto[10] is now spoken by more than 100,000 people in 83 countries. Its main disadvantage is that its words derive from European languages, although this could readily be modified. Otherwise it has many advantages. Words are pronounced as they are spelled, grammar is consistent, verbs are regular. Meanwhile English, estimated to be understood by 1 billion people worldwide, remains an obvious contender for world language status – a consideration which must suggest its revision to simpler and more consistent spelling and grammatical forms, and the continued evolution of 'quasi English' dialects such as Papua

New Guinea pidgin. Nevertheless, the language most commonly and fluently used is Mandarin Chinese, with over 1 billion speakers.

Oneworld would need to have the means to enforce the law. This would not necessarily involve an immediate surrender of all armed force by nation states. They would, however, eventually have to accept that the only major armed force would be that of the world government, while local police forces would continue to deal with internal crime. Professional soldiers from all nation states could enlist in this world police, and reasonable quantities of armaments would still need to be purchased, thus satisfying Axiom One. Control and direction of this force would be a major test of the ability of nations to work together. It would somehow have to reconcile two apparently opposed requirements – the need for international agreement on action, and the need for the armed force to act quickly in emergency situations. It was the failure of the United Nations to achieve this that contributed to the Rwandan tragedy.

The answer might be a previously agreed and detailed code of action, possibly along these lines: offending states would attract an established and escalating series of sanctions. Trade sanctions could be an initial penalty – they would be the more effective if imposed by all other governments. If these failed, the second level of penalty could be military measures to disable services rather than to destroy infrastructure or to injure or kill people. Ultimately, commando forces could have the power to enter a nation state, arrest offending government officials, and maintain a *de facto* authority until the people of the state could be consulted about their future.

Oneworld would need its own financial resources, and should not be dependent on voluntary contributions from member states. This became evident when, late in 1999, nations contributing to the United Nations owed it $3 billion in unpaid dues. Since one of its major activities would be dealing with multinationals, and evolving areas of world law covering their operations, a small tax on their turnover, allowing no deductible items, would seem appropriate. However, Oneworld could well be in the business of servicing, from which it would derive an income. International trade, tourism and promotion of new technology seem obvious areas. The World Commission on Environment and Development put forward another interesting possibility, 'revenue from the use of international commons, from ocean fishing and transportation, from seabed mining, from Antarctic resources, or from parking charges for geo-stationary satellites', also suggesting taxes on international trade.

OPTIMAL FUTURE HISTORY

- An international convention to devise changes that would give the UN real power as a world force, and define areas where nation states could initially surrender powers such as control of shipping, fisheries, genetic engineering, clean air and clean seas, to the world authority. Eventual authority of world government and world law.
- Turn swords into ploughshares – gradual multilateral evolution of annual reductions of all armed forces in the world, with particular reference to eliminating nuclear weapons, and the allocation of funds saved to the world authority for constructive purposes like alternate energy, poverty alleviation and disease control.
- Evolution of a body of world law, and a world police to enforce it.
- Development of a simple, easily learned world language, to be taught in all schools.
- Massive international exchange of young people as teachers, technicians, students and artists.
- Extensive development of internet 'communities', such as consumer organizations and experts of all kinds.
- Massive nagging, by email, mail and telephone, of those in authority, by people, to see these things get done. This means you!

CHAPTER 7

THE FOURTH HORSEMAN

Be warned. Much of what is in this chapter about war and weapons is unpleasant and frightening – nevertheless they are things you really need to know. But first, some good news. According to *War and Peace in the 21st Century*, by Professor Andrew Mack, of the Human Security Center in Vancouver, there has been a considerable decrease in the number of regional conflicts since the end of the Cold War. And a little publicized event of great importance took place late in 2005, when US president George W Bush removed funding for a new kind of nuclear weapon, the Robust Nuclear Earth Penetrator, so ending the programme, at least for the time being. It is tempting to hope that this may mark the beginning of a withdrawal from atomic weapons, and their eventual abolition. If you wonder whether this is prudent or necessary, remember that extinction of the human race remains an active possibility. All it would take would be the detonation of less than half the nuclear weapons now in the world, and a deadly cloud would extend to every corner of the globe and kill most of us from radiation sickness. The rest would succumb to famine as the sun dimmed and photosynthesis stopped. Our art, our buildings, our bridges and roads would crumble and return to the forests, our languages, writing and music would be forgotten, as indeed would be the human race, as if it had never existed.

This apocalyptic vision describes something that is possible – and soon. It indicates a need to consider the consequences of war coolly and rationally, with emotive issues like racial integrity, nationhood, ethnic cleansing, belief in religious exclusivity and narrow 'patriotism' resolutely discounted.

But plainly, reducing weaponry and limiting war will not be easy. Is it, indeed, possible? 'We have remained individually too greedy to distribute the surplus above our simple needs, and collectively too stupid to pile it up in any more useful form than the traditional mountains of arms.'[1] Jacob Bronowski's words remain as true of the human condition now as they were when they were written half a century ago.

The early years of Millennium 3 brought new and dangerous implications of war. The killing of almost 3000 people in New York's World Trade Center towers on 11 September 2001 revealed new kinds of enemies with which 21st century military forces seemed ill equipped to deal. Subsequent hostilities in Afghanistan and Iraq brought new and frightening weapons into prominence – among them devastating and controversial incendiary weapons of almost unimaginable ferocity, and aerial bombs each of which spawn 200 'bomblets' exploding into hundreds of fragments of shrapnel.

Are these kinds of weapons the ideal way to deal with the situation? The fact that 'the war against terror', according to most estimates, has killed more innocent Afghan and Iraqi civilians than combatants, at a time when many civilians were dying in Palestine, has led most of the world's 1.3 billion Muslims to see it as a war against Islam, and it is possible that a significant proportion of the world's population see it as a war against the poor. Whether either of these perceptions is rational or justifiable is beside the point – the evidence that they exist is so massive that they must be taken seriously. Given this situation, perhaps the most potent weapons in 'the war against terror' might not be military ones at all. Social and economic measures, designed to alleviate the poverty and despair afflicting the majority of humans, could prove far more effective. Speaking at a world forum on poverty in 2005 Pakistani President Pervez Mushurraf remarked: 'We are only involved at the moment in fighting terrorism frontally, the military perspective, the immediate response. But we are not addressing the root causes ... political disputes, poverty and illiteracy. '

During the closing decades of Millennium 2, armed forces were used increasingly in peacekeeping roles, and there was an appreciable reduction in the number of atomic weapons deployed. Even so there were still 27,000 in existence in 2005. An agreement concluded between Presidents Bush and Putin in 2002 proposes a reduction to around 4000 deployed by 2012 – a quantity still able to destroy all life on Earth many times over. Weapons withdrawn from deployment will, however, be stored rather than destroyed. This agreement appeared to exclude so called 'tactical' weapons, the numbers of which are estimated at between 5000 and 20,000. These, in the form of artillery shells, aircraft bombs and landmines, range in destructiveness from the equivalent of 100 tons of TNT to 50 times that of the 1945 Hiroshima bomb.

The *de facto* renunciation by the world's five major nuclear states – the US, the UK, Russia, China and France – of their obligations under the Nuclear Non-proliferation Treaty is a cause for major concern. More countries signed this treaty 36 years ago than any other international agreement – only India, Pakistan and Israel refused. It obliged nations without nuclear arms not to make them, and those with them to get rid of them. At the five-yearly review conference of the treaty in 2005 the US made it plain that, while it expected other nations, specifically Iran and North Korea, to abide by the treaty, it was not prepared to do so itself. In 1995, 173 nations agreed to reject nuclear weapons if the 'big five' agreed to work towards total elimination of their nuclear arsenals. Ten years later they have not done so. This 'double standard' is why there are still so many nuclear weapons in the world, and why, according to the British MI5 in a 2005 document *Companies and Organisations of Proliferation Concern,* at least 360 private companies, and government and tertiary organizations in 8 countries have bought goods or technology to make nuclear weapons.

Several recent events seem likely to guarantee their perpetuation. In January 2000, the Russian government indicated changes in its military doctrine which, for the first time, gave notice that it would use nuclear weapons when other methods had proved unsuccessful and not, as previously, only when the survival of the state was threatened. In 2002, a US Pentagon report to Congress indicated a dramatic increase in contingencies in which the US plans to use nuclear weapons.[3] Seven nations, including Russia and China, were named as potential nuclear targets. One nuclear arms specialist said the US shifting position on 'limited use' of nuclear weapons was encouraging other nations, like India and Pakistan, to consider them as part of their regular arsenal.[4] He commented: 'The Bush administration is reinvigorating the nuclear weapons force and the vast research and industrial complex that supports it.' In October 1999 the US Senate rejected the comprehensive nuclear test ban treaty, so signalling a renewed long-term escalation in atomic weapons. US plans to build a national missile defence system were widely regarded around the world as a contributor to a renewed arms race – 'a nuclear chain reaction among nations'.[5]

Nuclear arsenals represent such a serious threat to life – even to civilization – because of a 'modernized' array of specialized weapons, such as the neutron bomb, improvements in delivery systems, and the availability of atomic weapons to more and more states, including some in the 'rogue' category. A conference in Stockholm late in 2001 reported that a disturbing amount of the world's 4000 tons of weapons grade uranium and plutonium is going missing, that internal security over nuclear materials is generally lax, border controls inefficient, and that it would be relatively easy for terrorist groups to acquire radioactive materials.[6] Huge quantities of weapons grade material in the former Soviet Union – more than 600 tons – are the most vulnerable.

The problem of eliminating nuclear weapons is intimately associated with issues of security – even survival – in several parts of the world. The position of Israel, surrounded by Islamic enemies, is perhaps particularly eloquent. This small country of 6.3 million persons has built up a nuclear deterrent capability approaching Britain's – at least 100 bombs capable of being delivered up to 1100 miles by its Black air squadrons and Jericho 1 and 2 missiles – as a threat to any who may consider an all out attack on its territory. Pakistan fears India, therefore both countries are increasing their nuclear capability. China and the US, global rivals in spite of the rhetoric, are building up their nuclear armouries for the same kind of reasons. North Korea, distrustful of the US, is believed to have as many as ten nuclear weapons, and the capability to build more.

The 'refinement' of nuclear weaponry, that is, missiles designed for specialized purposes, appears to have been a reaction by planners to the perception that unspecialized weapons, especially hydrogen bombs, represent a chilling degree of overkill, with likely consequences, such as 'nuclear winters', that must rebound on those who use them. Something 'better' seemed necessary. What about, for instance, something that would kill everyone in a city, but leave it largely intact so it could easily be taken over later? Such a weapon would have to be designed to do minimal damage to infrastructure, have limited residual radiation, but be lethal over wide areas. Although it has had little publicity over recent decades, the enhanced radiation warhead, or neutron bomb, which does just this, is very much alive and well. These weapons, effectively small hydrogen bombs, are specialized so as to emit relatively small amounts of heat and destructive blast together with large amounts of deadly, but short-lived radiation.

Neutron bombing of cities, however, would have effects that are far from surgical neatness. It would result in millions of painful, undignified and unassisted deaths from radiation sickness, protracted over one to three weeks. Details of the bomb's effects are highly secret wherever it has been developed – and that is, probably, within all the nuclear powers. It is a matter of record that the US suspended development of the neutron bomb in 1978, but resumed it in 1981. China revealed in 1999 that it is developing it – it was stated to be among the nuclear secrets China had 'stolen' from the US, although China has denied this – and according to a recent statement by one of its scientists, India has the capability to build a neutron bomb.[7] According to antinuclear activist Helen Caldicott, the US is devoting $45 billion over the next 10–15 years to design, build and test new nuclear weapons.[8] Much of the emphasis will be on 'faster, stealthier, longer range delivery platforms, fully integrated into a 21st century "battlefield" controlled by satellite surveillance, remotely deployed sensor arrays and precision targeting'. According to Caldicott, England, France, China and Russia are already following a similar course, the British government in 2005 announcing a near tripling in funding of its Atomic Weapons Establishment at Aldermaston to more than £800 million by 2007. Caldicott believes 'within a decade, 10 more nations will have developed nuclear weapons, and, within 20 years, there will be nuclear war'. If this happens, it will largely be a war against people by machines, with no capacity for pity or mercy.

The increasingly dangerous proliferation of nuclear weapons is of course, closely associated with the nuclear power industry, which has produced as a by-product much of the world's 1855 tonnes of plutonium – enough to fuel almost half a million atomic bombs. This 'usefulness' to the weapons industry is without doubt the reason why governments have subsidized and protected the nuclear power industry, in spite of its dangers and inefficiencies. This deadly partnership, which continues to place the entire world and its inhabitants at risk, could probably only be checked by a Oneworld agency militarily strong enough to guarantee the security of individual states, and at least an approach towards this is needed before 2030. If not, it is more than possible that it will finally be an experience of nuclear war that shocks the remnants of humankind into a serious attempt at effective disarmament and world government.

If this does not sound forbidding enough, there are biological weapons. Perhaps most terrifying is the possibility that before 2030, genetic engineering will allow weapons to be developed that can kill only specific ethnic groups. This would mean that the main strategic argument against biological weapons – the likelihood that they could rebound on the user – would be removed.[9] Ironically, these 'designer diseases' could evolve as a spin-off from research into controlling cancer by identifying 'marker' genes on diseased cells, which can then be targeted while normal surrounding cells are not affected. Research on the human genome has already shown that ethnic groups can have distinctive 'marker' genes, making possible the development of disease weapons which would attack only those groups with the designated marker. The possibility of virus diseases being adapted to become almost universally lethal emerged in 2001 when a gene modification that greatly increases the amount of interleukin 4 in the body yielded an unexpected result – it totally suppressed the part of the immune system that protects against viral infection.

As many as 2.5 million Americans in uniform are being given vaccines against anthrax. Anthrax is normally communicated by contact between animals, or between animals and humans. As a biological weapon it would be dropped over armies or cities as an aerosol, or, as happened in the US in 2001, as a white powder sent in the mail. Everyone breathing it in would be infected. Its deadly spores can remain in the soil for as long as 40 years. In 1988, the Soviet Union attempted to destroy a stockpile of many tons of anthrax bacteria by soaking them in hydrogen peroxide, and then putting them into storage at an abandoned biological research station on Vozrozhdenuye Island in the Aral Sea, 1000 miles east of Moscow. Recent testing by US scientists given access to the stockpile showed that in spite of all attempts to render it harmless, many of the anthrax spores were still alive, with the potential to escape into the environment.

Former Soviet germ weapons specialist, Dr Kanatjan Alibekov, identified anthrax specially developed to be unusually virulent, a strain of plague resistant to antibiotics, botulism, smallpox and encephalitis as being among the disease weapons still under development by Russia as late as 1992.[10] In spite of an agreement with the US in 1972 not to develop biological weapons, the Soviet Union persisted with a major and secret programme during the

1980s. This included genetic modification of existing diseases to make them incurable and almost universally lethal. After the breakup of the Soviet Union and the economic difficulties that followed, almost all of the 25,000 scientists who specialized in biological warfare became unemployed. The whereabouts of many of them is unknown.

The idea that aerial bombing is now a precise science, using 'smart' weapons that can select targets with surgical precision, was heavily propagandized during the 1991 American war with Iraq – Operation Desert Storm. According to one writer, John Pilger, only 7 per cent of the 88,500 tons of bombs dropped were 'smart'.[11] Seventy per cent, mostly old fashioned 'dump' bombs, missed military targets and fell in populated areas, such as the strike on the Al-Amiriya bunker in Baghdad, in which 300 people, mostly women and children, were incinerated. According to one source, up to 250,000 Iraqis were killed in the American assault. Many were soldiers buried alive in their trenches by armoured bulldozers.[12] These machines are the forerunners of a totally new army of robots planned by the US which 'would give our forces concentrated lethality, available immediately', and which could be deployed by 2010.[13] Try and see past the Newspeak. That really means: 'Our forces will be able to kill far more people than ever before, without warning.' The nature of these metre high robotic soldiers, which go by the acronym of SWORDS, was revealed in 2005. They are mounted on tank tracks, have night vision, and mount automatic weapons able to fire more than 300 rounds a minute. Their efficiency is quite deadly – in quick firing tests they scored 70 out of a possible 70 bull's eyes.

It would therefore appear that our world faces potential military horrors which no reasonable person can consider acceptable. Almost any effort, almost any sacrifice, seems justifiable to achieve world disarmament and, especially, effective control of weapons designed for the mass killing of populations. The position of the arms manufacturers is central. Somehow, the power of the military industrial complex must be redirected to peaceful ends, and the uncontrolled supply of arms to whoever will pay for them must cease, since large numbers go to criminal and quasi-criminal interests and to those who want guns to terrorize and oppress their own people. 'There are 500 million illegally acquired guns and light weapons around the world, in the hands of everyone from child soldiers in Sierra Leone to drug traffickers in Colombia.'[14] This situation is made no better by the fact that the world's largest countries, including the 'democracies', are the major arms pedlars. The US was the largest provider, selling $12 billion worth of arms, almost half the world total, in 2005, with Russia next, at $5.8 billion.[15]

What do the war machines cost the world? The most conservative estimates are around a trillion dollars a year, almost half of this spent in the US: $421 billion in 2005, with plans for this to rise to $451 billion in 2007, according to the Center for Defense Information. The argument has been advanced that defence spending is justified because overproductive economies need an area of 'waste' outside the economy of supply and demand, to balance them. The huge costs of space research are seen as another such 'balance wheel'. Even if we accept the need for these 'balance wheels', it can be argued, just as persuasively, that this money could be more usefully devoted to a fund to combat world poverty, or to develop alternative energy systems. This issue is discussed further in Chapter 26.

The question of the cost of war cannot be left without a consideration of the cheapest and most prolific weapon of all – the estimated 200 million landmines which infest the world, and which every year cause thousands of deaths, and many more thousands of serious injuries, usually involving the loss of a limb. Children are probably the most numerous victims. In Cambodia alone there are 35,000 amputees as a result of landmines – the world figure is over a quarter of a million. Death and injury are not the only consequences of these weapons. Large tracts of agricultural land become unusable because they are too dangerous to enter. Mines cost only a few dollars to make, but it costs between $300 and $1000 to render each one safe and remove it. Modern developments, such as the plastic bodied mine, aggravate the difficulties of making them safe because they cannot be located by metal detectors. Hundreds of compassionate and courageous people are working to deactivate landmines, but with the facilities and technology now available it would take 1000 years and $33 billion to clear all the existing mines. Meanwhile, every year, between 5 and 10 million more are produced.

It is now considerably safer to be a soldier than a civilian in a war zone. The proportion of civilians killed grew from 52 per cent of all war deaths during World War II to 84 per cent during regional wars at the close of Millennium 2. In an article about the future of war, General Wesley Clark, who commanded Operation Allied Force in Kosovo, conceded that war has become potentially more lethal, and predicted that 'political restraints will be relaxed, and control of the actions will be delegated to on scene commanders. Unfortunately, significantly greater casualty rates can be expected among both military and civilian populations.'[16] However, he also remarked that due to 'global village' concepts 'war is increasingly constrained by law and the public's assessment of just causes and acceptable costs' and that there is also the option of a cyber war, able to 'scramble an enemy's military command or disrupt electricity systems without bloodshed'. Weapons researchers are currently developing the E-bomb, a device that produces a momentary flash of microwaves or radio waves powerful enough to disrupt or destroy the electronic systems on which almost all modern machines – military and civil – rely. Computers are especially vulnerable, and damage to them would generally be permanent. By 2005 it had become apparent that such weapons are feasible, relatively cheap and easy to produce. There also seem to be no possible mechanisms to control their proliferation. Being non-lethal, they will also attract less public fear and disapproval. Also under investigation is a microwave cannon, designed to inflict severe pain, but not to kill. Stun lasers are also being developed.

Behind war lie some of the most complex and destructive aspects of human nature – insecurity, an overweening desire for power, greed, nationalism, selfishness, a chilling lack of compassion, and the opportunity for warped mentalities to indulge in what would be unspeakable crimes within any normal rule of law. Those items might be regarded as fuel for the fire, but the match that so reliably lights it may come from a particular form of aggression, associated with a pleasure in killing, experienced by a minority of men. This is an area most people do not want to know about, but if it is close to the truth, careful thought is needed about just how extensive this pleasurable killing pattern is, who has it, and why.

Murders by people who take pleasure in killing and torturing their victims – often women – occur regularly all over the world. Is it then not reasonable to assume that armies, which are a cross section of society, also include such people? A highly controversial book by English scholar, Dr Joanna Bourke, indicates that this is so.[17] During her research, Bourke studied the large numbers of letters and diaries written by soldiers, held in the Imperial War Museum, and found in them many accounts of an intense pleasure at the time of killing. To stick someone with a bayonet, for example, was described as 'gorgeously satisfying'. A careful study of the history of conflicts, such as those in Bosnia, Rwanda and Cambodia, suggests that quite small minorities of humans plan and start them. The activities of these people in a normal state ruled by law would be regarded as criminal. They would be arrested and punished before their plans could become as destructive as they were in those regions.

If some kind of control mechanism does not exist, then indeed the fire can spread. Hence it is not enough to turn one's back on the fact that deliberate killers who find pleasure in murder exist. We now come into violently controversial territory. To what extent are such people the 'spark plugs' that fire up major wars and massacres? Should we attempt to influence this area, and seek the means of correcting the situation? Is it a genetic trait, which humanity should seek to eliminate? Is it, as has been suggested, associated with excessively high testosterone levels? Several studies of prisoners have shown an association of high plasma testosterone with chronic aggressive behaviour and with violent rape, but there seems no certainty of such a connection in the general community.

Most importantly, does such a 'killing class' exist? University of Iowa psychiatrist, Donald Black, believes it does, that it is different from the normal run of humans, and that its character-istics can be defined.[18] This 'antisocial mind', which results in cold blooded, depraved crime, is found in individuals who have had a lifelong pattern of bad behaviour, a willingness to break rules and hurt others, a lack of remorse and empathy towards others, and no sense of responsibility or guilt. The pattern is likely to have been manifest since childhood. Black estimated that there are probably 7 million Americans with this psychiatric condition, around 90 per cent of them men, and it is reasonable to conclude that they are just as numerous elsewhere. They seldom seek treatment, since they believe there is nothing wrong with them. Since men with this condition might well be attracted to military life, where they may find themselves free to indulge in atrocities against the civilians of an occupied country, a filtering mechanism which would ensure they did not become soldiers could be necessary.

Konrad Lorenz has shown that reasonable control of aggression is a major social bond for a wide range of species, including man.[19] Considering its potential, this control is one of the highest and most important attributes of a species. Its extension to abolish war must be an important area of study and action. However, there is nothing new about humans killing each other. Indeed we are the only species – except for rats in some circumstances – that kills its own kind in such numbers. Efficient modern societies have been able to control this powerful and unpleasant human quality, at least to tolerable levels within their own borders, through the rule of law. This law does not succeed only because of the sanctions it can force on individuals, but because the overwhelming majority of humans are 'law abiding' – they accept the rule of law, and allow it to override their basic aggressive and acquisitive instincts, because of perceived advantages in this to society as a whole and to them in particular.

When a husband travels home from his workplace in the evening, he can be confident that his house has not been sacked and burned, his wife has not been raped, and his children have not been murdered. Like all human institutions, the rule of law does not operate perfectly. An office worker might well come home one day and find that some of these unpleasant possibilities have happened. Crime continues to exist, but, in general, it is contained to the extent that most people can feel reasonably secure as they go about their day-to-day activities. Why, then, does this not happen outside national boundaries? What are the reasons for a significant majority of Londoners normally accepting that it would be wrong to bomb Oxford, Edinburgh or Cardiff, while at the same time considering that to do so to Paris, Berlin, Tokyo or Beijing in certain circumstances would not only be perfectly all right, but even laudable?

The answer to this is primarily nationalism – the idea that humans must be arbitrarily split up into regional groups who have linguistic and cultural differences that are so important that they justify dying for, in millions if necessary, and killing other people – women, children, even babies – in the most unpleasantly possible ways, such as burning to death, a normal consequence of aerial bombing.

Looked at coolly and rationally, in the 'global village', this concept must appear increasingly dangerous and absurd. War has traditionally been furthered by what is called 'patriotism', which means a belief that your segment of the human race is superior in all respects to the others. There can be no doubt that war has brought the most unselfish sacrifices from the many young men called upon to fight, and in no way should such heroism and devotion be undervalued. The tragedy is that almost invariably it has been betrayed by the ignoble purposes of those who committed their community to war, and who, for the most part, emerged from it unscathed and a good deal wealthier than when they went in.

These people have always touted patriotism as one of the highest human virtues. So it would be if it were directed to the human race as a whole – better still, to the planet as a whole.

OPTIMAL FUTURE HISTORY

- A progressive annual reduction of funding for war and weapons on a multilateral basis by all nations – the money saved to be devoted to more useful purposes like the reduction of world poverty and disease, and alternate energy infrastructure.

- Since there will not be another review conference on nuclear proliferation until 2010 some other world conference or organization will be necessary to see that nuclear weapons are at least substantially reduced each year. Immediate objectives could include an end to the production of highly enriched uranium and the reprocessing of plutonium. This objective could well be assisted by citizen organizations everywhere who regularly remind their fellow citizens of the catastrophic dangers of even limited nuclear war, and petition their governments to work towards these objectives and the eventual elimination of atomic weapons. I realize that this objective seems so large and forbidding it becomes daunting, but the issue is so important it warrants every possible effort.

- Abolition of the manufacture and sale of landmines, and major allocation of money and people to clear up what are there now.

- Scrupulous attention by military recruiters to the need to 'winnow out' psychopaths and those with a criminal record of violence and cruelty, at the enlisting stage.

PART TWO

DIRECTIONS

CHAPTER 8

WHICH WAY SCIENCE?

There is no doubt that the world has the skills and resources to cope with the 2030 drivers. The real issue is whether our productive institutions are moving in the right directions. If they are not, what do we need to do about it? The world's financial systems, the policies of the multinationals, the directions of science, the applications of technology, constructive and sustainable use of the land and the sea – all these things need to be assessed for their ability to recognize and cope with the drivers.

This question applies perhaps most importantly to science and technology. Their application must be decisive in coping with the drivers and carrying out the necessary reshaping before 2030. But are they being used to the best effect? For instance, it is claimed that almost half the world's scientists – some half a million people – are engaged in weapons research and production.[1] The Soviet Union maintained an establishment of 25,000 scientists working solely on biological weapons – such things as smallpox, especially virulent anthrax and antibiotic resistant plague. The words of David Suzuki and Peter Knudtson define an important part of the problem: 'The power to apply new scientific knowledge tends to reside not in the individual but in vast corporate and military organizations that possess the resources and expertise to harness novel techniques ... Motives of profit and military power should not be allowed to shape our society's technological priorities.'[2]

Genetic engineering seems to generate almost as many disadvantages as advantages. Even though more money and effort than ever before are devoted to medical research and the production of drugs, the benefits of these are heavily weighted towards the world's affluent minority, while major diseases like tuberculosis and malaria are killing millions. Huge and expensive particle accelerators, like the CERN Large Hadron Collider near Geneva, have cost billions of dollars. The International Space Station, the most expensive construction project in human history, has cost $40 billion already, with the final bill likely to reach $100 billion. The benefits of both of these projects to the immediate problems of most humans are doubtful.

Every 3.6 seconds someone in the world dies from starvation. Three-quarters of these deaths are children under the age of five. They do not die because the world is short of food – for the moment it is not – but because they can't afford to buy it. Millions die from preventable diseases, at least a billion more are made miserable and ineffective by chronic illnesses like malaria, AIDS and waterborne parasites. There is little room for complacency here. It is a fair conclusion that in spite of the 'progress' of science over the last century, more people die needlessly early, are ill, in poverty, ill housed or subjected to massive pollution than ever before.

However, any immediate conclusion that pure science should be abandoned for a crash programme of applied science to remedy the overall human condition is oversimplistic and needs to be viewed with suspicion. The history of science, with so many examples of important and practical results deriving from pure research, shows that the individual scientist thinking through a new idea can be of incalculable value to the world. If anything, the pendulum is swinging too far the other way, with increasing university dependence on business, and increasing pressure to deliver immediately marketable results. The new society might best be served by providing more facilities in terms of research institutes, perhaps within universities, that are immune from financial and other pressures from government and business, and are subject only to a reasonable audit from their peers.

In a world increasingly enamoured with materialism and gadgets, it may seem strange that growing numbers of people are tending to become less interested in things – in American 'stuff' – and are more interested in ideas, creativity, even what is now called spirituality. The necessarily more frugal use of energy must encourage this change in individual attitudes, but it will come mainly from lifestyles influenced – and altered – by 21st century science. It is well beyond the scope of this book to review relativity, quantum physics, chaos theory and modern cosmology in any depth. This, in any case, has been done very well already by Paul Davies and others.[3] The essential point is that modern physics has upset the materialist view that matter is inert and passive, governed by immutable laws – the 'clockwork universe'. Nevertheless, 17th century 'machine science' still informs our attitudes and conventional wisdom, in the words of Dr S J Goerner it 'changed the entire structure of western civilization, including the way everyday people lived their lives and experienced their world'.[4] Goerner and Davies contend persuasively that the 'clockwork universe' concept helped to shape our materialistic world, formed on the belief that everything proceeds in the cosmos according to fixed laws. The job of science was to establish just what these laws were and to learn how to manipulate them. This mechanistic view, still very much alive and preoccupied with material productivity, largely disavows creativity and free will, the mysterious, the spiritual. It works within broad, but limited, areas.

Science as a discipline has, of course, changed. Einstein provided totally new perceptions of space, time and gravity. Quantum physics implies that the apparently solid does not exist, except as energy, and perhaps as looped one-dimensional strings vibrating in 10, or 26, dimensions. 'Particles' appear to come into existence out of nothing and as mysteriously disappear again. Chaos theory, contending that systems which normally appear to be ordered can be perturbed by factors impossible to assess, depicts a universe partly of ordered events, partly of unpredictable ones.

A major part of the scientific view is toward the idea that the cosmos is organized on apparently random (dare we say it?) lines which may best be understood intuitively, rather than by reductionism and linear thinking. As Richard Dawkins points out, the best way to understand how a motor car engine works is to break it down into its component parts and understand those.[5] Whether this 'reductionist' principle is a tool one can apply to all areas of enquiry is now seriously in question. Many studies have been carried out into 'unconscious thinking' – intuition – leaving little doubt that the brain can sort information and present answers to problems without the owner of that brain being consciously aware of what is going on.[6]

The manufacture and ownership of material things is becoming less valued, partly because of individual alarm at high rates of pollution and the drain on the world's resources. The world's wealthiest man, Bill Gates, the founder of Microsoft, is now said to have more money than all but 25 world economies – and it is worth noting that he has given back billions to the world in a series of charitable foundations. This huge fortune stemmed from the development of the abstractions that lie behind modern computer science. The creative, the intangible, rather than the material, is coming to represent wealth.

Developments in cosmology and practical experience in space travel are bringing a greater humility and a saner realism to those areas. The science fiction concept of spaceships roaming to far off worlds, zapping aliens, terraforming planets, now appears more improbable and indecent than ever. Until 'warp drives' and the like begin to emerge from the purely fictional – and they show little sign of doing so – and assuming that the speed of light is the fastest that anything can move, journeys very far into space would require travel times of thousands or even millions of years. At current space shuttle speeds it would take 13,000 years to travel the 4.3 light years to Alpha Centauri, the star system nearest to us, and much longer to reach another habitable planet, if one exists, deeper in space. This would mean that thousands of generations of travellers would have to be bred aboard the spaceship. But research has already established that human reproduction over many generations could be severely impaired in space conditions, if indeed it were possible at all.[7]

Detailed research has shown space to be 'a sick environment', seriously affecting human muscle tone and the circulatory system, and exposing humans in space to huge dosages of cosmic rays, which cannot be stopped or avoided, and which cause genes to mutate.[8] This has already cast serious doubt on whether a projected human mission to Mars, lasting three years, is actually feasible.

Is there anything habitable for humans out there anyway? Two authors with respectable qualifications believe that there is probably not – the Earth is a rare 'Garden of Eden' among a myriad of environments that are 'terrible for life'.[9] Erratic energy sources, deadly cosmic ray bombardment, unstable or irregular orbits, unsuitable distances from their sun, and an almost certain lack of water, characterize most of the planets discovered so far outside our solar system. These seem mostly to be gas giants that could never be colonized by humans. Hence, the two authors say, we have a special responsibility to recognize the perhaps unique nature of the Earth and to give priority to preserving its welfare and its environment.

This matter then, comes down to one of priorities, and a general change in mindsets able to assist the most favourable outcomes. Viewed in this way, the idea that it is the destiny of humankind to 'reach for the stars' seems at best premature and unrealistic, and distracts our attention from the pressing but less spectacular problems of this world. Also, some silly but potentially dangerous notions have ridden on its back, such as the idea that it doesn't matter how overcrowded and ecologically damaged our world gets – we shall simply hop into spaceships and search for planets somewhere out there, and, having zapped the natives, will 'terraform' these places to suit ourselves.

With the passing of 30 years from the Apollo landings in 1969 without any further human landings on the moon or the planets, a more realistic assessment has evolved about what space technology is likely to achieve – certainly in the run up to 2030. This process has been assisted by the remarkable dispatching of a series of unmanned probes which have given us an accurate idea of what the other planets in our solar system are like. Mars seems, like the moon, a dead world, rocky, barren and pockmarked with craters which are generally assumed to be the result of meteor impacts on its surface, with huge dust storms driven by 200 mile an hour winds. It probably has water, locked into ice. Whether some form of bacterial life may exist there is still an open question. Under its shroud of yellow clouds, highly toxic with concentrated sulphuric acid, Venus is much the same, except that its surface is hellishly hot. Earlier ideas that our nearer neighbours might be inhabited, or might once have been inhabited, now seem unlikely. The huge outer planets are gas or ice giants.

Other bodies in our solar system which excite interest are two satellites of Jupiter, the intensely hot and volcanically active Io and the ice covered Europa. Is there a warm sea under the ice of Europa? There is some evidence that this might be so. Could there be, at the bottom of this sea, volcanic vents which might warm parts of the sea enough to sustain some primitive form of life, as they do at the bottom of Earth's oceans? A Europa Lander probe is scheduled for 2010.

Fascinating as all this effort and ingenuity is, the bottom line seems to be that little more can be learned or achieved by sending manned space missions to the other planets. In most cases the conditions are too harsh or toxic for humans to survive there. Mars remains the only possibility, but even there the technical requirements are huge, and even worse, colonizing the dead planet would require vast amounts of effort and energy which would have to be drawn from the scarce resources of Earth. When, in 1989, the then American president George Bush senior asked NASA about the practicalities of putting men on Mars, the space agency came up with a 30 year programme costing $450 billion. One shuttle journey to the International Space Station costs at least $250 million. Then there are the physical stresses on the astronaut – rapid bone and muscle loss, nausea, erratic heartbeat, displacement of body fluids and possibly fatal exposure to solar radiation among them.

In the light of the urgent needs of Earth for major scientific and technological fixes, it would seem reasonable to make space exploration less of a priority, at least until the major problems facing us before 2030 have been assessed and tackled, unless radical and at present unknown developments turn up that would make it feasible and useful. Such developments might include the capture and mining of asteroids – or the moon – for minerals, certain forms of manufacture which work better in space, and mechanisms to divert or destroy a space object on a collision course with Earth. The moon, for instance has considerable resources of helium 3, which is rare on Earth, and which could be a fuel for fusion reactors if that technology develops. There are also huge reserves of the rare earth metal titanium on the moon.

Developments in the areas of genetics and climatology are immediately important – these rate individual treatment in Chapters 4 and 9. But there are others areas – right at the front end of possibility – that warrant a hard look. Take, for instance, molecular nanotechnology. This jaw cracking label describes engineering measured in nanometres – one billionth of a metre – which, if it can be achieved, will amount to nothing less than modern alchemy – the ability to create almost anything by assembling atoms to make new molecules planned for specific purposes. These could be very tough and cheap photovoltaic cells, artificial antibodies and, on the downside, destructive new weapons so small they are almost impossible to detect.

The rapidly growing literature in this area claims the new technology could make diamonds from carbon – even windows might be sheets of diamond rather than glass. It could create microscopic 'submarines', capable of attacking bacteria, viruses, even cancer cells, while swimming in the bloodstream, and so supplementing and assisting the human immune system. The new photovoltaic materials might coat the surface of every sealed road or highway, providing all the electric power the world needs, other products dismembering dangerous pollutants like dioxins. Nothing would be impossible. Food, water, wood, gold and other metals, any physical substance could be synthesized from its component atoms.

The machinery which might achieve these things is visualized as molecular assemblers – minuscule devices themselves made from artificial molecules – resembling the manipulating arms of larger industrial robots. They already have a name: 'nanobots'. Nanobots are foreseen as machines with 'fingers' so tiny they can handle and assemble atoms into molecules. Miniature electronic brains would tell them how to do it. Right out at the leading edge are plans to make nanobots self replicating, so they could duplicate themselves in millions. Even grouped in those numbers they would still be invisible to the naked eye.

While manipulation of individual atoms has been carried out, whether it will ever be possible to make materials to order at the atomic level remains an open question.[10] Nevertheless, the possibilities of molecular nanotechnology are being given serious consideration – for instance, the powerful coordinating Japanese Department of Economics, Trade and Industry, METI, has identified 'control technologies for the precise arrangement of molecules' as a 21st century priority. Early in 2000, President Clinton announced American government grants of half a billion dollars for nanotechnology research, a White House statement at that time declaring: 'Nanotechnology is the new frontier, and its potential impact is compelling.'

If what is claimed for this possible new technology is barely half true, it would clearly represent a leap forward of the same order as the agricultural and industrial revolutions. Its potential to solve the 2030 problems would be immense. However, proponents of the idea also point out that new biological – and possibly physical – weapons of the most sinister kind, could just as easily result. There has been not unreasonable speculation about new areas of weaponry capable of destroying whole national populations. Such weapons are foreseen as being so tiny that they would be next to impossible to detect – hence defensive measures against them would be hardly feasible. Their construction, once the technologies were established, would also be very cheap. Large factories would not be necessary, and the amount of raw materials required would be minute by ordinary industrial standards.

Since the envisaged potential of nanotechology for good or ill is so great as to be almost unimaginable, what are we to make of all this? One option – that frequently favoured by modern governments – would simply be to wait and see what comes of it. The danger then might be that the technology had already been directed into destructive areas that, once established, could not readily be removed, as has already happened with nuclear science.

OPTIMAL FUTURE HISTORY

- Major diversion of money and expertise to practical world needs rather than to weapons systems and space travel.
- Establishment of a global authority to set priorities in this direction and advise on their inplementation.
- Assembly of a body of 'censors' to examine proposed new technology and identify areas that might be harmful, and of a world court to determine whether certain technologies can proceed.
- Establishment of research institutes for specific and practical purposes, with inalienable funding.

CHAPTER 9

IN THE GENES: NEW PLANTS – AND PEOPLE?

While the long-term promise of genetic engineering is considerable, the decades until 2030 are likely to present more problems than solutions. Forewarning people of a genetic predisposition to illness has been possible for some years, and will become more common. Finding and developing reliable genetically engineered cures is likely to take several decades. Genetic engineering of plants may provide more food in the developing world, but concerns remain about its consequences in the long term. After much discussion, UNESCO produced a Universal Declaration on the Human Genome and Human Rights which was endorsed by the United Nations in 1999, but support for it in many countries is conditional at best. These were among the issues raised at a major international conference of bioethicists in Salzburg in 2000, one of literally hundreds of meetings around the world presenting a remarkably diverse collection of views and attitudes.

Following the development of techniques to alter the basic nature of living things through genetic engineering, by removing or rearranging genes, or even by adding new genes to produce offspring with new characteristics, biology has become the science attracting the liveliest public interest. Since the discovery of the structure of DNA by Watson and Crick in 1953, intensive research has gone into mapping the genetic structure of the 23 pairs of human chromosomes present in every cell. Humans have about 35,000 genes, which have to be identified within 3.2 billion genetic 'letters'. The remaining 95 per cent – so-called 'junk' DNA, may well have meaning and importance, but this has yet to be researched. Genes, which are strings of four different molecular bases, are a code of instructions to the cell to make specialized proteins. These control the body's structure, development and maintenance. Physicist Freeman Dyson said that DNA can be considered, in computer terms, as software, whereas proteins are the hardware.[1]

When a gene is faulty or missing, the abnormal or missing protein can cause illness. The identification of genes which appear to trigger or predispose people to illnesses, such as osteoporosis, has already been achieved. Nevertheless, reading the 'letters' in this complex genetic alphabet is proving difficult and time consuming. Mapping the human genome, a massive task completed in 2000, was a necessary start to the even more formidable one of unravelling the human genetic code and establishing its significance – and its potential for improving health. An important area of this work involves identifying genetic 'markers', places where the genetic codes of different people vary by just one 'letter'. These single nucleotide polymorphisms, as they are called, are needed to trace genetic variations, which are often very complex, and which can predispose people to disease.

Nevertheless, Barbara Katz Rothman has noted the risk that 'we might be carried off to places we might very well choose not to go' – such as to developments of biological weapons which target particular racial groups.[2] 'Profit driven' genetic screening, especially for untreatable conditions, has attracted critics, who cite discrimination in the workplace or from insurers as an undesirable outcome. A simple mouth swab test to detect haemochromatosis, a condition in which iron builds up to deadly levels in the body, seems of obvious value, since this can be treated with blood transfusions. But is there any virtue in telling individuals, and their families, that they may lose their minds in

20 years' time because they have the gene for Huntington's disease, which is incurable?

These are just two of many lively controversies that genetic engineering has produced. Will genetic modifications simply carry out what scientists intend, or will they result in unintended, possibly dangerous, consequences? Will genetic crops 'contaminate' traditional or organic crops growing nearby through cross pollination? Will insecticides genetically introduced into food crops poison species other than insects, perhaps even humans? Will huge agrochemical companies acquire dangerous political power by controlling food production? To what extent do they already influence governments to protect them from opposition to their products? Could the power to choose the sex of a prospective baby create serious population imbalances? Could cloned humans be made in different lines, specialized as workers, prostitutes or soldiers, or be genetically altered to be unnaturally compliant, brutal or aggressive? Will a divorcement of sex from reproduction become common, causing profound social changes? All these possibilities have been canvassed.

The science of genetics has some doubtful antecedents. Eighteenth century botanist, Carolus Linnaeus, wrote of 'a great chain of being', a divinely ordained and immutable hierarchy of life which among other things, established white Europeans as a superior race, with the right, even the mission, to dominate 'inferior' races.[3] Racism, thus apparently sanctified by science, led on to the forcible shipping of 6 million Africans to America as slaves, and to the colonial empires which provided Europe with its power and prosperity as it entered the 20th century.

During the first decade of the 20th century a new 'science' called eugenics became fashionable. It evolved the ideas that super people might be created by selective breeding, and that some kinds of people were inferior to others. A number of American states passed laws forbidding marriage between different racial types; eugenics acts permitted sterilization of people in mental hospitals, many of whose problems had nothing to do with inherited qualities. The Nazi dictatorship in Germany carried eugenics to its ugly extremes, killing millions of Jews, sterilizing 400,000 Germans, and promoting breeding of pure 'Aryan' types – blonde haired and blue eyed – in a mission to create a eugenically 'ideal' German population. Hitler asserted that Aryans were 'the highest image of God among his creatures – it is the iron law of nature that the weak, diseased and wavering, be eliminated'.[4] Very similar sentiments extolling a need to foster 'the thrifty, energetic and superior stocks' were expressed by Winston Churchill when he was Home Secretary in 1910, but these beliefs 'were considered so inflammatory by succeeding British governments they were not made public until 1992'.[5]

It is important to keep this history of eugenics in mind, since modern genetic determinism can mirror it in significant respects, and because its ideas still appeal to some religious and racial extremists.[6] The problems of 2030 will be severe enough without the added complication of eugenic experimentation. However, genetic engineering does have the power to make eugenic 'experiments' more feasible and more extreme. For instance, some people are prepared to pay large sums of money to have 'attractive' children, as a 1999 auction of embryos from a selection of good looking models in the US demonstrates. By 2003, American companies were seeking 'eggs' from attractive, intelligent Australian women.

Controversies about genetics are concentrated in two main areas – manipulated changes in food plants, and in humans. An early technique in the field of plants was the addition of genes to major crop varieties that provide them with a built-in insecticide, or the ability to resist a herbicide that would destroy all other growing things in the sprayed area. These are seen by their proponents as valuable, because they eliminate or reduce the volume of crop spraying. In areas growing cotton, which is notoriously subject to pest attack, it has been possible to reduce aerial insecticide spraying by as much as 60 per cent. However, GM crops generally involve users buying seeds as part of a package that includes the same company's herbicides. Almost 80 per cent of those developed in the West are of this type. The policies of the giant agrochemical multinationals have been summarized this way: 'Today 70 per cent of genetically modified crops are engineered not to improve their food value, but to make them more dependent on the seed companies' own brand agrochemicals.'[7]

Opponents of genetic modification claim that the genetic changes might spread to other plants, including those grown by natural or organic growers, who do not use chemical fertilizers or poisons. Cases of weeds becoming immune to weedkillers by picking up genes from modified canola were reported in Canada in 2000. Just how high is the risk into the future? Jeremy Rifkin considers 'It is likely that we will be plagued by genetic pollution ... because of the volume of new introductions and because the introductions are so novel... My bet is that agricultural biotechnology is going to be one of the great disasters of corporate capitalist history.'[8] Among the products under consideration is a new class of seeds labelled 'terminators' – possibly the most disastrous choice of a product name in history. The objective is to create plants which sterilize their own seeds. Other seeds have had genes added from deadly venom-producing spiders, to create plants capable of poisoning insect predators.

At the root of much of the opposition to GM food has been the possibility that a few multinationals might come to control decisive areas of food production, because they, and only they, can provide the chemicals necessary to grow that food. The top five companies, controlling almost the entire Western market for genetically modified food, have the power to manipulate plants so they must be grown with the fertilizers and insecticides for which these conglomerates hold the patents. The possibility therefore exists of the price and supply of GM crops being manipulated if they come to be grown extensively – many voices have expressed the fear of an enormous and dangerous accretion of global political power to these multinationals.

These areas of concern became qualified by disclosures in 2002 that China already has a major independent genetic engineering capacity, second only to the US, with 600 workers and 80 DNA sequencing machines. China's completion of a draft sequence for rice was announced in that year. China plans to export GM seeds to other developing countries – a development of huge importance because by 2005, China was on the point of officially deciding to adopt mass production of genetically modified rice. Rice is the world's most important and most consumed food-grain. Experimental plots planted over the last few years are said to have improved yields 6 to 9 per cent, and reduced pesticide use by 80 per cent.

Cotton modified to resist pests and diseases is already being grown by millions of Chinese farmers. The fact that aquifers in many parts of the world have water too saline for food crops has opened up an important area of research. Salt tolerant tomatoes have been created, and work is proceeding on other plants. This includes the transfer of genes from plants that are already salt tolerant, such as mangroves. Technology of this kind is highly advanced in China, where scientists are working on plants resistant to salt, pests and cold; it represents a significant part of the total world effort on plant biotechnology.

GM crops may indeed help to alleviate malnutrition and disease in the developing world – provided the new crops are designed with that end in mind, and not to meet self-interested commercial motivations. This issue reached an uneasy stalemate early in 2000 with the Biosafety Protocol, the first significant treaty controlling international trade in GM organisms. This treaty recognizes the right of individual nations to ban imports of GM food, seeds and animal feed they consider might have an adverse effect on health or biological diversity.

But do we risk throwing the baby out with the bathwater? Trees that grow faster, leaner meat, food freed from its allergy causing qualities, useful crops able to withstand heat, salinity and drought, animals and plants more resistant to viral or parasitic predators, and above all, the promise of crops yielding bigger harvests – all these things have been promised by the proponents of genetic engineering. At the Hebrew University in Israel researchers have developed a gene which they believe may speed up the growth rate of food crops by more than 50 per cent. An American developer has bred genetically modified salmon that grow ten times faster than ordinary fish, and can become as heavy as an average man.[9]

One of the more remarkable and potentially most valuable successes has been a bright yellow rice grain which contains beta carotene – so called 'golden rice'. Beta carotene, the precursor of vitamin A, is present in the leaves and stalk of the rice plant, but is normally absent in the grain. Vitamin A deficiency, which reduces resistance to infection, is a widespread condition, leading in severe cases to blindness and subsequent early death of hundreds of thousands of children in rice growing areas. In 2005 golden rice[2] was announced, a new strain that provides 23 times more beta-carotene than the earlier one.

All these developments indicate that the genetic engineering of food is here to stay, and that it could be useful if it is properly controlled and directed. But is it the only way? Hans Herren argues that the huge sums being spent on genetic changes to make plants pest resistant are reducing funding for the study of natural predators, which would do the same job at less cost.[10] Herren was responsible for finding a natural predator to control the mealy bug, which had severely reduced the yield of cassava, a major source of carbohydrates in Africa.

Three of the most controversial possibilities of genetic engineering of humans are the manipulation of genes to create 'designer' babies of the sex and characteristics stipulated by the parents on an order form, the creation of human clones, and genetic changes which may alter human behaviour. Whether or not any of these things happen, legally or illegally, will be a matter of the greatest concern. There is a considerable risk that by 2030, they will take place illegally unless there is effective international policing of the technologies. The possibilities are endless and spill over into the wildest conjectures of science fiction – the creation of slave classes, even armies, made up of identical individuals, new individuals of strange, even bizarre, appearance and personality created for specific purposes, such as mindless repetitive work, prostitution, killing. Those who dismiss such conjectures as totally fanciful might be given pause for thought by some other apparently improbable happenings in genetic engineering which are already facts. University of Hawaii scientists have created mice from freeze dried sperm which can be stored, perhaps indefinitely, then used by simply adding water. By adding genes which make certain jellyfish glow green to this dried sperm, they created green mice.[11]

The much publicized 'designer baby' seems unlikely, since many desired attributes like intelligence and beauty have no single gene. Providing them reliably would prove immensely complex, and well beyond present technology. However, changing the 'germ line' of families in specific ways to eliminate hereditary defects, is a live issue. For instance: a technique called ICSI, intra-cytoplasmic sperm injection, developed in the early 1990s, makes parenthood possible for men unable to produce sperm in quantities likely to achieve natural insemination. Single sperm can be taken from the testicles and injected into the mother's egg in a laboratory. The danger comes from the fact that this basic infertility can be passed on to any son born of ICSI, due to defects in the transmitted Y chromosome, which only men can convey to male offspring. How will that son feel when he grows up, marries, and finds he and his partner are unable to have children?

This could be corrected by 'germ line gene repair', according to a leading reproductive specialist, Professor Roger Short, so that the defect in the Y chromosome conveyed to the son would be corrected by adding the missing genes.[12] This, unfortunately, brings us to the very edge of the taboo. Once particular germ line changes are accepted, the path lies ahead to others aimed at 'designing' children.

However, persuasive arguments for germ line gene repair have been advanced by the Professor of Fertility Studies at the University of London, Robert Winston.[13] Lord Winston points to the possibility of eliminating diseases with hereditary elements, like diabetes, Alzheimer's, even heart disease, by removing the causative genes. The fact that some people carry powerful protective genes against many diseases has opened up a whole new potential for medical treatment, based on transferring these 'protectors' to the germ line of people who lack them, so their offspring can be born free of the potential for those illnesses. Professor Winston has also identified factors that are likely to make 'designer children' a less than attractive proposition, including uncertainty as to the results, the imposition of traits which might seem attractive now, but which may not seem so in the future of that family, and the complexity of the genetic basis to 'desirable' qualities such as beauty and intelligence.

The provision of children of the sex required by the parents is already on offer in several countries. The sex of the foetus can be determined in time to permit early abortion. This has already caused trouble in the world's two most populous countries, India and China, where cultural influences make boy children preferable. Indeed, such testing is now illegal in India, where the proportion of girls in the total number of births has dropped significantly in recent decades. There is already a shortage of women of marriageable age in China, for similar reasons.

The whole issue of children being conceived other than by sexual joining has been controversial on a fairly general and emotive basis – 'scientists should not play God' – since the birth of the first 'test tube baby', Louise Brown, in 1978. But since then more than half a million children have resulted from the technology, to the benefit of parents who would otherwise have remained childless. These procedures involve treating the woman with hormones that result in her producing perhaps 15 eggs. These are fertilized with sperm from the father or a donor, and produce embryonic human beings, several of which are implanted into the mother's womb several days later. A normal pregnancy then ensues, and all being well the mother gives birth to a healthy child, or in many cases, several children. The unused embryos are frozen, a state in which they remain viable. If the initial pregnancy does not succeed, or the couple want more children later, the spare embryos can then be used. However, in almost every case not all of the frozen embryos are required. Should they be returned to room temperature, and allowed to die, or should they be kept for other purposes, for example to be donated, or sold, to another couple? The embryos could also be used for research, such as to provide 'lines' for stem cell research, but whether or not this should be permitted is a source of major controversy.

Prenatal genetic diagnosis is now becoming common. Its purpose is to establish whether an embryo in the womb has serious abnormalities, for example, Down's Syndrome, to allow parents the option of informed early termination. Selection of embryos for in vitro fertilization procedures are also possible to ensure 'disease free' children. The evolution of DNA 'chips' to screen hundreds of genes at a time will allow such a check to become much more comprehensive. The world will need to decide at what point rejection of an embryo is acceptable. Where a disability like Down's Syndrome is involved the issue seems fairly straightforward, but what about the presence of genes considered to predispose for suicide or alcoholism? Studies of twins who have been brought up separately indicate that as much as half of human behaviour has genetic origins.[14] Could such traits in individuals be altered by genetic engineering and, if so, should they be? Genetic engineering modifying behaviour in an animal was achieved in 2002.[15] Mice, which tend to be cautious and not particularly social in their behaviour, were made bolder and more sociable by transferring a single gene from another rodent, the prairie vole, which is gregarious.

Genetic research opens up the possibility of cloning – a clone is an individual genetically identical to another individual, as is the case with identical twins. The successful production of the world's first artificially cloned mammal, Dolly the sheep, in 1997, immediately aroused extensive controversy, and the banning of experiments into human cloning in most countries. The process of cloning turned out to be relatively simple technology, requiring the removal of the nucleus from the egg cell and its replacement by a fragment of material from the animal to be cloned – in the case of Dolly, from the 'mother's' udder. It became apparent that cloning other animals, including humans, was feasible.

But, on present knowledge, cloning is done at an enormous cost – there were 276 failures before Dolly was produced – and she began to show signs of premature aging in 1999. Her life was ended in February 2003 after being diagnosed with progressive lung disease; she had only reached half the lifespan of a typical sheep. Later experiments in animal cloning have also resulted in a high wastage of embryos, a high spontaneous abortion rate, a large number of malformed foetuses – so much so that a veteran of cloning described it as 'incredibly inefficient, and also dangerous'.[16] According to some estimates, as many as 400 eggs might be needed to produce enough embryos to create a human clone. Fifty surrogate mothers would be required. Perhaps eight to ten pregnancies would result – and one normal baby 'might' eventuate. Also, as Lord Winston points out, the exact cloning of humans may not be possible in any case, since significant amounts of DNA in the cell occur outside the nucleus, and because nurture and environment play such a large part in the development of an individual.[17]

Perhaps the most promising and exciting area of cloning does not seek to reproduce individual humans or animals at all. This therapeutic cloning uses embryonic stem cells, which can develop into almost any of the specialized cells that make up the human body. In theory this technique may be able to provide replacements for diseased or malfunctioning organs – kidneys, a liver, or more immediately, specialized tissues such as the dopamine producing cells of the brain, the lack of which appears to cause Parkinson's disease. The area has been controversial because the stem cells have had to be extracted from week old aborted human embryos. However, it is now possible to reproduce stem cells in a culture, and they have been found to exist in adults, taking much of the force from this objection. The technique involves taking the nucleus of a non-reproductive cell from the patient, and placing this in an unfertilized egg from which the nucleus has been removed. The resulting embryo will begin to produce stem cells, which can be reproduced and perhaps specialized. The big advantage of these tissues grown from stem cells is that they are unlikely to be rejected by the recipient. Research is already well advanced in Finland, the US and Brazil, into the means of directing stem cells to produce human teeth. Persons otherwise forced to use dental plates or implants may be able, quite literally, to grow a third set of teeth.

Nevertheless, it is fair to say that this work has a long way to go, and that, based on the rate of success by 2005, it would be premature to predict the successful manufacture of replacement organs from embryonic stem cells in the foreseeable future. The first are likely to be dopamine producing brain cells designed to treat Parkinsonism – 'we are talking a five to ten year timeframe'.[18]

This science needs time and room to develop. Because of this, any attempt to set priorities 'what needs doing', would be inappropriate and presumptuous. However, it is not too difficult to imagine dangerous and grotesque consequences from uncontrolled genetic engineering – and great advantages from the science if it is well directed. Lay women and men ought at least to know something about it – because it has such huge implications for the future world. A body of knowledge in society could help ensure a proper degree of transparency in the technologies, and the necessary controls, which could both be most efficiently organized at the international level.

CHAPTER 10

THE VALUES OF THE SEA

Fish populations are declining in most parts of the world, but as with other problems, there is a feasible answer. According to Dr Colin Roberts of York University, when fishing is forbidden in about a third of the area of a fishing ground, populations recover – so much so that yields can double in as little as seven years. Speaking at an international conference on marine protected areas in Melbourne in 2005, Dr Roberts said research had established that it was worthwhile for governments to subsidize fishermen while fish stocks recovered in these protection areas. And indeed, in 2003, an earlier conference had advocated protecting a third of the world's oceans by 2012. The bad news is that barely 1 per cent of marine habitats are so protected, and there has been a major increase in the number of large boats, many registered under flags of convenience, carrying out illegal fishing. Humanity seems determined to maltreat the oceans and their denizens.

This is not good enough – recent discoveries and research are signalling that much needed materials for the infrastructure of sustainability, and perhaps much of the additional food protein the world will need, could come from that 70 per cent of the planet's surface which is sea. Hence there are very good reasons to protect it from further damage, and exploit it responsibly. The idea that we know more about the outer planets than about the ocean deeps is now due for change with the development of robot drilling and exploration probes, which can operate miles deep in toxic environments no human miner could approach. Investigations using modern machinery already indicate that a great deal of the world's mineral reserves are under the sea[1] – global assets that can only be valued at trillions of dollars. At least three submerged sites 'probably have values in the billions of dollars'.[2] These assets, and the increasing feasibility of mining them, bring into question earlier predictions that the world is within decades of exhausting its stocks of essential minerals.

Nevertheless, most undersea minerals will be expensive to mine, requiring technologies yet to be developed, able to operate in oceans as much as 2 miles deep. It will be some time before these new mineral and energy reserves can come on stream, but there is no doubt they will be needed. Because of this, they warrant major development as soon as possible. It has long been known that virtually every mineral, including the rare and precious metals, occurs in minute quantities in seawater. There are rich deposits in the silts in deep pools in the Red Sea. One of these alone, the Atlantis 2 Deep, is estimated to contain billions of dollars worth of gold, silver, zinc and copper in 94 million tons of metal rich muds. More concentrated resources exist in millions of sea nodules, mineral laden objects typically about the size of a tennis ball. These, containing up to 35 per cent manganese, as well as copper, nickel and cobalt, litter the sea bed in huge quantities, but at great depths – as much as 3 miles. Those in the Pacific Ocean alone have been estimated at 1.5 trillion tons.

But most promising of all are the fantastic environments where submarine volcanic vents create tower-like seabed structures rich in minerals. In parts of the Pacific rim, such as Indonesia, chains of active volcanoes frequently extend beyond the coast onto the ocean floor. Mineral deposits, silver, copper, zinc and gold among them, are formed when very hot mineral laden water emerges into deep seawater that is close to freezing point. The minerals have accumulated into towers and chimney-like structures, sometimes as high as 200 feet (65 metres). No human diver could stay alive in these sulphurous, toxic areas, bubbling with methane gas, where mineral eating microbes may have been the first life on Earth. However, mining using robot machinery remotely controlled from a ship on the surface may be possible, and if so, will help to maintain the world's supply of the scarcer metals. The prototypes for such robot machinery already exist.

It is not yet possible to assess the quantities of minerals available around volcanic vents on the ocean floor, other than the general statement that they must be very large, and that most have not yet been located. However, two large deposits near Japan are estimated to contain minerals worth $16 billion. Other big resources are being investigated around seabed volcanoes northeast of the Indonesian island of Sulawesi,[3] and in waters around Papua New Guinea. The richest concentration of minerals ever seen has been reported in a field in the Bismarck Sea, which contains gold and concentrations as high as 10 per cent of copper and 20 per cent of zinc.

Submarine volcanic activity arises from the fact that the ocean floors are not static. Movements of the tectonic plates on which the continents float are continuous, creating not only earthquakes but also volcanic emissions – magma, smoke, even geysers – miles below the surface. These have brought, and will continue to bring, minerals to the ocean floor – a perpetual metal factory.

Much of this vast mineral wealth exists under the high seas – ocean areas outside national territorial waters. Who should be entitled to mine them, and on what terms? This could only be decided by a world authority – indeed, the 1982 Law of the Sea agreements, which extended the exclusive use of the seas to 200 miles off the coasts of maritime nations, also foreshadowed the necessity for some form of global authority over high seas mineral deposits which are the 'common heritage of mankind'. As a result, the International Seabed Authority, representing 135 nations, was established and in 2001 began 'to organize and control all mineral related activities in the international seabed areas beyond the limits of national jurisdiction'.[4] Formulating regulations for prospecting deep seabed metals was well advanced by 2005, with an implementing target set for the following year. Interested contractors will be required to respect the marine environment.

Coordinated use of this huge asset could be vital to the construction of the new energy infrastructure which will be needed before 2030.

The increasing level of pollution and exploitation of the sea and the creatures that live in it remains one of the more alarming attacks by humans on nature. For instance:

- Around 700 million gallons of oil get into the oceans each year. Tanker accidents are always big news because they can cause heavy pollution and disproportionate damage to the environment in limited areas. However, they are responsible for only a small percentage of ocean pollution – around 40 million gallons. Three times as much comes from tankers illegally washing out their tanks at sea. The largest single source of pollution is from industrial activity on the land, oil runoff from roads and improperly disposed of motor oils – well over 300 million gallons.[5] Oil well explosions and blowouts are also a major cause.

- An estimated 1 million seabirds and 100,000 whales, dolphins and seals are killed each year when they try to eat, or are entangled in, the hundreds of thousands of tons of plastic dumped into the sea annually. Since most of this plastic is not biodegradable, it continues to be a permanent danger. Discarded plastic fishing nets and lines account for 150,000 tons of this. About half the world's salt marshes and mangrove forests, major fish breeding areas, have already been destroyed,[6] and as much as 30 per cent of coral reefs are in a critical condition.

- Current fishing practices result in the waste of about a quarter of the world's fishing catch of around 90 million tons a year, and cause the destruction of hundreds of thousands more dolphins, turtles and seabirds. More than half the marine fish populations in US waters is overfished – this means they are depleting faster than they can replace themselves, even though the US imports 40 per cent of its fish.

- 'Toxic tides' all over the world are resulting in warnings that fish caught on coastlines are too poisonous to eat because of high concentrations of contaminants like mercury, DDT and PCBs (polychlorinated byphenyls).[7]

The planet's smaller seas, generally bordered by highly populated areas, suffer most from pollution. The Mediterranean, which is almost tideless and has little natural self cleansing capacity, remains heavily polluted, in spite of an extraordinary plethora of plans and commissions of enquiry. The North Sea is another problem area. The nations bordering the North Sea are concerned, but there is little evidence of adequate practical efforts to improve matters. Large quantities of pollution are still carried into the sea by the Rhine River. Russia's Aral Sea is considered virtually dead, its fishing boats are rusting skeletons in the lifeless shallows, its waters are heavily polluted by pesticides and fertilizers.

The dumping of nuclear waste in the sea was banned in 1983 when it became evident that radioactive plumes in the oceans did not remain localized, but could spread immense distances. The classic case is that revealed by the Sellafield Study. During the 1970s the Sellafield nuclear reprocessing plant in Britain discharged caesium 137 and iodine 129 into the Irish Sea. This was later identified in large amounts – greater than the background level from nuclear weapons testing – in Arctic waters as far east as Canada. The plume had been spread by the Norwegian current north of Scandinavia into the Barents Sea.

Pollution of the sea has driven some marine species to extinction or close to it, although efforts have been mustered to protect and breed endangered species in captivity. Probably the most important development in marine species preservation has been the international agreement in 1985 to prevent whaling, although some nations, such as Russia and Japan, still hunt whales, allegedly for 'research' reasons.

Commercial fishing demonstrates a need for much more rigorous control by an international authority than is the case at present. Properly managed, fish are the best way to provide adequate protein food for the world. Already 25 per cent of the world's fish comes from controllable fish farms, and a large extension of this figure is desirable, provided it is not maintained by unsustainable exploitation of small sea fish to feed the farmed fish. It has been estimated that sustainable fishing of the oceans for food might be approximately 100 million tons a year – not a great deal more than the 90 million tons now extracted. However, that figure could only be maintained by careful evaluation of the breeding stock of commercial fish species, and especially by eliminating present wasteful methods of fishing.

In mid 2003, a review of several studies concluded that the world's fisheries were 'in a far worse state than anyone thought'. Each study 'told a similar story of fish stocks crashing within years of the arrival of industrial fishing'.[8] These conclusions derive in part from a 10 year research study showing that fish caught now are much smaller than those taken 50 years ago – typically as little as half the weight.[9]

Tuna often swim in close association with dolphin. When the less scrupulous commercial tuna fishermen see dolphin they put out large areas of nets to catch the tuna swimming beneath and behind them. The dolphin are caught with the tuna – more than a 100,000 dolphins a year are killed this way in the east Pacific fisheries. Huge nets and 'longlines' – as much as 80 miles long with tens of thousands of hooks – are undiscriminating killers of fish, mammal and bird life. Overfishing of North Sea herring brought stocks almost to extinction by 1975, resulting in the necessity to shut down the fishery until breeding could provide a natural recovery. The cod fishery, producing 300,000 tons a year in the 1980s, had fallen to around 100,000 tons in 1999 due to stricter fishing quotas, but in spite of that, and possibly partly due to climatic reasons, cod numbers continued to decline. By 2002 the European Union Fisheries Commission was forecasting the probability of a virtual shutdown of the cod fishery, although by 2005 it had been decided the fishery could continue with reduced quotas. These diminishing catches represent an economic disaster for the villages and towns that have relied on fishing as an industry for centuries. Forty years ago there were 50,000 fishermen in Britain – by 2002 this had declined to 16,000, with further heavy reductions imminent. Overfishing of the Atlantic cod cost the jobs of 30,000 Canadian fishermen after the Grand Banks fishery was shut down in 1992.

Unfortunately the lessons from these fishery failures have not really been learned. Governments set fishing quotas, but these are regularly exceeded. Modern methods – using heavily capitalized and mechanized fishing boats – can destroy entire fish populations in large areas of the sea. Many use fine mesh nets, which kill small fish as well as large, severely restricting the quantities remaining to breed for the future. There are twice as many fishing boats than the world's fisheries can support.[10]

Is the answer to 'farm' the oceans, simply by dropping nutrients into the water, and waiting for plankton, and the food chain stemming from it, to increase? Would this be a lavish source of cheap protein for the developing world and at the same time help to sequester carbon dioxide in the oceans? At least seven patents and four initial experiments in this area existed by 2002. Research groups in Norway and Japan are studying this idea, and three major universities are working on it.[11] The spokesperson for one group claimed that each floating factory, designed to make ammonia from the air and ocean water using solar technology, could stimulate the growth of 370,000 tons of sardines a year. This would provide adequate protein for 3 million people at a cost of about 8 cents ($0.08) a day per person.[12]

Michael Markels, an American chemical engineer, says that 60 per cent of marine life occurs in the 2 per cent of the ocean surfaces that is nutrient rich.[13] He estimates that 25,000 tons of fertilizer – iron, trace elements, nitrogen and phosphorus – would result in increased fish production of 50 million tons. Markels has concluded an agreement with the government of the Marshall Islands, in the south Pacific, to lease almost 2 million square miles of its exclusive economic zone, an area virtually devoid of fish, to experiment with the technology.

It has, however, already proved controversial. While phyto-plankton in the seas do absorb as much carbon dioxide as all the trees on Earth, and could be vastly increased by fertilization, some ecologists warn of decreased biodiversity in the oceans and the possibility of a depletion of fish in the tropics if the Southern

Ocean, perhaps the most promising area, is fertilized extensively. One study says: 'If implemented on a large scale ocean fertilization would, by design, change the ecology of the oceans ... the long term consequences of which are a cause for great concern.'[14] Some marine scientists warn that fertilization could create domination of algae that produce toxins, or reduce oxygen in seawater, resulting in the mass death of fish. Nevertheless, the potential to dramatically and cheaply increase the world's supplies of protein – always a scarce commodity – seems so great that this technology, if it can be properly controlled, could be important. Meanwhile ocean warming has resulted in a significant drop in the number of phytoplankton in the world's oceans.

All these concerns return us to a recurring theme, the need for proper international supervision of human affairs – in this case a global Authority of the Sea. Among other things, it could regulate and control present areas of sea pollution, establish mandatory minimum standards for oil tanker design, closely supervise nuclear facilities and other industrial sources of pollution, establish safe and sustainable standards, if possible, for large scale fish farming by adding nutrients in present 'barren' sea regions, and farming of krill at levels which do not deprive species higher up the food chain. Such requirements suggest the diversion of much of the world's navies into a maritime police force, Oceanguard. And there is one other – like slavery, sea piracy is very much back in the world today, so much so that the US deputy assistant secretary of state, Matthew Daley, in 2005 referred to the sea as 'the most unregulated of spaces'. In that year there were more than 200 attacks on merchant ships, and 300 seamen were killed, kidnapped or disappeared. Ships, their crews and cargo, regularly vanish completely as a result of attacks by organized pirates, using fast motor-boats and modern weapons.

OPTIMAL FUTURE HISTORY

- Establishment of a Oneworld agency with access to a sea force – Oceanguard – made up of elements seconded from the world's navies. This might be an extension of the International Seabed Authority with greater powers, including control of illegal oil dumping from tankers and illegal fishing, and prevention of piracy on merchant shipping.
- Supervision of fish and krill populations and effective control of takes to maintain sustainability.
- Development of fish farming technology and ocean fertilization at sustainable and safe levels.
- Control and eventual repair of ocean pollution.
- Financing and establishing extensive marine protection areas with the objective of increasing current fish stocks.

CHAPTER 11

MULTINATIONALS: GOOD BUSINESS OR BAD?

Multinational corporations have the power and resources to introduce the sustainable manufacture required for necessary change. How much are they likely to cooperate? On present showing, not much, other than some elaborate public relations exercises. The world power groupings of which they are such a significant part seem more inclined to push their own short-term interests, to favour 'islands' of prosperity, rather than engage the needs of humanity as a whole. In this area, perhaps more than any other, a fresh start is necessary, using strategies compliant with both axioms.

One doesn't have to research too far to find that multinationals generally get a bad press. It is a part of conventional wisdom that there are faceless management hierarchies out there that are interested only in dominating as much business as possible worldwide, making as much money as possible, and doing as little as possible to the benefit of the world in the meantime. Crimes ranging from harassment, massive tax evasion and even murder are convincingly attributed to them. If there is doom to come, then in the popular view the multinationals are probably hastening its arrival. Novelist David Cornwall – who writes under the name of John le Carre – after considerable research into the area, said: 'The biggest delusion of our times is that great corporations have an ethical centre. They have absolutely no ethical or moral centre. I think we are dealing with an octopus that really must be attacked by public opinion. Multinational companies are beginning to replace nations.'[1]

There is substantial evidence to support these views, and evidence also of limited and essentially self damaging business policies. Is this due to insufficiently trained management? Too much specialization? While a cost accountant is perhaps good at changing three brass screws to three steel ones and saving a few cents in a $100 appliance, he may not have enough knowledge of, or interest in, long-term issues that affect the organization's future. So what? If the steel screws rust out and the gadget falls apart, why ... that's good for business! But is it, in the long term?

Perhaps corporations are so large, so amorphous, that they are unmanageable. Is there any other reason why some multi-nationals adopt policies that effectively increase poverty and damage the environment, when good management would see that, even in the shorter term, these might affect their own interests, among many other things, by steadily eroding their markets? This was regarded as a factor in the decision by Coca-Cola to cut its staff globally to an unprecedented extent early in 2000 – thereby reducing the market even further for its product, and other products. Falling demand in many places, but notably in Russia, was one factor in the dismissal of 13 per cent of Coca-Cola's 29,000 staff. 'Downsizing' in a host of other enterprises has been attributed to falling markets. A move by British soap giant Unilever into home cleaning and other services was in part ascribed to 'markets in the developing world [that] are not growing fast enough to compensate for stagnating performance in the developed world'.[2]

Large industry in its present state can scarcely be described as efficient. The world is awash with overproduction – for instance, at the turn of the millennium, many car makers were operating well under capacity. An unkind, but perhaps just, assessment could be that many multinationals are keeping afloat by having things made cheaply in the developing world and selling them with very high markups in their home markets.

A little later in this chapter we shall look at some of the bad and good manifestations of transnational corporations. But there is an initial caveat: while it is human nature to seek something generalized – and preferably mysterious – to hate or to blame, it is misleading to look on the world's 500 plus multinationals as birds of a feather. They vary widely in their size, their usefulness, their rapacity and their degree of concern for public welfare. But one and all they are concerned with making money. Grant them that, and assured and growing markets, and much might be done.

Of the 150 largest global economies in 2005, 95 were multinational corporations, although the top 21 are governments. Topping the corporations is the American Walmart Stores, worth almost $300 billion.[3] Multinationals are, accordingly, businesses with the power to influence the world decisively, and no amount of demonstrations, banner waving and fulmination is likely to change that. If they are capable of the degree of flexibility necessary through self regulation, so much the better – if not, control by a global economic authority would become necessary, and would be absolutely justified. This authority would need to be very tough, with clear and definite powers, but in terms of Axiom One it would need to be structured to benefit the multinationals, coordinate their work, help find them new business, and offer them subsidies where needed to make sure useful things are done which might not otherwise be done. The huge Japanese instrumentality METI could provide a structural model.[4] Such an authority could make a careful assessment of world needs, not only at present but also in the future, and ensure efficient meshing of supply and demand through the development of new and useful areas of manufacture. Since predictable and reliable demand drives business, this does not seem unreasonable.

How then, might Axiom One apply in a detailed case? In Chapter 2 the possibility of a major new industry for poor countries producing fuel hydrogen via solar generated electricity is canvassed. If Axiom One is to be taken into account, the extent to which the financial interests of oil companies – among the world's most powerful multinationals – are affected is likely to be critical. Existing pipelines could be converted to move hydrogen gas, and existing oil tanker fleets modified to ship it to markets in the metropolitan powers in liquefied form. Planned shifts in direction, say from defence weaponry to alternate energy technology, carefully managed and executed, are therefore feasible if multinational corporations do not see themselves as threatened by the necessary social and economic changes.

Highly ambiguous in this context are the factories built by multinationals in the hundreds of 'free trade zones' around the world. Along the Mexican side of the border with the US, in Latin American states like Honduras and Guatemala, and in Asian countries like Sri Lanka, huge industrial complexes have sprung up in which millions of workers, mostly young women, work long hours in bad conditions for wages that are only a fraction of those paid to workers in the home states of those multinationals. Typical examples are the *maquillas* of Latin America, where wages are as low as $50 a month for 12 hour working days. These zones are characteristically in 'poverty belts' where a lot of cheap labour is available – cheap labour that is expected to work without complaint, often in crowded, unhealthy, even dangerous conditions. As many as 20 million people are now employed in the free trade zones. According to John Pilger, an Indonesian worker is paid 40 pence to make a pair of fashionable sports shoes that sell in London for £100.[5]

Apologists for the system make one simple point in justification: if it were not for the free trade zones these people would have no work and no money at all. They are not compelled to work there, they do so by their own choice. The argument is plainly not unreasonable. However, the further consequences must be considered. People working for low wages compete with others elsewhere, contributing to unemployment, falling wages and falling demand in real terms globally. Mandatory doubling of wages and improved working conditions in these places would add very little to the eventual retail prices of the products. A ruling such as this would necessarily have to apply equally to all corporations throughout the world. It might be done by self regulation, assisted by trade boycotts against offenders, but on present showing this seems unlikely. Probably only a world trade authority able to show its teeth could do it.

While it has been said that any publicity is good publicity, this is not really true, as events in Italy in 1976, and in India in 1984, demonstrate. Driving north out of the industrial tangle of Milan towards the lakes and the mountains one passes an exit from the autostrada to the town of Seveso, where, on 10 July 1976 a chemical reactor at a company called ICMESA – a subsidiary of the Swiss chemical multinational Hoffman La Roche – overheated. That reactor was used to produce TCP (trichlorophenol), from which was made hexachlorophene, a proven harmful disinfectant, the use of which had by then been restricted in many parts of the world. TCP was also used to make a weedkiller, 245T, which was to become notorious as one of the main ingredients in Agent Orange, used by the US during the Vietnam war to destroy vast areas of Vietnamese forest. TCP is very toxic and is still causing horrendous birth defects in the third generation after the war in Vietnam. But when it is overheated, it produces a dioxin which is far more dangerous still.

As the Seveso reactor overheated a safety valve opened, releasing a huge light grey cloud into the air. Very soon, dust-like particles dropped from it on to everything below, condensing into minute white crystals.[6] Meanwhile, the cloud also settled over much of Seveso and the surrounding countryside, causing an intense acrid smell, and burning the eyes and throats of the people exposed to it. It was nearly a week before it became known that the harmful element was a dioxin that is the most toxic substance known, more dangerous than cyanide or arsenic. It is odourless, invisible and tasteless. Soon hundreds of people were ill. Children developed masses of ugly skin rashes – chloroacne – others had blinding headaches, nausea and dizziness. Domestic animals and fowls began to die in the hundreds. Large areas had to be evacuated. A medical survey in 2000 revealed that men exposed to high levels of dioxin in Seveso had fathered only 44 per cent of male births, compared with the normal 51.3 per cent. For men younger than 19 at the time of the accident, the percentage of sons born was only 38.

In December 1984, 40 tons of a poisonous gas, methyl isocyanate, were released from a factory in the central Indian industrial city of Bhopal, run by a subsidiary of Union Carbide. The consequences of this, the worst industrial accident in history, were appalling. As the poisonous gas drifted through the densely populated residential areas around the factory, as many as 8000 people were killed, according to one estimate.[7] Around 50,000 more were disabled by breathing problems and temporary blindness, and by 2000 as many as half a million people were considered to have suffered some after effect. Investigations revealed the insecticide plant to be understaffed, with substandard safety and operating procedures. Union Carbide was ordered to pay $470 million in compensation.

These are by no means isolated incidents. There have been many others, among the more notorious the poisoning of thousands of people in the Japanese coastal town of Minamata by mercury wastes from industry, and the Love Canal contamination in the US.

By contrast, the Merck and Co drug company has, over the last 18 years, given free treatment to 40 million people in 35 countries against a major developing world scourge – river blindness. Bites from a small black fly infect humans with millions of tiny parasites, which sooner or later affect the eyes and cause blindness. When a Merck researcher found a drug, Mectizan, that could combat the condition, the company decided, in 1987, to provide it free for as long as it took to control river blindness worldwide. Since then more than a billion Mectizan tablets have been provided free. As a result perhaps 2 million people have escaped blindness, and areas of agricultural land estimated to be as large as Britain can be used again. In 2001 Merck announced that it would donate $50 million towards HIV/AIDS control and care in Botswana, in coordination with a donation of the same amount by the Bill and Melinda Gates Foundation – one of many such from the Gates family.

Ray Anderson was the co-chair of President Clinton's Council on Sustainable Development. He is also chairman and chief executive of a multinational corporation, Interface Inc, which is one of the world's largest carpet makers, manufacturing in 33 centres in 6 countries and selling into 110 countries. Speaking on an Australian radio programme in 1999 Anderson said: 'The economy is the wholly owned subsidiary of the environment and there's no way the economy, the child, can prosper without a healthy parent. The parent is constantly infusing capital into the child. The economy draws natural capital from the environment, from the Earth. No CEO with a subsidiary that required a constant infusion of capital would keep that subsidiary very long, and nature is a better manager than any CEO I know, and capable of being far more ruthless.'[8]

Anderson defined seven objectives his companies were working towards:

1   To eliminate waste.
2   To ensure that any manufacturing emissions were benign.
3   To close the loop on materials – basically to recycle materials, to 'harvest yesteryear's carpets and bring back ... those previous organic molecules'.
4   To drive all these processes with renewable energy.
5   To make transportation services more efficient.
6   To involve customers and distributors in the recycling process.
7   To literally reinvent commerce itself.

Toward this final objective, Interface uses a business device mentioned in the introductory chapter of this book – to lease goods rather than sell them, and in doing this make recycling virtually automatic. Its EverGreen Lease 'sells the surface the carpet delivers. The colour, the texture, the comfort underfoot, the acoustics, the cleanliness, the functionality, those are the reasons that people want carpet.' So 'we retain ownership and ultimate liability for the product, intending to convert that liability into an asset ... bringing those carpets back at the end of their useful lives and giving them life after life'.

Anderson estimated that 'in our supply chain over the last four years the amount of material taken from the earth and processed to produce a dollar income has declined almost 26 per cent ... but the hard part still lies ahead'. Much of this hard part involves replacing materials derived from the petrochemical industry with natural products. However: 'We think there's been enough carpet already made and we should not have to take another drop of oil from the earth, once we learn to recycle those molecules... We want to mine the landfills instead of fill the landfills because there's a vast source of feedstock from carpet that's already been produced.'

He concluded: 'Business is the largest, most powerful and most pervasive, wealthiest, most influential institution on earth and the one doing the most damage. It's incumbent on business to take the leadership and begin to undo the damage to restore the earth.'

The Japanese multinational Fuji-Xerox has also embarked on a programme in which it leases photocopiers, fax machines and computer printers rather than sells them, and reconditions worn out machines to 'new or better' in the interest of conservation. The programme, which guarantees spare parts to keep machines in use indefinitely, is consciously designed towards sustainability, but also resulted in significant cost savings to the company during 2000 and 2001.

There are indeed signs that some major multinationals are beginning to respond to public concerns – if only because the general population has the power to affect their finances through mass boycotts. Millions of people worldwide still refuse to buy any Nestlé product because of its campaign to persuade mothers in developing countries to give up protective breast feeding in favour of a Nestlé bottle feeding product. Boycotts throughout Europe and elsewhere of service stations owned by Europe's biggest business enterprise, Royal Dutch Shell, resulted from its proposal in 1995 to dump a redundant oil rig, Brent Spar, into the North Sea. Shell was also involved in controversy because its oilfields in Nigeria were having a detrimental effect on people living in Ogoniland, in southern Nigeria, and because of the suppression of protest by the military government of Nigeria. This culminated in worldwide concern over the execution of writer and activist Ken Saro-Wiwa and eight other people, and claims that Shell had not sufficiently used its influence over the Nigerian government to save them.

The Nike shoe organization has conceded that it found it necessary to respond to consumer criticism of its manufacturing operation.[9] Nike began taking global steps to improve its work environment: 'Changes have been put in place partly because of the negative publicity the company received.' Nike had been subjected to a massive consumer boycott because of bad working conditions in factories making its product, especially in Indonesia.

Consumers of coffee, the world's largest selling commodity after oil, can now identify whether it has been grown under economically just conditions or otherwise. More than 300 democratically run cooperatives, involving more than half a million of the world's four million growers, are part of a non-profit network in 41 countries which polices the coffee market and controls Fair Trade Certified labelling. Fair Trade Certified coffee is sold directly by growers rather than through middlemen, at prices that are at least twice as profitable to the farmer. After discussions with Friends of the Earth and other consumer organizations America's largest gourmet coffee chain, Starbucks, like hundreds of smaller outlets, decided in 2000 to market Fair Trade Certified beans. This followed earlier and similar initiatives in Europe, where trade certification is also being applied to cocoa, tea and bananas. However, by September 2002, when the price of coffee slumped to 43 cents a pound, well below production costs of about 80 cents, fair trade coffee amounted to less than 1 per cent of world sales. It has since grown to 3 per cent, and two of the four global coffee majors, Nestlé and Proctor and Gamble, have launched fair trade products in some areas.

Use your spending power as a vote. Business, after all, is competitive – there is little sympathy for rivals for whom things go wrong. The stick, then, can be wielded effectively by consumers who have organized themselves to do so, by concentrated boycotts on businesses which offend. The world already has hundreds of consumer organizations, small and large, who are exerting considerable influence. The internet offers them the opportunity to exert a great deal more influence, provided they can combine to that end. Combined internet 'power buying' deals (see Chapter 22) offer a powerful weapon. These could be promoted very readily by consumer organizations.

It is up to governments, local and world, to serve up the carrot – a judicious mix of tax incentives and penalties, subsidies for useful research and even price subsidies for good products finding their way on to the market, benefits and security for companies ready to take part in major coordinated programmes. The concept of 'the greater good' has been raised from time to time in this book. This is not seen as a moral attitude, but rather as a hardheaded measurement of ideas, actions and commodities in terms of their long-term value to the majority of people. A confederation of citizen and consumer groups could post a greater good index, graded from one to ten, on the internet, to help people choose where and how to spend their money.

Consumer action can indeed provide both the carrot and the stick – the good business gets the action and prospers, the bad one goes to the wall.

OPTIMAL FUTURE HISTORY

- Establishment of a world coordinating body with decisive authority over multinational corporations, designed to promote fair wage and industrial policies, but also to direct industry towards products likely to benefit the majority of humans; these measures to be taken in ways that assist the profitability and productivity of industry globally.

- Establishment of a coordinating body for consumer organizations with a responsibility to maintain a 'common good' index, rating manufacturers on such things as value for money, reliability, durability and utility of product and costs of service and spare parts.

CHAPTER 12

THE TROUBLE WITH MONEY

Money is the key to solving most of the problems of the planet, the universal solvent, the fluid connecting global productive effort. Plainly, the way money is used and distributed is basic to the task of eliminating poverty, but most money use seems to increase poverty rather than otherwise. Is this inevitable, or are there better ways of using money?

In 1976 a practical idealist who happened to be a Bangladeshi, the professor of economics at Chittagong University, decided to do something about poverty. Muhammad Yusuf founded and developed the Grameen Bank – Grameen means village – with the simple gesture of making capital totalling $27 available to 42 hardworking and competent people who were, in spite of their efforts, living on the edge of poverty. Yes, that figure was $27. Their poverty, as is the case with millions in the developing world, was due to their oppression by petty but extortionate moneylenders who exact interest rates as high as 10 per cent a week. It all began when Yusuf talked with a young woman, supporting a family of three children, whose livelihood was making bamboo stools. He found she depended on a petty capitalist to supply her with materials, which she could not afford to buy, on the basis that he bought the finished product back from her. Her 'profit' from continuous and unremitting hard and skilled work was the equivalent of 2 cents a day. This pittance, just enough for the bare necessities of life, ensured her continued poverty and quasi-slavelike state.

Yusuf's conviction that small amounts of capital made available to the very poor could transform their lives got scant support from conventional bankers. The poor would not repay the loans, they said; the poor have no collateral. But Yusuf's faith was amply justified. In 2004 the Grameen Bank had 3.7 million borrowers, with average loans of $150. Of these, most are women. Its repayment record – around 98 per cent – is better than most conventional banks. It operates in 46,000 villages, more than two-thirds of all the villages in Bangladesh, with a staff of 12,000.[1] It has inspired almost 200 similar banks in 58 countries. An important aspect of these banks is the provision of support networks, including business advice and training, to the people given loans.

However, Yusuf's vision did not end with the Grameen Bank. His declared objective is nothing less than the elimination of poverty throughout the world by 2050. A first step in this direction was the Microcredit Summit in Washington in 1997, attended by 3000 people from 137 countries, designed to reach and help 100 million of the world's poorest families by 2005 – that is, those with an income of less than $1 a day. While this objective was not quite reached, spectacular progress was made, with 2931 micro-credit institutions established, providing for more than 92 million clients, by the end of 2004. The next summit meeting is due in 2006. Yusuf firmly declares that charity is no solution to poverty. It is necessary to give every human being a fair and equal chance. In a 1998 report[2] the United Nations acknowledged the value of Grameen type schemes, but pointed out difficulties reaching 'the poorest of the poor', including the relatively high interest rates and rapid repayment times required by many grassroots banking institutions.

We are at rock bottom here when it comes to assessing necessity. Death, disease, blindness come only too easily and early to the world's poorest. Millions die each year before they reach the age of five. Consider the desperation that drives hundreds of thousands into selling their children into bonded labour or prostitution. These things are, or should be, unacceptable in the world of the 21st century – they should disappear from our history of the future.

Access to economic building blocks – the material facilities to help villagers out of their abject poverty – seems a necessary first step. This is the rationale behind the Billion Artifacts programme described in Chapter 26. Beyond this 'pump priming', interest free loans to individuals – even outright grants – could bring the kind of economic freedom provided by the Grameen Bank and others like it. Each amount would probably be quite modest in Western terms.

Using money in these ways plainly has useful and humane results. Contrast it with money's predominant influence now. Its political impact, now greater than ever before in the world, is perhaps its most dangerous aspect, because it is fundamentally irresponsible. Big business freely acknowledges that its basic concern is not public welfare, but to increase profits to shareholders. Yet even this limited objective is often betrayed. Concealing or misrepresenting the movement and use of money has become a major industry, resulting in mass transfers of funds from the public and shareholders to insider traders.

The collapse of the American energy giant Enron in 2002 prompted this comment: 'Enron hid billions of dollars in debts and operating losses inside private partnerships and dizzyingly complex accounting schemes that were intended to pump up the buzz about the company and support its inflated stock price.'[3] 'Greed is good', as they say on Wall Street. However, the only true wealth of the world comes from someone, somewhere, making, creating or growing something. The tendency for such people to get less and less money, and for the manipulators and middlemen to get more and more, has caused severe economic and social distortions at a time when innovation and rapid material development in new directions are becoming very important. *The Economist* in an article on February 19, 2005, discussed attempts to make business practice into an academic discipline, with special emphasis on MBA degrees, and quoted Canadian business professor Henry Mintzberg as saying 'the MBA trains the wrong people in the wrong way with the wrong consequences.' This and other academic criticisms in the article revolved around the idea that modern business teaching is for mechanistic, immoral attitudes based on low standards of corporate responsibility.

If the current bias toward the finance, insurance, distribution and service sections of economies continues, with vast accretions of 'paper' wealth, the damage will become painfully obvious. The new society must be efficient and innovative, yet frugal enough to keep pace with the need for rapid and constructive change. Its use of money will almost certainly need to be rechannelled and modified. This might include controls on currency and share market trading, bimonetarism – in which money as a means of exchange and as a means of investment are separated – the provision of capital loans and grants without collateral to poor nations and people, and new approaches to company financing. There is increasing support for the ideas of economist Silvio Gessell, with a number of successful experiments in the issue of 'local money' which, instead of attracting interest, depreciates in value over time so there is an incentive to spend and circulate it, rather than saving it. This has already proved to be a potent accelerator of local economies.

'This new order has no democratic mechanisms for representation, as nation states do, no elections, no public forum for debate. The rulers are effectively blind and deaf to the ruled. Protesters take to the streets because this is the form of expression available to them.'[4] The phenomenon thus described – globalization – attracts major criticism because of the problems it causes in national and individual finances. The essential nature of globalization is perhaps best expressed in these words of billionaire George Soros: 'It's not trade that makes it global, it is the movement of capital... There is a need for some international political cooperation to match the globalization of markets.'[5] Writing in 2002, Soros remarked on the need for 'powerful international institutions devoted to ... social goals such as poverty reduction and the provision of public goods on a global scale'.[6]

Even in the world's wealthiest countries, most of the pile is going to very small groups of people, often enough by questionable means. For instance, executives of Enron sold more than 1 billion dollars worth of share options they had been granted in the 2 years before Enron collapsed, while thousands of shareholders lost money as the same shares became almost valueless.[7] One of America's biggest and most respected auditors and some of the biggest US banks were complicit in the Enron affair.

The gap between top executive's rewards and their workers is growing steadily – business executives are regularly voting themselves incomes that are huge by any previous standards. The vast majority – 84.5 per cent – of the wealth in the US is in the hands of the top 20 per cent of the population, compared with 3.6 per cent at the disposal of the poorest 20 per cent.[8] Much of the wealthiest business is in the retail and service areas. The US retail chain Wal-Mart was the world's largest, turning over almost $220 billion in revenues and sales in 2001, at times over $1 billion in a single day. The richest people in the world in 2005 were the Walton family, of the Wal-Mart chain, with $97 billion, Bill Gates, of Microsoft, with $46.6 billion, and Warren Buffet with $44 billion.[9] There are almost 587 billionaires, with total assets worth $2.2 trillion, well over the annual income of half the global population living in the 48 least developed countries – a situation described by UN planners as 'grotesque inequality'.

In Asia, the financial crisis of 1997–1998 barely touched the elite,[10] a group estimated at 3.4 million and located in the major capitals. This figure represents less than 0.1 per cent of the Asian population and contrasts with severe disadvantage, often amounting to poverty, among the remaining 99.9 per cent. This financial elite was almost entirely urban, ranging from 17.5 per cent of the population in Hong Kong to 4 per cent in Djakarta. In the US during the last years of Millennium 2, according to economics professor, Robert Frank, of Cornell University[11] 'the people at the top are getting most of the growth in income'. Approximately 36 million people in the US go hungry regularly. They are mostly working poor on the minimum wage.[12]

During the 1990s, large American corporations cut their tax payments by $70 billion through the use of tax havens and other evasion systems – money which had to be raised by increased taxes on individuals.[13] In 1992, corporations paid 23 per cent of total corporate and individual tax. By 1999 this had fallen to 20 per cent.

The basic ideas behind an economic system transcending national boundaries seemed persuasive when they became influential three decades ago. Free market forces and the laws of supply and demand would set prices, wages and working conditions. There would be 'a level playing field', protectionist policies such as tariff barriers would disappear, and the country best equipped and specialized to make certain things would do so, and sell them to the rest of the world. In the long run, everyone would be better off.

A yawning gap in this reasoning has been that while economies have become more and more globalized, there has been no global political system able to counterbalance and control them. The proposition that more money at the top creates a 'filter down' effect to the poor has not been realized – the reverse has happened. 'Market forces' have made industry less efficient in terms of the real needs of the world, and its products increasingly inappropriate. Fewer and fewer people are working longer and longer hours under increasing pressures, while the numbers unemployed or underemployed worldwide are growing steadily.

The free market concept has also lost credibility because its main advocate and the world's largest economy, the US, has persisted with protection of its own industry, notoriously its agriculture. By mid 2002 this protection had increased to the point where almost half of American farmers' income was coming from other taxpayers. These subsidies, totalling many billions of dollars a year, allow US farm products to compete unfairly on the world market, to the detriment of farmers elsewhere, and especially in the developing world. Huge agribusinesses are getting the lion's share of this transfusion from the American taxpayer.

In 1997, the spectacular collapse of the economies of Korea and almost every southeast Asian country, an enormous run of bankruptcies, a fall in the value of Asian stock markets of $2 trillion, and an increase of tens of millions unemployed, brought the issue to a head. Although this catastrophe was due in large measure to cronyism and inappropriate spending of borrowed money in the Asian countries, it was seen in those countries as being due to meddling by Western 'free market' interests in their currencies. Such transactions make it possible for interests controlling enough money to use 'market forces' to alter the value of a national currency up or down to the benefit of the manipulator, and to the detriment of that nation and its people. Some estimates place the value of this 'wandering money' as high as $4 trillion.

The idea that market forces, if left to themselves, can solve economic problems is not new – it lost credibility in the 1930s during a long and seemingly intractable world depression. An alternative economic theory was put forward by John Maynard Keynes, who said that what he called 'aggregate demand' was the determinant of business prosperity and employment rates. Aggregate demand, the total spending of governments, business and individuals, could be increased by greater government spending, financed by budget deficits. Monetary policies, making credit available at low interest rates, would stimulate business spending. Thus overall prosperity would be increased, encouraging individual consumer spending.

Probably the most famous Keynesian enterprise was the American New Deal, designed to lift the US from the consequences of the 1929 stock market crash which led to massive bank and business failures and huge unemployment. When he took office as American president in 1933, Franklin D Roosevelt put forward a radical new package of legislation during the 'first hundred days' of his presidency, setting out an unprecedented level of government intervention in the economy. Failing banks were assisted, farmers subsidized, and massive public works, such as the Tennessee Valley hydroelectric scheme, commenced. Millions of the unemployed were given work in government financed public works and conservation schemes, the Works Progress Administration and the Civilian Conservation Corps.

Keynesian solutions nevertheless came to develop their own problems – a tendency for governments to prefer deficits to less popular economic solutions, thus adding to national debt, and, typically, high inflation and high interest rates – stagflation. These factors led to extensive abandonment of Keynesianism in the 1980s in favour of the current 'free market' system or monetarism, which was promoted by two economists, Austrian Nobel Prize winner Freidrich von Hayek and Chicago academic Milton Friedman. It has been criticized as effectively a reversion to unfettered capitalism, 'the respectable economic excuse for removing protections and benefits exacted painfully from unwilling governments after decades of struggle by the labour movements'.[14] This is one point of view. An advocate of the free market would claim, with validity, that it broke the chains of high inflation which had brought stagnation to many world economies, and has made business more efficient with the reduction of state regulation.

'Planned' economies – especially those in the former Communist world – involved close government supervision, and generally included state ownership of the means of production. These typically led to low standards of living and scarcity, poor quality commodities, and crippling inflation. On the other hand, free market capitalism typically leads to high unemployment, large income disparities, and the creation of what will sell rather than what is needed. Because its gurus insist that state enterprises must be 'privatized', this has often resulted in assets being almost given away, as with the extraordinary loans for shares deals done between private capital and the Russian government in 1996. Free market economic practices have also had a regrettable tendency to impoverish large numbers of people, as has notoriously been the case in the former Soviet Union and Argentina. In these countries, much of the community was reduced to poverty at virtually developing world standards following conversion to 'free markets' directed by American advisers.

So do we damn both planned and free market economics out of hand? Not necessarily. The ill effects listed above arose from the regrettable tendency of humans – especially 'experts' – to favour extremes. All this indicates that successful economic policy, like much other policy, is unlikely to succeed if it is driven by narrow or extreme philosophies. The market needs to be free enough to move and work efficiently, but controlled enough to prevent the inevitable urge to loot. This Axiom Two tendency must be restrained from damaging reasonable social and economic standards. One thing is certain – a better world economic system is needed than the one we have now. Granted a balanced approach and compliance with the axioms, it should not be too difficult to achieve.

Perhaps the kindest overall assessment of modern economics is that it is classically reductionist, concerned with money in one form or another, with little regard to who possesses it or the social consequences of that, with gross domestic product (GDP) no matter how it is distributed, and with 'market forces' no matter how destructive or irresponsible their effects might be. The advocates of globalization point to a growth of 500 per cent in world production of goods and services in the second half of the 20th century, without apparent regard to the fact that almost all of these economic advantages have been to the benefit of a minority of humans – probably well under 20 per cent – and have contributed to high pollution rates and an alarming and massive wastage of natural resources. 'Productivity' levels, if they are made up largely of luxury or wasteful artifacts, or driven by planned obsolescence, harm the world rather than helping it.

Accurate and realistic perceptions of economic matters seem necessary. Are they available? How honest, for instance, is the concept of GDP, generally touted as the standard yardstick of economic prosperity? According to three American economists[15] GDP 'is a crazy mismeasure of the economy that portrays disaster as gain ... by the curious standards of the GDP, the nation's economic hero is a terminal cancer patient who is going through a costly divorce. The happiest event is an earthquake or a divorce.' Since GDP is a simplistic measure of all goods and services output, without taking into account the reasons for this, these criticisms seem apt enough. Further distortion results from allocating manufacturing income in a developing country to that country's GDP, when in fact most of that money returns to a major industrial power as profits or dividends. Apparently dramatic rises in GDP in Asian 'tiger economies' were largely due to this method of calculation.

But is there a better way? Is it possible to cure massive unemployment, unused industrial capacity, weak consumer confidence – all basic world economic problems at the time of writing? Looking back through history, the example of Germany after Hitler came to power in 1933 is interesting. Germany, by the winter of 1932, had an unemployment rate of 30 per cent – some 6 million out of work – and industry, hard hit by the onset of the world depression, was operating at under 50 per cent capacity. Germany's foreign trade declined by two-thirds between 1929 and 1932. Three years later gross domestic product had doubled, unemployment was under a million. Germany actually had a labour shortage by 1937.

This apparent miracle was wrought by two things – the financial abilities of the Minister for Economics, Dr Hjalmar Schacht, and the rigid authoritarianism of the Third Reich.[16] Schacht, an admirer of Keynes and the New Deal, persuaded Hitler to throw money into the economy in huge amounts – this was the time when the great *autobahns* were built, Ferdinand Porsche designed the Volkswagen – the people's car – and German armed forces were hugely increased. These were Keynesian solutions, and, initially at least, were financed by printing new money. Conventional wisdom would assert that this should have created a major wave of inflation. However, this did not happen because the 'slack' was taken up by unused industrial capacity and by reducing unemployment. Prices and wages were controlled, taxation remained high. As earnings increased, so did government tax revenue. Industry was subsidized, the labour force was strictly controlled. One lesson for the new society to learn from this example could be that massive new investment in reasonably labour intensive programmes to benefit the developing world could result in greater prosperity and falling unemployment worldwide, without undue inflation.

Since a massive diversion of money towards real needs will plainly be necessary to avert the worst effects of the 2030 drivers, let alone serve the purposes of the ensuing new society, how might this be achieved within the terms of Axiom One? A self regulating decision by multinational corporations to return agreed, standard and adequate proportions of their profits to the nation in which they operate by way of tax, to their workforce in the form of higher wages, and to a global fund to address world problems, would be a good start. Provided this applied to all corporations, there would be no competitive disadvantage to any – rather the prospect of rapidly expanding markets in a higher income world. Organizing such a system ought not to be beyond the powers of the World Trade Organization. If effective self regulation is not forthcoming, mandatory payment of a turnover tax, not subject to deductions, to a world fund, could have the same result.

Strict international regulation of tax evasion schemes such as tax havens and transfer pricing, the global imposition of a wealth tax on all personal income beyond $1 million a year, and on all proceeds of currency speculation pending world controls on predatory currency trading, and a guaranteed UN income stream from global commons, would also serve to provide necessary revenue. Cancellation of developing countries' debt, readily financed by small reductions in armament spending on an agreed and uniform worldwide basis, would permit poor nations, now struggling, to make progress – there would be a stable base on which to build decent societies.

OPTIMAL FUTURE HISTORY

- Get money diverted to developing world needs in large chunks – immediate reallocation of 10 per cent of World Bank funds to micro-credit schemes would be a good start.
- Start a subsidy fund to generate income producing businesses in the worst poverty 'hotspots', especially in regions where the sale of children to bonded labour and prostitution is demonstrably common.
- Get rid of tax havens, currency trading, developing world debt, agricultural subsidies and any other legal but immoral devices which channel money unfairly from the poor to the rich. The world could be transformed by this one measure alone, which national governments, acting in consultation, could readily legislate for.
- Replace GDP with quality of life indices.
- Audit of company accounts by a statutory authority, not private firms.
- Senior executive salaries determined by vote of shareholders.

PART THREE

UPGRADING THE INDIVIDUAL

CHAPTER 13

THE PURSUIT OF HAPPINESS

In 2004 The Economist Intelligence Unit used a complex formula in an ambitious attempt to rate quality of life – happiness – in 111 countries. Ireland came out on top, but perhaps the most illuminating result was that the top seven nations were all small ones – Ireland, Switzerland, Norway, Luxembourg, Sweden, Australia and Iceland. Of the world's largest nations the only one to rate reasonably high was the US, in 17th place. The UK was 29th, China 60th, India 73rd and Russia a dismal 105th. Why is this so? Is it because the circumstances of the basic unit of humanity – the individual – seem to be taken into consideration by planners less and less, especially in bigger countries? If so, this must be recognized as an important negative tendency, if only because future needs will require balanced, competent and motivated people.

For several decades, some futurists have held that a 'remake' of the human species will be necessary if we are to cope successfully with the era of great and rapid change on which we are already embarked. Charles A Reich called for 'a new way of living – a new man, a higher transcendent reason', promising 'a life that is more liberated and more beautiful than any man has known'.[1] The much maligned behavioural psychologist B F Skinner believed 'we need a technology of behaviour … we need to make vast changes in human behaviour', because 'things grow steadily worse, and it is disheartening to find that technology itself is increasingly at fault'.[2]

Neither of these theorists express very clear ideas about how this transformation is to be made. Nevertheless, the central idea, that the state of the overall human condition depends on the individual, her or his stability, his or her happiness, is important. A more practical approach came from philosopher Bertrand Russell and his wife Dora, who opened a 'progressive' school in 1927 at Beacon Hill in Sussex to demonstrate that children learn better when they are free, happy and non compliant. This school, with its contemporary, Summerhill, was widely criticized by the establishment of the time – it is alleged that a visiting clergyman was met at the door by a little girl, stark naked, who shouted 'God does not exist!', then slammed the door – but was the forerunner of many established since.[3]

These people, among many others, saw that somehow we are failing at the individual level; our educational methods are producing large numbers of illiterate, unbalanced or unhappy people; our medicine is orientated towards the affluent Westerner, while the major killing diseases are gaining ground; our gadgets are delivering disappointing results. Our complex technology, its unforgiving speed, the dilemmas of population, war and peace, government, pollution, productivity – all these things require management by balanced, self confident, healthy individuals, yet as time goes by we demonstrably have fewer and fewer such people. Instead, depression rates have increased worldwide to epidemic proportions.

Negotiating the perilous course to 2030 is, then, involved at the most basic level with the welfare and happiness of individuals. There are abundant research results that link creative productivity and a positive approach to problems with individual happiness and welfare. Hence there is a huge and demonstrable economic benefit for the world if as many people as possible are happy, healthy and well adjusted.

What is it then, to be happy? The *Concise Oxford Dictionary* gives a fairly cursory 'lucky, fortunate; contented with one's lot'.

Much of the popular media view of happiness equates it with personal and immediate sensual and material gratification, although there is plenty of evidence that satiation frequently results in discontent and unhappiness. The Dalai Lama believes the basic purpose of existence is 'a happy life, happiness, joy'.[4] This would not come from material goods, but from the use of intelligence to understand and resolve problems.

A 2001 study showed a consistent view that self esteem, connections to other people, personal competence and autonomy are regarded as major ingredients of happiness.[5] The safest definition is perhaps the absence of depression. Viewed this way, happiness becomes of massive human importance. Depression rates are increasing – it is soon likely to be the world's most common ailment after heart disease.

Is it regrettable that a lot of people don't feel cheerful? Rather more than that. According to some research even mild depression can be a killer.[6] This research has established a clear link between depression and heart attacks, indicating that healthy people with no history of heart disease are twice as likely to have a heart attack if they are depressed, even if the depression is at mild levels. However, death from heart disease is by no means the only depression killer – suicide, a disabled immune system and an unhealthy influence on a whole range of diseases, including cancer, are part of a 1999 World Health Organization prediction that by 2020 depression will be the second largest killing disease.

Happiness is a commodity sought in the world as never before. Drugs are developed and eagerly used which, it is hoped, may deliver happiness. Psychologists earnestly study the physiological effects of laughter. Write a book entitled 'How to be Happy' and you can be pretty sure it will sell, regardless of its content. The extent to which happiness is desired and pursued confirms that a great many people are not happy. It also shows a lack of understanding of the fact – and it is well documented – that the elusive happy state is indeed just that – elusive. It is unlikely to derive from taking a pill, it cannot be bought regardless of the amount of money spent, it does not necessarily follow success or achievement. Sexual love, it would appear, is by no means a guaranteed source.

Indeed, the experience of falling madly in love shows such strong correlations with some forms of mental illness as to confirm the time honoured label of 'love sickness'. Research showed biological parallels between the love sick and those who suffer obsessive compulsive disorder, a condition in which sufferers feel compelled to go on repeating certain actions, like checking that doors are locked or washing their hands.[7] In both cases, low levels of the brain 'feel good' neurotransmitter, seratonin, were observed – around 40 per cent less than in normal people. The same Italian subjects observed a year later, after they had become sexually accustomed, appeared to have recovered – the levels of seratonin in their blood were back to normal.

There is evidence that in stressful situations optimism strengthens the human immune system, and extends life. A study of 839 Americans over 30 years to 1999 has shown that pessimists – defined through a careful selection process over several years – had a 19 per cent higher death rate.[8] University of California psychologists studied 90 young law students.[9] Those who had an optimistic attitude towards their studies showed higher counts of protective T cells and killer cells than the pessimists. Optimism in this case amounted to expectations that they would succeed, and a positive belief in their own abilities.

Laughter, commonly regarded as an outward expression of happiness, is now recognized by most hospitals as a positive factor influencing healing, to the extent that there are now specialized laughter therapists. Laughter has recognized physiological benefits – stimulating the immune system by activating the T cells that kill viruses and cancer cells, reducing the 'stress' hormone cortisol, releasing 'feel good' endorphins and improving respiration.

It has frequently been observed that the people who make an effort to help the world are often happy – those who are unhappy are likely to be too preoccupied with their own affairs, too inward looking. Research in this area suggests that people who are happy don't think about happiness much. Being happy, they simply take that condition for granted. American social psychologist David Myers describes the experience of happy people as an 'unselfconscious "flow" state' and warns that a self preoccupied pursuit of happiness can detract from that.[10] Happy people, he says, are 'flow' absorbed in a task that challenges them without overwhelming them.

So it becomes important to enquire why all this should be so. Are the depressed people 'constitutionally' unhappy, in the sense that it has always been their normal state? Do their conditions of life make them unhappy? Is there some physiological basis for their condition? Or is it just because they are much too concerned with themselves and not enough with things outside them? Most modern research into happiness – as opposed to unhappiness, or now more popularly, depression – shows that people who say they are happy are almost always doing something. They are enthusiasts, caught up in what they are doing. There are countless autobiographical testimonies that the act of creation, of achievement, tends to be more valued than the result. Happy people tend to be realists – Bertrand Russell commented: 'The key to happiness is accepting one unpleasant reality every day.'[11]

An American researcher, Robert Franks, believes that increasing affluence contributes to unhappiness.[12] Things that once were luxuries reach the stage where they are everyday occurrences. Broadly the same area of research in Britain also indicates that increasing affluence does not bring happiness.[13] On the contrary, mild depression has become more prevalent in Britain, affecting almost one-third of the population.

Some theorists believe children can learn unhappiness from their parents – if they see their parents in a permanently unhappy state they may well conclude that unhappiness is something you can do nothing about. And because children tend to see everything in terms of themselves they might blame themselves for their parents' unhappiness. American psychologist Martin Seligman used experiments with dogs to demonstrate what he calls 'learned helplessness'. Faced with unpleasant experiences – mild electric shocks – about which they could do nothing, the dogs simply gave up, and passively accepted the pain. Seligman and others evolved a theory that human depression comes from a confirmed pessimism about life and its events.

There is abundant evidence that physical activity induces a sense of well-being, even to the extent of increasing 'happiness' endorphins. Creativity also has a strong association with happiness. A study of the autobiographies of creative people confirms that a deep sense of satisfaction comes from the act of creation – even belief in a link with an inscrutable outside power, sometimes identified as the divine.

How does creativity start? Chapter 16 discusses the effect of schools on native creativity, and the evidence that it can be suppressed or nurtured early in life. Children and their toys become relevant here. It is likely that the child who painfully hammers three sticks together into an 'aeroplane' may become a happier person than the child who is given a bagful of plastic toys. Although the first child might acquire a few sore thumbs, the basic creative urge has been nurtured. The aeroplane, once made, brings a sense of achievement, and the urge to create things in childhood is likely to be carried forward into adulthood. Dora Russell observed this at Beacon Hill. All this suggests that those attitudes towards life which could be collectively called happiness may well be set in childhood and substantially maintained throughout adulthood. A child who is, for instance, subjected to constant bullying in school without any apparent recourse or means of escape may well react like Seligman's dogs.

Harvard University psychologist Daniel Gilbert consulted more than 100 academics about their emotional state of mind, specifically their degree of happiness. He found that good and bad things that happened to them had no permanent effect on their usual happiness level, which fairly quickly returned to what was normal for them. A University of Illinois researcher, Edward Diener, noted that for events like being promoted or losing a lover, most of the effect on mood had gone in three months, with not a trace left in six months. Lottery winners were found to be no happier a year after their win. It becomes, then, important to investigate how and why that 'default' happiness level is set.

There is some consensus that a genetic element is involved, but opinions differ about how important this inheritance factor is. A behavioural geneticist, following research involving 1500 pairs of twins, considers that about half the happiness default is due to genetic influences.[14] Other psychologists say the size of that factor is not yet reliably assessable.

Those seriously mistreated by life usually – but not always – feel less happy. Ill health, poverty and unemployment can cause depression, rather than the other way round, and it is probable that those with a low 'default' happiness level suffer most. Young people who can't find work feel rejected, their self esteem drops; divorce and relationship breakups often lower the happiness level of almost all the people involved. Modern conditions of living, especially urban living, can generate stress and unhappiness. There is a relentless association between unhappiness and proneness to illnesses, and between unhappiness, social disadvantage and crime.

Nowhere is this evidenced so starkly as in the position of Australian aborigines. Although indigenous people comprise only 2 per cent of the New South Wales population, they account for around one-third of the number of juveniles in detention, one fifth of women prisoners, and one-seventh of adult male prisoners. Outrageous statistics of this kind, which are echoed elsewhere in the world, are evidence of the disposition of governments to lock people up, and build, at high cost, more and more prisons, rather than make any serious effort to deal with the underlying social stresses we are considering in this part of the book.

Have those who seek to remake humanity, to create 'new women and men', got the right idea? Probably not. Most of the evidence shows that human nature has a remarkable resistance to such basic, rapid and dramatic change. But there is another possible approach: to look critically at the conditions in which humanity lives – its habitat, education, relationships, religion and work – to assess what imperfections lie there. It seems an obvious requirement to identify and seek the means of mitigating the miseries, deficiencies, perversities and adversities which society somehow seems to inflict at the personal level. There are a number of reasons why these things happen. Many of them are readily identifiable and therefore susceptible to correction.

Since such an effort is unlikely to come from governments or bureaucracies, which generally remain obsessed with narrow economic considerations – and, more recently, 'terror' – the responsibility may well rest with you. Improvements in law, housing, education and conditions of work will probably emerge from what look at first like small individual efforts. Perhaps 20 families might be prepared to avail themselves of the high prices of urban properties to sell out, pool their resources, and attempt social structures similar to those we shall now go on to consider. One shopping cooperative might decide to boycott the goods of a corporation that offends the greater good. One group of parents will seek for their children a different and more creative education. Such things are already happening, and must be nurtured, since these groups then cease being powerless and ineffective, and instead exert a positive influence. Provided they can muster the intelligence and determination to succeed, they will, in time, seed others like them.

The rest of this section of the book then, deals with those social areas which impinge on the life, welfare and happiness of individual people, and what might be done about them.

CHAPTER 14

LOVE, FAMILY AND FREEDOM

Perhaps the most significant, and often disruptive, changes going on at the individual level are in relationships between men, women and their children. 'None of the changes now are as important as those going on in our personal lives – the most difficult and disturbing changes of all', British sociologist Anthony Giddens has remarked.[1] The conventional family, in which the man is the master and leader, respected and obeyed by his wife and children, is fast disappearing. It was a creation of social and economic conditions now almost superseded in the Western world, and becoming so elsewhere.

When life was physically harder, and the accumulation of property usually slow and difficult, family coherence and loyalties were in everyone's long-term interest. Sex and fertility were closely linked. Because of this, sexual relations had major social and economic implications – so much so that in most societies the choice of marriage partners was not left to the individuals, but was arranged or heavily influenced by families. This remains the case in much of the developing world. 'Love' in the sense of spontaneous sexual attraction became especially suspect as a basis for marriage, because of its often ephemeral nature. The marriage, which was intended to last throughout life, must be based on more permanent things – family allegiances, money, property. Such marriages attempted to 'protect' women from extramarital affairs, because of the importance of property being inherited by 'legitimate' heirs.

The new system of cohabitation has been described by Giddens as 'coupledom', based on emotional attachment and requiring 'emotional democracy', an equality not only between the man and the woman, but also between them and their children. 'Coupledom' acknowledges the often short-term nature of sexual attraction. The relationship may well not be for life – it probably won't be.

The 'breakup' between partners is now a familiar aspect of many societies, and can cause a great deal of pain where expectations and early conditioning in one or both partners has been for a permanent, marriage-like state. Social and legal frameworks are still, in many ways, geared to the traditional family system, habitat is still substantially based on one man, one woman and children living together. There are still traditional families like this which are apparently successful, still powerful elements of government and society which stress 'family values', which see a return to those values as the answer to the problems of society.

Does the implicit contract of 'coupledom', that the relationship lasts as long as 'love' lasts, conflict with the needs of any children of the union for a continuous, stable and reassuring background with adequate material support for as much as two decades? There is considerable evidence that it may do so. Research from Britain indicates that families with cohabiting parents break up four times as often as married ones.[2] In Australia the rate of relationship breakdown in cohabiting couples has been assessed at about double that of married couples. One researcher found that a quarter of cohabiting relationships lasted a year, and that three quarters had ended in four years.[3]

There is a prolific amount of research indicating that the children of single parents can become disadvantaged educationally and socially, and suffer higher levels of personal danger. A 1999 study in the US, Canada and Australia indicated that children of divorced parents end up with around one year's less education, with a dropout rate in high school about 60 per cent higher than in children in stable married relationships.[4] Children seem to do better if the sole parent is working, with one survey showing that 40 per cent of the offspring of welfare dependent single parents showed low learning skills, compared with 20 per cent of the children of working parents.

There are those, however, who have a different view. After surveying more than 1000 major studies of divorce, Australian National University academic Bryan Rogers objects to simple statistical associations leading to assumptions that it is divorce that causes the problems.[5] Rogers' assertion is that it is rather the problems within the family that led to the divorce that should be blamed, and that conflict, physical violence, sexual abuse, mental health problems, substance abuse and poverty are likely to be more damaging than divorce itself.

However, research in two countries does suggest that children in cohabitational families are likely to be in higher personal danger. A British study found that children living with unmarried biological parents were 20 times more likely to be subject to child abuse than those with married parents; in those living with a mother and a *de facto* boyfriend the rate rose to 33 times.[6] In Australia, child murder figures in 1994 showed that 'the proportion of suspected child killers in *de facto* relationships was six and a half times higher than in the general population'.[7]

Barbara Ehrenreich remarks: 'The real paradigm shift will come when we stop trying to base our entire society on the wavering sexual connection between individuals. Romantic love ebbs and surges unaccountably; it's the bond between parents and children that remains rocklike year after year.'[8] Ehrenreich suggests the establishment of adult contracts, not to live or sleep together, but to take joint responsibility for children. In view of the crucial role of children as heirs and eventual controllers of the new society, this suggests automatic and adequate financial levying of both parents from the birth of their child to 18 years as a minimal requirement. Disputes over male parentage would be resolved by mandatory paternity testing, now cheap, easy and readily available.

Despite its problems, coupledom, with all its implicit social mobility, appears to be here to stay, and with the imminent arrival of an effective male hormonal contraceptive pill, sexual 'wandering' can only increase. In most parts of the Western world, coupling now normally precedes marriage – that is, when marriage occurs at all. Marriage, as a later phase in a relationship rather than the beginning of it, has become very different. Its social, extended family element is much reduced; it is a more personal affair, motivated by an intimacy and sense of rightness demonstrated in the preceding coupling, and acknowledged by both parties. The eventual marriage is also less overtly a 'till death do us part' contract in most cases. It is tacitly accepted that if love goes, the relationship ends. This is an acknowledged part of 'handfasting', the marriage ceremony used by the burgeoning Wiccan spirituality, where couples 'vow to remain in partnership as long as love lasts, after which each is permitted to leave the relationship and go their separate ways'.[9]

Traditional marriages, of course, often at least, *seem* to be successful, although almost all careful and apparently honest accounts of family life within them reveal many tensions – and that goes for almost all cultures. Popular Chinese traditional novels, such as the *Chin P'ing Mei*, which was written in the 16th century, make this abundantly clear. That novel, the story of a mandarin and his six wives, describes almost every conceivable form of chicanery and villainy from false witness to murder within that single large family.

In the past there has been a strong inculcation of family values into children. Religions have typically stressed them. There are many picture books for small children showing 'families' of animals – and this brings us to an interesting point. The modern science of ethology – the study of animals in the wild – has evidence indicating that the 'family' does not exist among most other living creatures. If there were to be any comparison with human affairs, the lives of other primates would seem most useful. According to Robert Ardrey, there is no sign of a family unit among the higher primates – and many live in elaborate, conscious societies.[10] He points to observations of many life forms – even schools of fish – where the individuals are nearly all the same size, and presumed to be much the same age. Ardrey quotes well documented and respectable research concerning the other primates indicating that the bond between mother and infant is broken quite soon after a younger sibling is born, and that the elder offspring then becomes a member of its peer group. Large troops of baboons studied in southern Africa all seem to have been very much of the same age. Young animals need their peer group, and their 'play' is an important part of their maturing to normal adulthood. Ardrey quotes experiments in which primates deprived of peer contacts grew up to be 'neurotic' and sexually inadequate.

The work of the ethologists indicates that human behaviour is much closer to that of other animals – especially other primates – than has been popularly acknowledged, in many ways. But more of this later. For the moment, the peer group research ought to make us stop and think, especially those who shake their heads forebodingly when the human child begins to shun the influence of its family for that of its peers. Is this a 'natural law'? The evidence seems strong enough to support strengthening, reinforcing and helping the peer bond rather than deploring it as a disloyal, ungrateful and transitory part of growing up.

CHAPTER 15

HABITAT: THE DILEMMA OF THE CITIES

One in three of all city dwellers in the world lives in a slum, and the number is growing fast. These points were made by the UN secretary-general, Kofi Annan, in a statement on World Environment Day, 5 June, 2005. By 2020, according to the UN Environment Programme, more than two billion people – at least a quarter of all mankind – are likely to be in 'improvised slums and informal squatter settlements which are neither legally recognised nor serviced by city authorities'. But even in the prosperous Western cities some ominous hints of a chaotic future are emerging, such as the virtually uncontrolled violence, including the burning of more than 7000 cars and scores of public buildings and businesses in Paris and other French cities, during several weeks of rioting in 2005. Even in these more 'developed' cities, high housing costs, transport bottlenecks, air pollution, noise, urban crime, difficult and stressful child raising, abrasive contacts with neighbours who are close – all these and more are only too familiar.

Nevertheless, the urban problem is at its worst in the developing world. In most of the world's biggest cities, as many as half the inhabitants live in an untidy skirt of unspeakable slums.[1] In Kolkata, in India, a third of the population literally live, eat and sleep on the streets, often renting small areas of pavement from criminal gangs.[2] Other cities with populations of over 10 million that have similar problems are Sao Paulo, Djakarta, Manila, Dakar and Karachi.

These consequences have arisen from a tenfold increase in the urban populations of the developing world since 1940, combined with a lack of the resources to maintain infrastructure even at inadequate existing levels. Natural disasters combined with dense urban development and inadequate construction standards can make the increasing numbers of high rise apartment buildings in some of these cities lethal traps. Such was the case when a major earthquake struck Gujarat state in India in January 2001, killing more than 20,000 people. In another earthquake in a highly populated area in Turkey in August 1999, tens of thousands of people died when their apartment blocks collapsed around them at three in the morning. About 27,000 buildings – half of those damaged – had to be demolished completely.[3] Subsequent government reports estimated that more than half of the deaths were due to buildings having inadequate foundations and steel reinforcing, and too little cement in the concrete. Buildings, including, tragically, many schools, collapsed in hundreds when an earthquake and its aftermath struck Kashmir in 2005, killing as many as 100,000 people.

Such deathtrap buildings are common in much of the world, due to economic pressures and inefficient governments, which are usually authoritarian. However, they even occur in densely populated, earthquake prone Japan, according to a Japanese professor of concrete engineering, as a result of a longstanding corrupt conspiracy between some Japanese parliamentarians, bureaucrats and a cartel of big construction companies.[4] This circumstance prompted a major scandal in 2005, when many apartment blocks and seven hotels, including a 260-room Tokyo tower, were closed because cost cutting and shoddy building made them liable to collapse in even a moderate earthquake.

Cities, then, are highly vulnerable to natural disasters, and in times of war. The higher the rate of urbanization the more dangerous this factor becomes. Air pollution, so severe that it presents a major health hazard, has become characteristic of most major cities, although many have been forced to regulate the causes of pollution simply to remain habitable. Such was the case in London after four terrible days in December 1952, when smog laden with sulphur dioxide became so thick that air, road and river traffic could scarcely move. Visibility was reduced in some parts of London to as little as one foot, buses had to be guided by a man walking in front with a lighted flare. Those four days of pollution killed at least 4000 people.

As energy becomes more restricted and expensive, can we actually afford to maintain the cities? In most of them, basic infrastructure like water supply and sewerage, much of it built 100 years ago or more, has not kept pace with population growth, or is in increasing disrepair. Fewer than 300 of India's 2500 cities and towns have sewer systems, and most of these lack treatment plants – sewage simply flows into lakes, rivers or the sea. Two-thirds of urban dwellers lack sewerage.[5] As energy becomes more expensive, the cost of such infrastructure, and of 'urban renewal' projects, escalates. Yet as cities grow larger, they become increasingly vulnerable to the consequences of the breakdown of these facilities. And even modern Western cities have an average reserve of food for only five days.

Predictions that the mega-cities will continue to expand may, however, now have to be qualified. UN census statistics in 2002 indicated that urban growth may now be faltering, apparently because of inadequate infrastructure and the appallingly unpleasant conditions of life in so many cities. In Mexico City, Kolkata and Buenos Aires, more people are leaving than arriving, although high birth rates will continue to push their populations higher.

Architects and designers see the need for changes in the nature of buildings. With the liberation provided by computer assisted design, the 'monolith' type building is giving place to structures of formerly impracticable shapes and proportions, like Gehry's Guggenheim Museum in Bilbao, Spain, Libeskind's addition to the Victoria and Albert Museum in London, and the National Museum in Canberra. The ability of modern automated manufacture to build complex computer designed shapes should allow this freedom to extend to housing. Already, mass produced composite panels and prefabricated concrete modules that slot into each other can accommodate an almost indefinitely varied range of houses, in which the straight line and the right angle are no longer obligatory. Automated housing systems now in use employ fibre reinforced modular panels with wiring and plumbing already in place for walls and roofs, contain no timber or steel, claim to be vermin, fire, earthquake, corrosion and hurricane resistant, and can be put in place more quickly and cheaply than conventional housing. The pressure on land is becoming so extreme in The Netherlands that plans are in hand for housing, businesses and even roads floating on water. At least 100 such houses will be built in Ijburg, a new up-market suburb of Amsterdam, and a floating city to house 12,000 people near Schiphol Airport is at the planning stage.

An almost universal opinion is that living spaces must become smaller, and thus need to be more flexible. The concept of apartments or houses being a set of rooms is giving place to one of neutral containers into which pre-manufactured modules, like bathrooms, kitchens and sleeping quarters can be located, and even moved around to suit the whim of the occupant. Even furniture is envisaged as being multipurpose – curtains might contain solar cells that would charge during the day, and emit light at night. Light switches would turn on and off as you looked at them; materials such as bedding could sense variations in temperature and change their molecular structure to become denser or lighter.

Much of this is speculative, but it has one major point of interest: there is an expectation of a radical change in the nature of habitat, so radical that it is difficult to see how it could be accommodated in most existing city infrastructures, which can barely cope with present population densities. Most architects realize the need to get away from grey suburbs of uniform apartment blocks that almost totally lack anything that grows naturally. Some contemplate buildings in which whole floors are devoted to manmade forests or parks; others attempt, by going ever higher upward, to devote more of the available ground space to gardens and sporting facilities such as pools and tennis courts.[6]

There are a number of problems with these ideas. Because their economic rationale is based on an artificial but only too influential factor – the high cost of urban land – they turn out to be expensive, attainable only by the wealthy. Such schemes are likely to be built in any quantity only in a small minority of the world's cities, and they cannot solve the basic intractable problems outlined earlier in this chapter. It is more reasonable to seek those solutions in totally new habitat areas.

A high priority, then, is to evolve at least some decentralization from the large cities and into carefully planned regional complexes that can offer living conditions less demanding than those in the cities, and that are more suited to groups and families. Away with everyone then, to arboreal villages? This idealistic view, which one comes across in one form or another in hundreds of comments in all the media, seems to be one answer – and indeed many people actually do it. Waiheke Island at the entrance to Auckland Harbour in New Zealand has large areas virtually denuded of native vegetation after decades of sheep farming. Here 15 families have established, on 300 acres, 'a place where we live in harmony with the land, conserving and enhancing the land and its ecosystems'.[7] Agriculture is to be organic – no artificial fertilizers or insecticides – and sustainable. To protect native wildlife, no dogs or cats will be permitted. The internal politics of the community will be based on consensus, not majority voting. Dwellings are planned in three clusters around a community house. This is a rural variation of the urban 'co-housing' concept which is popular in Europe, and is rapidly gaining adherents around the world.

Such ideas also exist within the 'voluntary simplicity' movement, which has attracted hundreds of thousands of people, especially in the US. Its principles include a reduction in the amount of time spent working for material possessions, in order to make time for better personal relationships and individual accomplishments, closer communion with nature, and living more frugally and sustainably so there is enough for all to share. One popular US bumper sticker reads: 'Live simply, that others may simply live.' 'Common cause economics', in which individuals take into account the community interest as well as their own, is seen as part of this, and perceived as being easier to achieve in small communities than large ones.

Business likes people to be in cities because business is there, and it is convenient to have the workforce, like other commodities, neatly packaged in boxes nearby. The urban jungles of today are indeed a product of industrialization. When mass production of goods developed it was economically desirable to have workers conveniently near. So whole new suburbs, rows of terraced houses in the main, were built to accommodate them. Blocks of modern high rise apartments are designed for the same purpose.

Is this pattern of life natural, and does it have to be permanent? It is worth remembering that it evolved quite recently in terms of human history. Before the industrial era, men generally worked on the land where they lived, along with their wives and families. In many parts of the world this is still so, and it could become possible again in Western societies. Nevertheless, community size is important – very small habitat areas languish for lack of facilities and social interest. The challenge is to create urban areas which are optimal in size, providing lifestyles at least as attractive as those in large cities. For most people, the work element is vital. Their job is in the city. If they don't want to take on the arduous burden of commuting long distances, it is easiest to live near their work. Then there is fun. The big entertainment and sporting venues, the places people want to be seen, are usually in cities.

Yet even these considerations are receding. Millions already work from home – telecommuting – without being close to, or even visiting, 'the office'. 'Outsourcing' is creating millions of small contract businesses which are replacing the huge factories of the past. For most people, electronic media are fast becoming the major source of entertainment, and these can be enjoyed anywhere. Gardening is becoming immensely popular – surveys have shown that in many countries it is the preferred hobby. Such influences tend to favour smaller, more decentralized habitat areas specialized to suit modern needs and preferences.

A second difficult area is the physical infrastructure of the megapolis. Many of these problems are simply due to the fact that almost all cities are old, can no longer cope with modern conditions and exploding populations, and are no longer suitable for modern lifestyles. Narrow streets block traffic, but the surrounding property is so valuable it becomes uneconomic to widen them. Even if widening does become possible, traffic levels soon seem to be as bad again. There are problems with other infrastructure. Sewerage, water supply, electricity, gas, telephones – all these services become increasingly difficult to repair or extend to cope with rising populations. These are almost universally acknowledged problems. Can the cities solve them, and provide a genuine *habitat* to the individual – I use this word in this context to mean circumstances that give an adequate and satisfying quality at all stages of life – from childhood to old age?

The answer seems that, without considerable modifications, the city probably will not offer an adequate habitat, except for specialized groups, such as the very wealthy and childless, and perhaps for young people who have not yet started families. A major retarding influence is the increasing cost, in real terms, of even minimal urban housing. A 20th century phenomenon almost everywhere was a large increase in the cost of the land component of urban housing. This means that dwellings become less and less affordable, smaller, closer together, and more isolated from nature. This economic factor is perhaps most evident in Tokyo, where the majority of people live in tiny apartments, where businessmen sleep through the week in capsule hotel 'rooms' which are tubes not much larger than a coffin, and go home only at weekends because of the pressures on public transport. Such developments bring to mind the science fiction nightmare of individual humans conditioned to living in isolated cocoons, surrounded not by real things, but by virtual reality.

The fact that urban living has already commenced that conditioning is disturbing. The small size of most apartments, their closeness to neighbours, the frequently poor sound insulation, polluted air and generally unnatural surroundings, their difficulty of access to schools, playgrounds and other children, all militate against the normal development of our children. There is nowhere for them to wander and play experimentally except the street, which is too dangerous, and the apartment is too small for many indoor play opportunities. Noisy games – and all children need to be noisy sometimes – are impossible because the neighbours will complain. Parents have little time to relax with their children because they are too busy making a living, ferrying the children through dense traffic to school or some activity centre. Traffic gridlock, lack of parking places, pressures on time – these things conspire to make the apparent advantages of urban life less and less attractive. Inevitably, children are forced from the earliest age to watch TV, play electronic games and tinker with computers. The road toward the isolated cocoon is already under our feet.

So where do these considerations lead us? Toward forms of housing that do not have a high land cost component, that are large enough to provide all the necessities for a natural and creative childhood, that encourage peer group activity among children, that can accommodate modern 'coupledoms', that can help to absorb the shock of relationship breakups, that can provide effective social reinforcement, that can provide habitat of the highest order, and which are energy efficient. A large order, but not impossible – although it should be said that the last thing habitat planning should do is to force people into set lifestyles. Modern urban development is doing that too often now. If families want to live in their own house, houseboat, tree house, or whatever, that should be possible.

Less than two centuries ago the village, consisting of a number of mostly small houses and at least one central communal gathering place – perhaps a pub, perhaps a church, perhaps a community hall – was the normal dwelling place for most humans. In those communities everyone knew everyone else. But satellite towns, designed to provide cheaper land, with more open space, have not been notably successful. Most of them have been mere 'housing estates', providing pretty minimal housing at that, with little thought for the social infrastructure, both behavioural and physical, that is most desirable for any community. The village concept seems more promising, and is becoming more feasible with the development of new technologies, better and faster public transport, and the opportunity for more people to work from their homes at computer terminals. More than 100 years ago Ebenezer Howard published an immensely popular book describing in detail proposals for 'garden cities' – decentralized habitats which nevertheless offered the advantages of concentrated urban life.[8] Many of his ideas have more force now than when they were written.

Envisage a wide circle of large 'houses', each big enough to accommodate, say, 20 adults and as many children, each group within it occupying its own self-contained module, in comfort and privacy, but sharing facilities like a swimming pool, a music room, a library. Each house could be added to at need with low cost modules mass produced on robotized production lines.

The people living here might be couples, with or without children, unattached adults, grandparents, even orphans, who live close to each other because they want to. The accent would be strongly on flexibility, especially within the modules, which would offer as much or as little space and facilities as the occupant wanted or could afford. The location would be an attractive seacoast or country area, and the town is one of a number linked to an urban, largely automated, industrial, mass entertainment and storage centre by fast maglev trains.

Because good quality land would be cheap and freely available, much of the food used by the community could be 'homegrown', fresh, wholesome, and probably organic, produced either by individuals as a business or cooperatively. Drinking water would come from roofs; sewerage systems might be replaced by composting toilets, which are now a well established and successful technology, 'waste' water would be recycled into gardens. Much, if not all of the community's electricity would come from renewable sources, including amorphous photovoltaic cells on roofs and other surfaces, perhaps even the roads and lanes that serve the community.

Each 'household', because of its cooperative financing and low land costs, could afford virtually any leisure, sporting or cultural facility, to the especial benefit of the children. These children would have at all times the support of their peer group, as well as access to proxy 'mothers and fathers' and a wide range of educational, sport and hobby activities. Relationship changes would be cushioned by the existence of a supportive network of friends. It would remain possible for both parents to continue in the same habitat after a relationship break. The young mother suffering from postnatal depression would have readily available help, as well as the means of relief from 24-hour-a-day baby care. Most people's work would be carried out without leaving the town.

Within the perimeter, in which no powered vehicles would be permitted, there would be social and leisure facilities, for example tennis courts and swimming pools, and the junior school, located in such a position that even small children could make their way to it on their own feet. Higher education by expert, gifted communicators would be largely at computer terminals and specialized seminars. Companionship for adults and children, entertainment, social and educational facilities, and most forms of sport, would be available cheaply and within walking distance. The need for vehicle use – and these vehicles would be quite unlike today's cars – would be minimal. One writer postulates such a community in 2786: 'the new president's inauguration will be attended by all five of the mixed sex, multi-racial commune that raised her. She will establish sizable tax reductions for couples or groups of any size that create stable households for their children and other dependents. Peace will break out.'[9]

Communities somewhat like this, of course, do exist – there are 270 of them in Israel. *Kibbutzim* still produce 35 per cent of Israel's agriculture, run the nation's largest network of hotels, holiday villages and country lodgings. There is also a national orchestra and theatre company based on them. While many are adapting away from the early concept of completely communal living, they remain a key element of Israeli society. I can remember spending a couple of days in one – the Leon Blum *kibbutz* not far from the Syrian border. There was extensive sharing of facilities – most people used a pool of cars rather than owning their own, meals were available in a communal dining room or could be prepared at home. Orchestras, a theatre, library – all these were fostered by the community as a whole. This place was obviously prosperous; most of the people there said they were content with their life. However, human nature being what it is, such communes can prove too safe, too predictable, provoking a degree of dissatis-faction, especially among young people.

Why not, therefore, plan into the habitat complex 'pads' in the reworked cities where acquaintance with other boys and girls, 'fun' and adventure, and the means to try differing work styles, could be available? Disused city infrastructure could readily be adapted to this purpose, and to live entertainment.

There are without doubt many people to whom such ideas would be anathema, possibly because of the influences of their own upbringing. Changed methods of education, developing social contacts and skills very early, might well reduce their numbers. Chapter 16 looks at this aspect of the idea. Also, those starting their first relationship might well prefer to live alone for a while. But for those who choose the true community, the advantages are obvious. Granted that they are intelligent and enlightened, as they probably would be, they would acknow-ledge the power and importance of peer group influence on their children, and would offer that peer group creative and satisfactory pursuits simply by providing them with the facilities likely to encourage this.

At present, of course, many Western children are brought up with concepts like 'privacy', 'staying in one's own backyard', and 'keeping oneself to oneself', which may or may not be natural. Rebuffs to early social questing are a painful part of almost every childhood. It seems likely that children brought up in a freer, more cooperative way, in which peer group influence and the mentoring of adults are acknowledged and nurtured construct-ively, would more readily see the advantages of the 'village' when they became adults. And the village, of course, would be a much safer place than a city, especially for children, who would almost always be close to a range of people they know. Those who have read Aldous Huxley's last novel, *Island*, will recognize some of the ideas set out here. Perhaps we should also include his thought that every child should have access to a second family, to whom he or she can go when for any reason they are at odds with their parents for the time being.

CHAPTER 16

MAKING EDUCATION WORK

No teacher discipline, no exams, no formal lessons, no set curriculum or textbooks – such is the pattern for the Met school in Providence, Rhode Island, arguably one of the world's most successful places of education. In spite of the fact that about half of the students are from poorer homes, and had limited previous learning skills, *every* one of the first two graduating classes were accepted into university. Three quarters of these were the first in their families to go on to higher education. Less than half of the students are white, 38 per cent Latino, 18 per cent African-American.

So successful are this school and its clones now developing rapidly in America that Microsoft billionaire Bill Gates in 2005 donated $52 million to establish 70 more Met schools across America by 2007. Gates commented: 'America's high schools are obsolete. Until we design them to meet the needs of the 21st century we will keep limiting – even ruining – the lives of millions of Americans every year.' The school is attracting worldwide attention – 50 Dutch school principals have already come to look, 50 more are due.

Established by teacher Dennis Littky in 1996, the Met school is based on groups of 14 who stay together for 4 years with a teacher adviser, pursuing largely individual goals. In Littky's words 'The main thing is not to be boring'. The major objectives are to teach students how to learn and think, and to pursue their own interests and abilities in an individual but purposive way. Peer interaction and freedom from iron-clad curricula and 'discipline' motivate learning, what is learned is closely related to the real world.

The new society will need the best methods of education possible – designed to develop socially adequate, innovative, happy people who recognize their own abilities and ambitions and are confident in them. These requirements suggest that considerably more money and effort should be devoted to education, and that some quite basic changes in approach are necessary. These might include a better appreciation that the process of education begins, and is perhaps at its most important, early in life.

A number of recent studies have confirmed what women have always known – that effective 'mothering' is highly important in the earliest development of the individual. Close physical contact between mother and child, facial expressions, such as smiling, even baby talk, seem necessary to create an optimal brain network on which later knowledge, and indeed the means of social stability, can be built. Significant implications are that adequate paid maternity leave is something more important than mere convenience, that the care and nurture of children is vital work worthy of fair recompense, and that any economic requirement that mothers return early to the workforce is socially damaging.

It is salutary that the framework of most present day education systems is almost 2500 years old. The Greek philosopher, Aristotle, believed that from the age of seven children should be educated in ways which moulded them to suit the needs of the state – a new idea at that time.[1] After puberty would come 'liberal' schooling, in many ways similar to modern tertiary education. 'Education must be one and the same for all.' Aristotle wrote: 'The oversight of education must be a public concern, not the private affair which it is now, each man separately bringing up his own children and teaching them just what he thinks they ought to learn.'[2] This was the model followed by the developing Western world. It is still much in evidence today.

Nineteenth and early 20th century concepts of education, at their most extreme, saw a school as a 'sit stillery' in which organized and largely arbitrary areas of learning – 'subjects', such as geography and mathematics, were taught. Much virtue was seen in rote learning, which was thought to stimulate the mind and memory, and rigid discipline, enforced by punishment, was seen to have moral 'character building' values. Then, at the beginning of the 20th century, came an influential reformer, an American professor, John Dewey.[3] In Dewey's view societies could develop only if education became less rigid, permitting children to form their own ideas and develop their natural creativity. Within this reasoning, fixed, ordered curricula become obstructive, even dangerous. Activity and experiment should replace rote learning and set 'subject material'. These ideas quickly became popular, especially in the US.

Austrian born Ivan Illich was an ordained Catholic priest who, in 1969, was relieved of his priestly duties because of Vatican disapproval of his ideas about education. These were that schools should be abolished altogether, and that education should become experience in real life situations.[4] Illich vigorously attacked schools as dangerous, unbalanced institutions which do more harm than good. His alternative was a loose acquisition of useful experience from peers and elders, as well as practical experience with things. In a sense, teachers would continue to exist, but they would be guides facilitating the learning process, which would not follow a curriculum, but would serve the individual's needs and curiosity. There are striking similarities between these views and actual practice in the Met schools.

There is a note of despair evident in much of what teachers and 'experts' are saying about conventional schooling. 'In education, the more skilled the teacher, the better the performance. Yet the education industry everywhere is using the same techniques that were common 150 years ago: students in groups from 10 to 50 being taught by a single teacher. The challenge will be to make education less labour intensive by using fewer teachers better.'[5] The following quote comes from one well researched and considered Canadian paper: 'Schools are generally intellectually boring places, uninteresting both for the students compelled to attend them and for adults hired to work in them... And there is not a single educational reform in the 20th century that has changed this fact... The educational establishment, including most of its research community, remains largely committed to the educational philosophy of the 19th and early 20th centuries.'[6] Alvin Toffler remarked: 'Mass education was the ingenious machine constructed by industrialism to produce the kind of adults it needed... Our schools face backwards towards a dying system, rather than forwards to the emerging new society, which will require people who have the future in their bones.'[7]

Different individuals do indeed respond best to different methods of education. Some children will amicably learn a pre-defined curriculum in a group, although the long-term benefit of this to them is doubtful. Others rebel against it. Some work best alone, some need more time than others to complete a task. Why, in the light of this background of thought, and the demonstrably differing needs of students, has the traditional school hung on so long? Social structures provide much of the answer. Class systems in which 'the working class' is expected to 'know its place', in which 'the deserving poor' are seen as inevitable, are still very much alive in many places. Since increasing numbers of women now work in most parts of the world, schools have acquired a significant function as places for children to 'be' while both parents are at work. Many religious schools around the world tend to be conservative and to teach what suits the dogma of that particular religion.

Education, then, has two major and often conflicting objectives: first to mould children to fit society and suit its purposes; second, to provide information and conditions for the free development of the abilities and ideas of young human beings. These alternatives lie behind much of the very considerable body of current comment on education. There is a view that the 'progressive' should prevail and many private schools are informed by it. Then there is the opinion that since human societies function under the rule of law, which protects individuals and offers them collective benefits, education systems should train children to accept the obligations and restrictions society requires.

Ordinary commonsense indicates that an amalgam of both influences is reasonable, with most considered opinion and practice tending towards less restrictive education for younger children in particular. It could reasonably be argued that the most useful and productive social conscience is likely not from conformity, but from people thinking and speaking freely and innovatively. The heresies of one generation are frequently the gospel of the next.

What might ideally be taught to four to eight year olds as the first requirements of their education? There are plenty of ideas on this subject, many of them stemming from the thousands of 'progressive' schools, both private and public, around the world. Among them we may find the following:

- Respect and love for the planet, all its life forms and its ecosystems. This, to be taught largely by seeing and doing things, becoming involved with nature early in life in hands-on activities such as gardening, caring for animals, involvement in environmental causes.
- The ability to handle personal relationships within the constraints of society. There have been successful experiments in 'classroom democracy', using ideas like the right to equal treatment, opportunity and responsibility, the concept that no person 'owns' or should dominate another person.
- Nurturing and encouraging individual human abilities. Children often show an early interest in painting, music, dancing. It should be automatic for them to assume that every human has the right and the obligation to explore her or his potential, to know what it is and develop it to its full extent, that a basic value is to be creative, and that the products of human creativity are important, with great potential for good or bad.

Accordingly, the age at which children should be introduced to abstracts like mathematics and literacy is controversial, and while there has been some reaction from the formerly accepted ideas of Jean Piaget that their teaching should be linked to maturation, and that children should be tasked when they are 'ready', those ideas are far from being abandoned.[8]

The Early Learning Goals system officially promoted in Britain, obliging nursery schools to teach an approach to reading, writing and mathematics, has been considerably criticized as 'hot housing' and 'battery farming'.[9] The organization Let Children Play, suggests on its website that formal teaching should be delayed till the age of six or seven, as is the case in Switzerland.[10] This site quotes an international study, conducted in 32 countries, which found that children taught literacy later have, at the ages of 9 and 14, better reading skills than those taught earlier. Professor Anne Locke claimed the Early Learning goals were clearly beyond the maturity of some children, presenting 'a real danger that at the very least we will turn children off learning because they will not succeed and will be conscious of failure'.[11] She also quoted the European experience 'where children are not introduced to this kind of work until they are much older, but learn a lot more quickly'. According to one report, the Swiss system teaches the basics of reading in two terms, compared with three years in Britain.[12]

The need for knowledge is growing rapidly in today's flexible and fast moving patterns of work and relationships. If students are going to master larger volumes of new knowledge, some things may have to be left out to make room for this. Cheap, easy to use calculators diminish the need for rote learned 'tables' and basic arithmetic. Once voice actuated computers become freely available – and that will be soon – even the basics of literacy, particularly handwriting, could well be questioned. Should laborious rote learning, which has been made largely irrelevant by technology, yield priority to learning how to 'tap into' the vastly increased bank of modern information?

Advanced education, then, might also become a departure from the traditional classroom where on-the-spot teachers of varying ability lecture to students, to a much more flexible and experimental mode making extensive use of audio visual methods, especially visual recorded 'lessons' from unusually good communicators. What is a school, after all? The Greek word meant 'leisure'. Originally a school was a group of people who voluntarily gathered at the feet of a great thinker, who came and went as they felt they had acquired what they needed from his wisdom.

To what extent might this influence the use of modern communications technologies in schools, rather than simply providing computers and saying: 'Okay. Now sit down in front of those, do as you're told and become smart/smarter/smartest'? Teaching mere computer literacy achieves the means without the objective. But, properly used, computers offer the chance of bringing the talents of a gifted teacher to thousands – even millions.

How do children learn? Research into successful home schooling indicates that they learn naturally by asking questions about what comes into their minds, and that these do not follow each other in any organized 'curriculum' way. 'Why is the moon yellow?' 'Why is sugar bad for you?' 'Do cats think?' The evidence is that children have a natural ability to learn this way and then to fit all these things together into a coherent picture of the world. It is probably the way all human children learned prior to the introduction of mass education systems.

To what extent are traditional schools the product of the 'clockwork universe' ideas of the 19th century, which assume that a standard and arbitrary body of knowledge, administered compulsorily to everyone in an 'organized' way, regardless of their differing abilities and capacity, is best? To what extent does boredom act as an abrasive in the machinery of learning? Many textbooks are badly written and unattractively presented. They are frequently mechanistic, loaded with often unnecessary charts and diagrams, insufficiently related to life experience. Their connection to anything 'real' may seem obscure, especially to young children. On a visit to China, I was impressed by a 'Children's Palace' in Shanghai. These craft and activities centres are not only designed to stimulate curiosity and creativity in children, but also to permit observation of the particular talents and interests of the individual, so these can be encouraged and nurtured. There may well be scope for this approach in schools everywhere.

Certainly a downgrading of 'curriculum' considerations, allowing much greater freedom for individual development, and much looser time frames, seems desirable. The objection that this makes formal examination more difficult is acknowledged. But this is, or should be, a secondary consideration to providing a good education. Employers want examination results, but would these not be more useful if the exams were organized and provided by employer groups to assess the specialized knowledge and skills their businesses need in potential employees?

School time could offer students the freedom to select, from books and audio visual materials, things they want or need to know. There is also scope for electronic presentations of inter-active sessions with teachers of proven ability, originality of mind and demonstrated communication skills, even if these verge on the charismatic. Open-ended learning schedules, rather than fixed terms ending in examinations, would allow students to approach excellence in their studies in their own time.

An essential problem of 'mass' schooling is its influence in maintaining inequalities.[13] Children of affluent and educated parents go to 'good schools' which, because they are good, attract the best teachers. Student motivation is usually high, and because of these factors, the quality of the school is maintained. These factors do not generally obtain for schools with a high proportion of deprived children. Here difficulties of discipline and a general contempt for the learning process become common, and the schools are frequently unable to teach even basic literacy universally. Eventually 'working class kids get working class jobs' – or no job at all. The power of modern communications technology to redress this balance is obvious.

Ivan Illich claimed most schools have a hidden curriculum, based on the discipline and regimentation they impose on children, 'to know your place and sit still in it'. Illich's concept of a framework of educational resources which would give individuals the choice and opportunity to learn what is most useful to them, widely considered impracticable when he wrote, is rapidly becoming less so as information technology advances.

In general, schools, and indeed universities, promote a culture of half learning when they are organized into fixed terms of study interspersed with regular examinations. These generally have an acceptable pass mark, as low as 50 per cent. The majority, who never even approach the highest marks, are finally passed out as being educated in their subject area when in fact they probably know little more than half of it. Liberal subject choice in examination questions tends to reinforce this effect. The student responds to what he or she knows, and what is not known is tacitly ignored.

By contrast, modern electronic 'open' universities, now developing in many parts of the world, accept that a student should study a subject for as long as it takes to at least approach excellence, that her or his study should involve a great deal of individual choice of material, no matter how long it takes. Students are encouraged to draw their own conclusions, criticize, and put forward new ideas, not just sit and listen. They can then be examined when they feel they are ready. Education along these lines could be the subject of experimentation at many levels.

OPTIMAL FUTURE HISTORY

- Education to produce original, even dissentient thinking, rather than conformity.
- Education for excellence, rather than to lesser standards.
- Education for individual aptitudes, rather than fixed curricula.
- Motivation by practical goal-seeking, rather than by imposed 'discipline'.
- Considerable freedom for students to choose areas of knowledge they feel happy with, consistent with their abilities and purposes.
- Maximum use of modern technology to convey knowledge from the best teachers, rather than average class teaching, and designed to inspire enthusiasm for learning.

CHAPTER 17

HEALTH AND WEALTH

Globally, the war against disease is going badly. This is regrettable enough in itself, but it becomes all the more serious because increasing human incapacity, if unchecked, will accelerate the 2030 drivers. Chronic illness or disability affects as many as two in three people, premature death takes millions more. Some African countries are virtually crippled, as AIDS destroys as much as 40 per cent of the workforce. Major killing diseases, recently considered under control, are again exacting a toll in the millions. The worst effects are being felt in the developing world.

And most of those millions of premature deaths, more than half of them of small children, are preventable – quite easily and cheaply. Western nations justifiably wring their hands and lament for years when calamities such as the September 11 disaster strike. If one has tears for the 3000 people killed in the World Trade Center, why not some for the 10 million children who die each year, whose only crime is to be born in a developing country and not the affluent West? What is happening here?

Indeed, the accident of birth can have fatal consequences: well over half of humanity lives in conditions of poverty and malnutrition that favour the quick spread of disease, in places where the research effort and money devoted to health care are minuscule compared with that directed to a small affluent minority in the West. Classic instances are the appalling rate of multi drug resistant tuberculosis infection in Russia – especially in the prisons – and the slowness with which an effective anti malarial drug, *qinghaosu*, is being developed, more than 20 years after its value was established by Chinese research. During that time 45 million people have died from malaria.

Three major diseases – malaria, tuberculosis and gastric infections in infants, take 13 million lives every year.[1] A fourth new and incurable disease, AIDS, had killed more than 25 million by 2005, and in that year more than 40 million people worldwide carried the virus. In 2004, 3.1 million people died of AIDS, and for the first time, in many areas, the number of women affected exceeded men. In South Africa it was estimated that 22.8 per cent of pregnant women were HIV positive, and that around a third of the children of these women would be born with the virus or would be infected while breastfeeding.[2] Over the next ten years this African disaster is likely to be repeated in south Asia, the former Soviet Union, Indonesia and possibly China. And there is still no cure, no cheap, effective treatment to halt this global pandemic, and no united world response to a killer of humans in numbers now seen as likely to exceed the death toll of the Black Death. There are 6.5 million people in the world who need AIDS drugs – less than a million are getting them.

Infections like tuberculosis, malaria and pneumonia, once considered reasonably under control, are dangerously expanding their incidence. In 2004, deaths from tuberculosis were estimated at over 2 million.[3] The disease is the leading cause of death for the world's young women – around three quarters of a million a year;[4] 70 per cent of all cases are in the developing world. The world's renewed tuberculosis epidemic has close links with AIDS, with estimates that AIDS increases tuberculosis infection by a factor of 30.

The death rate from curable or avoidable illness in the developing world contrasts sharply with the affluent West, where people are healthy and long lived compared with those of even a century ago. As late as the 19th century, barely half of all children born survived into middle age, many dying at birth or soon afterwards. In 1900 the average life span in Western countries was still under 50. The change over a century has been dramatic. In 2004 the European mountain state of Andorra had the highest life expectancy of 83.5 years. Japan was next with 81 years, the US was 46th at 77, and Britain 38th at 78. Due mostly to AIDS, ten sub Saharan African countries were rated lowest; Zimbabwe's healthy average life expectancy was 32.9 years, Sierra Leone's was 25.9[5] – 'levels we haven't seen in advanced countries since medieval times'.[6]

But the news is not all bad. Global attacks on disease, carried out by the World Health Organization and the United Nations Children's Fund, have had some spectacular successes. The disfiguring and often fatal smallpox, for so many centuries a scourge in the world, appears to have been eliminated in 1977, when the last case was reported in Somalia. Until the vaccination programme began in 1967, 15 million people a year had smallpox. Of these, 2 million died. A similar campaign against poliomyelitis – infantile paralysis – made significant progress during the last decade of Millennium 2, when cases reported in the world fell from 350,000 in 1988 to just 600 in 2001.[7] Deaths from measles and gastric disease also declined substantially. The rates of heart disease – the world's largest killer – dropped by around a third in much of the developed world during the last decade of Millennium 2, due mainly to lower consumption rates of tobacco, alcohol and fat, and a fashion in the West for exercise regimes. However, these lifestyle improvements were chiefly among the wealthy and educated.

Forecasts of life expectancy in the 21st century as high as 400 years exist,[8] based on expectations of the powers of genetically engineered drugs, and on 'bionic' devices – effectively human spare parts.[9] These estimates are speculative at best. However, perhaps more significant areas of research are based on theories that the life expectancy of a species may be influenced by the proportion of energy devoted respectively to reproduction and to self repair. The life span of fruit flies was doubled over 100 generations by permitting only eggs laid at a late age of maternal life to reproduce. Genetic engineers were able to double life spans in nematodes by manipulating a single gene. Researchers are now looking for the equivalent gene in humans, and believe that quite soon future generations may live 150, possibly 200 years. The morality of extending life spans in an already overcrowded world is, however, questionable.

At present around one in 10,000 people in the industrialized world reaches 100; around 30 per cent are physically and mentally competent into their 80s and 90s.[10] Most are women, none is obese, virtually none smoke. Several countries have claimed the world's oldest person, but probably the most credible when she died late in 2003 was Elizabeth Israel of Dominica in the Caribbean, then aged 128. Only two others have reached 120 or more. Elizabeth Bolden, of Memphis, Tennessee, was considered the world's oldest person late in 2005 , aged 115.

The essential – and controversial – problem with health care is its extreme variability. Do not get sick if you are poor. But if you are poor, you are much more likely to get sick. These statements reflect the strong association of good health with high economic status and degree of education. This is most sharply obvious when health and prosperity in the developed nations are compared with those in the developing nations. For instance, annual private and public spending on health in Kenya is $8 per person, $5 in Nigeria, $3 in Ethiopia, compared with $1500 in the US and $4000 in the US. For every 10,000 people, Kenya has 1 doctor, Germany 35, the US 25.[11] Drugs often cost much more in developing countries, due to 'market forces'. Nevirapine, which prevents AIDS transmission between mother and child, costs $430 in Norway, but $874 in Kenya, where it is desperately needed;[12] a course of first line tuberculosis treatment would cost a Swiss worker 1 hour's wages, a Tanzanian labourer would need 500 hours'.[13]

However, this rich–poor division and its effects are also evident within the wealthier nations. A survey of 1000 people in each of five countries, the US, Britain, Australia, New Zealand and Canada, showed that 29 per cent of those with below average incomes reported fair or poor health compared with 10 per cent of people with above average earnings.[14] How does the connection between health and wealth happen? In many cases, as in the prisons and refuges for the homeless in many countries in which tuberculosis, hepatitis and HIV/AIDS are rampant, the link is due to almost ideal conditions for cross infection and debilitation caused by poor food and cramped living conditions. Any initiative seeking to remedy this situation will find factors extending well outside the 'health' area into economics, habitat and education.

The major, preventable problems persisting in the developing world are exacting an appallingly high cost. Of the world's 45 million blind people, 90 per cent live in poverty stricken areas of Asia, Africa and Latin America. Of these, 80 per cent could have kept their sight through established, relatively cheap procedures. For instance, virtually all of the 20 million with cataracts could be cured for around $20 each, the 6 million blinded from trachoma could have been cured by a $25 operation – lid rotation surgery. Many of these blind are children, who usually die within two years.[15] The commendable battle to combat river blindness by US drug multinational Merck and Co by providing free medication for the past 17 years is described in Chapter 11.

Largely due to an array of new and expensive diagnostic machinery and medical drugs, health budgets are increasing steadily in all Western countries, running into billions of dollars a year, but there is insufficient funding for the simplest and most necessary health measures in poor countries. Cheap vitamin A supplements, which can prevent the blindness threatening millions of children, could be provided for around 50 cents a child, but are still not generally available in the developing world.

Tropical disease rates are on the increase in developing countries, and even in 'second world' nations such as Brazil, where malaria has increased twentyfold in recent years to a figure approaching 1 million infected people. Malaria, perhaps the world's most damaging infectious disease, is spreading rapidly, now affecting around 45 per cent of the planet's land surface. Global warming is expected to increase the areas prone to malaria to 75 per cent of the planet by 2050, including parts of the US, Europe and Australia that are now malaria free. The situation has become more dangerous because the single-celled parasite which causes malaria, and which is transmitted by *Anopheles* mosquitoes, has developed resistance to almost all drugs. This applies in particular to the most feared cerebral strain, *Plasmodium falciparum*, which is responsible for the majority of fatal cases.

One in 15 of all humans has malaria – as many as 500 million people – around double the 1980 figure. It kills more than 2 million people every year.[16] People infected with malaria can suffer as many as 15 recurrent and disabling bouts a year. Those who die are predominantly pregnant women and children. The most promising treatment is derived from a Chinese plant called *Qinghao*. A ten-year field trial involving over 100,000 people on the Thai-Burmese border has shown that the extract, known as *Qinghaosu*, is almost 100 per cent effective in preventing malaria deaths when used in association with established anti malarial drugs. The active agent, artemisisin, is, however, in short supply because there is not enough of the *qinghao* plant. However, a team of international researchers are developing a synthetic version of the drug, OZ277, and are now working on getting the costs of the drug combination down to no more than $1 a tablet. It is hoped it will become available in quantity in three to four years. Only three tablets would be needed to effect a cure. Since it kills the parasite in the bloodstream it can also prevent people from getting the disease. The World Health Organization estimates a global need for 132 million courses of treatment of ACT – the combined artemisinin and other anti-malarials.

One of the most dangerous and feared disease threats to the world is influenza – not the common strains which annually afflict millions of people, but rare mutations against which there is little general resistance, and frequently no protection from specific flu vaccines. These are capable of causing pandemics like the one which killed an estimated 40 million people in 1918 and the severe acute respiratory syndrome (SARS) outbreak in China which caused global panic in 2003. The influenza strain commanding world attention in 2005 was H5N1. A little publicized outbreak of this virus among chickens in Hong Kong in 1997 brought the world dangerously close to another such influenza epidemic, with the potential to kill 100 million people.[17] Influenza is common in birds, and aquatic wildfowl carry the viruses. While the birds do not always become ill themselves, this avian virus pool can mutate and transfer to other species, such as pigs, and thence to humans. In the event, efficient detective work by the world's virologists, and the subsequent slaughter of more than 1.5 million chickens, appeared to have controlled the Hong Kong outbreak. But by 2005 H5N1 had again become a major threat, killing 60 people in several Asian countries and 3 in Turkey, prompting expenditure of billions of dollars to stockpile the only anti-viral drugs likely to be useful, Tamiflu and Relenza.

Then there are the new illnesses which have inexplicably become much more widespread than they were 50 years ago. Hay fever, apparently quite rare a century ago, has now reached epidemic proportions, and since it can develop into asthma, which may be fatal, it can be dangerous. Typically it results in streaming eyes and noses, a bad attack of the snuffles, and general misery for millions of people. Millions? Well, yes, tens of millions even. As many as a third of Americans, a quarter of Britons and 40 per cent of Australians, now suffer from hay fever regularly. Why now? Theories vary from disturbances to the immune system caused by mass vaccinations, to air pollution, to less exposure of children in developed countries to infections and dirt during childhood. Another persuasive case has been made that planting high pollen producing trees like cypress and alders in streets and gardens is also a contributing factor.[19]

Huge costs accrue to national health services because of the effects of harmful and addictive products such as tobacco, alcohol and, to a lesser degree, 'illegal' drugs like marijuana and heroin. The failure of the tobacco industry to market a fire safe cigarette – one which will go out if it is dropped or discarded – is estimated to kill 1000 people a year in the US alone. While this should be noted, these fatalities are negligible compared with the 4.9 million killed annually by lung cancer and other tobacco related illnesses, as estimated by the World Health Organization. Nicotine is as addictive as heroin or cocaine, and smoking should be regarded as a serious drug addiction 'second to no other', according to one 2000 report.[20] A commentary on this report defined smoking as 'a deadly and pervasive addictive drug syndrome covering a quarter of the population ... not just some innocuous or quirky lifestyle habit'.[21]

There are time honoured fiscal reasons why the world's two major killing drugs, alcohol and tobacco, responsible for close on 10 million deaths a year, do not attract the odium and legal prohibition of other recreational drugs such as marijuana. They provide massive tax income to governments. The tobacco industry is at its largest in China, where there are estimated to be 320 million smokers, of whom 800,000 a year die from tobacco related diseases. The national tobacco monopoly in China provides the government with around $20 billion a year in tax revenue, employs at least 8 million people, and produces more than a quarter of the world's 6 trillion cigarettes.[22]

Meanwhile, smoking related deaths in the developed world have grown over the last 50 years more rapidly than population increase, especially for women – from 26,000 in 1955 to 476,000 in 1995. Deaths worldwide are three times the number of road fatalities – and are estimated to grow to 10 million a year over the next few decades as smoking increases in the developing world. There seems, therefore, a reasonable case for an additional special tax to be levied on the manufacturers of products of this type, which are legal, to cover their huge costs to public health systems.

Early in 2000, a World Health Organization investigation found 'an alarming spread of drug resistant infections in many impoverished countries', with drug resistance also increasing in the wealthy countries due to the overuse of antibiotics. There was, accordingly, 'a very real possibility that today's antibiotics would be rendered useless in 10 to 15 years'.[23] The use of antibiotics in food production is widely suspect. They are commonly administered in meat-producing industries, such as factory farmed chickens, to prevent the infections which would normally kill off creatures reared in such unnaturally close proximity, and also because they can promote extra growth. The issue is not an easy one, because there has been no definite proof that these antibiotics are transferred to the human consumer. However, there is a disquieting amount of circumstantial evidence.

The basic rules for staying healthy are, or should be, fairly generally known by now. It is suspected that not eating too much – actually feeling hungry much of the time – can add to life span. Some researchers are even putting figures to the number of years certain dietary and lifestyle measures may extend your life. Not smoking heads one list at eight years, avoiding saturated fats rates six years, a good night's sleep and regular small doses of aspirin around three each, small amounts of alcohol two years.

Responsible recent research has not suggested that moderate meat eating, less than 140 grams a day, is harmful. More than that can be, especially if the meat has a high saturated fat content. Of interest too, is some very respectable research by the Institute of Public Health at Cambridge University, which has been monitoring the health of 9000 people from all parts of Britain, and from a wide range of social sampling, for more than 15 years. The major result showed that those who ate salads, raw vegetables and fruit had much lower rates of heart disease and cancer.

Foods seen as desirable luxuries, such as ice cream, frequently contain large amounts of sugar and fat. High fat content makes food seem more desirable – it is known to induce a sense of stomach satisfaction. But there is also, of course, the economic factor. Fats, especially the most dangerous saturated and trans-fats, are present in the cheapest ingredients, such as palm oil, frequently used in processed foods of all kinds. Their use is almost automatic – it becomes a part of economic competition. Such processed and 'fast' food frequently becomes the most easily afforded by families on tight budgets, who are virtually compelled to buy it for economic reasons. Cheap margarines can contain large amounts of transfats.

Food and water are the basic necessities of life. It is possible to control their quality effectively by regulation, and this will need to be a high priority for the new society. Already, civil law is intervening in the situation, with more and more successful cases against purveyors of substances which are demonstrably damaging.

OPTIMAL FUTURE HISTORY

- Major development of health maintenance co-operatives, designed to prevent illnesses.
- Development and production of life-saving drugs by a world authority, not by private pharmaceutical companies; this authority also providing necessary micronutrients such as vitamin A wherever they are needed.
- Diversion of millions of dollars now spent on medical 'machinery' and new drugs often no more effective than their predecessors to drugs to prevent and cure the world's major killing diseases.
- Mass production of mobile health clinics and operating theatres to provide a basic travelling medical service in developing countries.
- Training schools in the developed world to provide health workers able to cope with most ailments, as with Chinese 'barefoot doctors', and with the knowledge needed to recognize and refer more difficult conditions to specialized areas.
- Taxes on producers of harmful substances, including foods, sufficiently high to cover the medical costs to the community of their effects.
- Mandatory requirement for doctors trained in developing countries to stay there, rather than agreeing to be 'poached' to a more affluent society.

CHAPTER 18

RELIGION: THE CEMENT OF SOCIETY?

Most humans are religious in one way or another. There are more than 2 billion Muslims and Hindus – for almost all of these people their religion is an intimate and essential part of their daily lives. Thirty-six per cent of Americans believe the Bible is literally true.[1] There is an instinct for ritual, an important element in most religions, among many life forms, including humans. This tends to indicate that religions are indeed a basic social cement, if only because they cater for that deep- seated human need for ritual, for the mysterious.

But there is also the view that the conservatism of religions, their insistence on dogma, their subjugation of the human mind to an inscrutable 'divine will', and their tendency to become extremist, damage human society to an extent that outweighs their merits. Fundamentalist religious extremism has certainly been an element in conflicts that caused several million violent deaths during the 20th century, and many of which have continued into the 21st. In the fertile and beautiful Maluku islands of eastern Indonesia in 2001 Muslim extremists forced thousands of Christians to convert to Islam, brutally killing those who refused, and, almost as brutally, compelling circumcision on those who agreed, regardless of age and sex. But this was far from one sided. Christians retaliated just as savagely, beheading Muslims.

Disputes between Hindus and Muslims in south Asia have killed millions. Believers in 'the rapture' assert Christ will stand alongside those 'saved', watching everyone else crushed in huge fissures that will open up in the ground, or killed in a multitude of other hideous ways during seven years of tribulation. During the 200 years from the 16th century, hundreds of thousands of women and young children were burned as witches by both Catholic and Protestant Christians after 'confessing' under torture.[2] Religions, therefore, especially those parts of them driven by assertive and inflexible dogma, can without doubt be forces for evil. This dangerous extremism is likely to increase in circumstances of increasing global hardship – not only in terms of the numbers recruited to religions, but also in its potential to do harm.

Traditional religious belief that humans are fundamentally different from other animals, and thus divinely authorized to exploit other species, is showing signs of softening as the influence of the environmental movement extends. Extreme and now largely unacceptable Christian ideas, such as a Heaven somewhere in the sky and a Hell in which the evil are tortured by eternal fires, have all but disappeared. Such images of sitting on clouds playing a harp or frizzling forever were decently interred by statements from Pope John Paul II that Heaven is 'not an abstraction, nor a physical place among clouds, but a living relationship with the Holy Trinity' – and Hell 'the state of those who freely and definitely separate themselves from God'.[3] Islam and some Protestant Evangelical Christians, however, still hold that there is a Hell after death, a definite place of punishment, and even torture.

All the world's religions include people who earnestly seek adaptation to the changing world. There is increasing evidence of greater cooperation and efforts at mutual understanding between world religions – a trend defined by the awkward word 'ecumenical'. A significant, and largely unreported, ecumenical initiative, the Parliament of the World's Religions, brought together more than 6000 people from over 100 religious communities.[4] All the major religions, Islam, Hinduism, Buddhism, Judaism and Christianity, were represented at this massive assembly. One of its major concerns was the absence of any moral basis for globalization.

Anyone who has visited one of the great medieval cathedrals must marvel at the patience and persistence that allowed relatively small communities, using primitive hand tools, to create structures of such size, complexity and inspired design. These apparent miracles were not confined to Europe. Almost everywhere in the world, and thousands of years back in time, such testaments to faith can be found – and generally the standards of craftsmanship, even of artistry, are so high as to indicate a deep devotion to purpose by the builders. Religion and ritual appear to have been a powerful influence in human communities, as far back as history can be traced.

Rituals, common to almost all religions, may well prove much more important than the rationalist view regards them – essential to individual and social stability. Ethologists have identified a need for ritual as one of many qualities once idealized as exclusively human, but actually present in the behaviour of other species, among them the courting habits of birds, and the communication forms of many species. While some animals are solitary, many assemble, live, fight and hunt together in packs where social rituals can be observed. Children walk along a footpath touching every third paling on a fence, or hop over paving stones in a definite order. Left to themselves young children tend to accumulate in gangs, which readily acquire simple forms of ritual – almost the beginnings of primitive religions. William Golding has given a sensitive and penetrating illustration of this.[5]

It is, of course, not possible to leave the matter at this simplistic level. Overlaying this apparent instinct for ritual are spirituality and faith, attested to by millions of people as major influences in their lives, and historically the basis for most systems of law, ethics and morality. The practice of meditation, which means clearing the mind and, it is believed, opening it to an outside, benign influence, has been common to most religions for so many centuries it is impossible to ignore it. The fact that millions of people all over the world practise meditation regularly appears to indicate two things: that there is individual awareness of, and attraction to, the spiritual, and that this is frequently exerted outside the limits of conventional – church orientated – religion. Indeed, in what was claimed to be the world's largest survey of church going Christians most of those between 15 and 25 expressed some dissatisfaction with the church experience.[6]

Thinking in the Western world from the 18th century onwards evolved rationalism, a group of ideas which advanced the primacy and independence of the logical, intelligent individual and the reductionist methods of science, economics and technology. All this greatly reduced the grip of both ritualized religion and the family on societies, altering social patterns and greatly reducing the power of the Christian churches over their congregations. However, it seems unlikely that these social changes can, in the long run, override the need for spirituality and ritual that seem so deeply imbedded in human consciousness. The popularity of the many TV series based on 'magic', the prevalence of fortune tellers and astrologers offering their services, interest in witchcraft, Taoism, the I Ching, astrology, etc, all testify to a nostalgic desire for the occult, the mysterious, the ritualistic. *Feng shui*, the Chinese craft of spiritually orientated and designed buildings, is in extensive use in the West. Sinologist Orville Schell commented on a Western urge 'to give parts of ourselves to a way of living in which belief rather than rational-ism reigns'.[7]

Albert Einstein argued that science and religion were necessary to each other – 'science can only ascertain what is, but not what *should be*... Science without religion is lame, religion without science is blind.'[8] Einstein considered people could be religious without necessarily believing in a personal god, but by achieving 'a far reaching emancipation from the shackles of personal hopes and desires', and thereby attaining 'that humble attitude of mind towards the grandeur of reason incarnate in existence and which, in its profoundest depths, is inaccessible to man'.

The Chinese government's crackdown from July 1999 onwards on the Falun Gong movement shows how persistent ancient rituals and customs can be in the face of rigorous campaigns to suppress them. Falun Gong, which insists it is not a 'sect', does use elements of Chinese Buddhism and Taoism, as well as ancient breathing and meditation techniques designed to induce tranquility and good health. Claiming to have as many as 100 million adherents worldwide – but mostly in China – Falun Gong recruited many Chinese officials and soldiers, some of them members of the Communist Party. The banning of Falun Gong and the arrest and imprisonment of thousands of its members may well drive this movement underground, but is unlikely to suppress it totally.

Accumulation of, and insistence on, dogma – a body of beliefs all members of a faith are required to accept uncritically – is perhaps the area in which organized religion is most criticized. One of its consequences is the controversy between Darwinian evolution and creationism. Creationist Christians believe that the account in Genesis describing how God created the world in six days is literally true,[9] and that the theory of the evolution of species is wrong and blasphemous, while neo Darwinists strongly support the evolution theory.[10] During 2005 there was a major campaign advancing 'intelligent design', claiming that species were created by a mysterious and supernatural intelligence, rather than evolving through natural selection. During the last half of the 20th century fundamentalist sectors of Islam, Hinduism and Christianity, motivated by rigid and selective bodies of dogma, gained substantial influence, and at times acquired terrorist overtones. There is, however, evidence that poverty is a causative factor in religious fundamentalism, with at least one economist asserting that economic losers retreat into religious extremism.[11]

To the observant, it is a daily miracle that the Earth spins millennium after millennium, poised in space, never too hot nor too cold to maintain life of some kind, maintaining a breathable atmosphere, a reliable water supply, and in innumerable other ways sustaining ecological balances of great complexity through what seem to be largely automatic processes. Why? For most people this question may initially seem pointless – they simply take the planet's performance for granted. But not everyone does so.

In the 1960s, astronomer Fred Hoyle, studying the way carbon
– which is the basis of life on Earth – is made from helium inside
large stars, concluded that this 'monstrous series of coincidences'
suggested 'a put up job', some kind of deliberate design.[12] In 1972,
geophysicist James Lovelock suggested that the Earth behaves
almost like a sentient organism in which physical and biological
systems cooperate to maintain these delicate and improbable
balances. Speaking in Tokyo in 1992, Lovelock redefined his
proposition to the following: 'The whole system and its material
environment is self regulating at a state comfortable for the
organisms.' On that occasion he made it plain that 'a sentient Gaia
able to control the Earth consciously' was not intended, remarking,
'This was never some trendy New Age pseudo science.'[13]

The Gaia hypothesis – the name comes from the ancient Greek
earth goddess – has certainly become well known, and has been
extended by other people into areas well beyond Lovelock's
original proposition. These extensions resemble animism, the
earliest known human religion, based on the worship of the Earth
and the forces of nature. Hence, for the sake of this discussion, the
name neoanimism can be assigned to the mystic and arcane
beliefs that have sprung from the original Gaia hypothesis, and
which in various forms constitute one of the world's fastest
growing religions.

Lovelock's original idea was set out in a paper postulating an
influential control over the Earth's climate by some of the planet's
smallest creatures – algae. The essential proposition is that tiny
fragments of a substance called DMS,[14] emitted by algae, seed
clouds. Hotter conditions breed more algae, which means more
clouds. When it becomes cooler, as cloud cover increases, the
algae decrease. This was instanced as one of the planet's many
self regulating mechanisms.

The neoanimists assert that 'primitive' human faiths based on
worship of natural forces and the planet and its life forms, contain
elements of a religion relevant to present world conditions and
those of the immediate future. In a widely publicized statement in
2000, Prince Charles approached this view, calling for greater
reverence for nature and awareness that humanity is a part of

nature. However, while ancient animism was driven largely by fear of natural forces and the need to placate them, neoanimism is motivated by knowledge and respect for them. It could well become a major evolving religion in the new society, perhaps as part of a greater pantheism.

One of the influences of most traditional religions, including Christianity, has been the idea that humans, in the image of God, are masters, free to destroy its other life forms, indeed the fabric of the Earth itself, to create what seems to be a favourable environment for themselves. This influence has assisted the total obliteration of thousands of species, and created environmental conditions to the overall detriment of the planet. Concern about these issues is the driving force behind the worldwide environmental movement, which seeks the preservation and protection of natural things.

If current religions do not adapt themselves, especially to a greater regard for other life on Earth, they may well find themselves replaced by a neoanimist religion, as likely as not to accumulate around those aspects of the Gaia idea which promote respect for and empathy towards the world, all its living organisms, and its natural systems. Its beginnings – such groups as the Dragon Environmental Network in Britain, which asserts the sacred nature of the Earth, and Progressive Wicca – are already established. In June 1999, a new Australian Protestant hymn book with strong environmental influences was launched, including such hymns as 'Touch the Earth Lightly' – 'we who endanger, who create hunger, agents of death for all creatures that live, we who foster clouds of disaster, God of our planet, forestall and forgive.' The first edition of the new hymn book sold over 1 million copies. Biologist and philosopher Charles Birch describes what he calls a 'pan experientialist' position – a perception of God in the total of the subjective experiences of all organisms.[15] He believes humans must make a real effort to understand the subjective experiences of other people and other life, and to assess their implications.

It has been estimated that the fastest growing religion in the world is Islam, which, with 1.3 billion adherents in 75 countries, is gaining ground on the largest, Christianity, with a theoretical 1.7 billion, many of whom are not active. Said to be the fastest growing in the US is Paganism, whose adherents often call themselves witches. Such a Wicca coven prospers at America's largest military base, Fort Worth, with the tacit approval of military authorities, who point out that the US constitution defends the right for any religion to be practised.

The basic tenets of Paganism are neoanimist, and are most commonly represented as gentle and noninterventionist. They involve a worship of the Earth, of nature and all its manifestations, and respect and care for these things, and have distinct and established rituals. These include the Sabbats, eight seasonal festivals and the monthly meeting, the Esbat, generally held at full moon. However, according to the high priestess of one coven, modern witches do not fly on broomsticks, hold sacrifices, worship the Devil, or indulge in orgies. Indeed, it is highly unlikely that witches, the 'wise women' and healers of old, ever did these things.

OPTIMAL FUTURE HISTORY

- There is a demonstrable human need for some consistent and sustainable moral background of the type that religions have traditionally provided. This should encourage religions to adapt themselves to contemporary realities, present a united worldview as far as possible, and identify and actively promote influences contributing to the greater good.

- There is a need for religions to recognize the reasons for and dangers of extremism, do their best to make these generally known, and take whatever steps necessary to control unreasoning fundamentalism.

- There is a need for religions to become more flexible, to adjust their attitudes more accurately to the needs of the modern world, to be aware of the growing influence of the 2030 drivers, and to direct their influence towards more favourable outcomes.

- There is a need for religions to recognize the extent of ecological damage to the planet, and the viewpoint of people who are concerned about this. This may require far reaching philosophical changes, towards accepting the Earth as a place of value and happiness in itself, rather than merely a proving ground for some future life. Assuming the world was made to a divine plan, derogating its status to a place of misery and trial – 'there'll be pie in the sky by and by' – could be seen as the ultimate blasphemy.

PART FOUR

THE NEW SOCIETY

CHAPTER 19

THE MECHANICS OF CHANGE

It is possible for us to decide what we want for our future with reasonable precision. First, in the light of what we've considered so far, what sort of new society do we want? By looking at the facts of today and considering the options, it is within our power to influence the future in important and useful ways, set priorities, get new areas of thought and action moving. It is even possible to set down a broad outline of what shape our society might take in 20, 30, 40, 50 years' time. But this needs to be done in a practical way – there seems little point in visualizing new societies that are derived from idealism or uninformed speculation. There are plenty of Utopian visions around that are just that. The new society needs to be pragmatic, evolving from intelligent and feasible responses to the 2030 drivers and their dangers. Whether we like it or not, its creation must involve some very large changes to social and economic patterns and the adoption of simpler, more frugal, lifestyles.

The transition will happen when there are enough well planned political and economic pressures on the establishment from the grassroots – and this will inevitably build up as the influence of the drivers increases. But that will not be enough. The actual building of the necessary new social and physical structures will need the best efforts of people as individuals and as purpose oriented groups, and a lot of innovative thinking at the cutting edge. A recurring theme in this book has been this basic need of the new society for planners and thinkers capable of innovation and originality, and empowered to exercise these capacities. This need is not served by current trends in which many academics, who should be at the front line of new thought, are increasingly trammelled by real or perceived threats to their tenure, short-term commercial considerations and undue peer pressure, which naturally assembles at the lowest common denominator. Pyramidal business and bureaucratic management structures often seem to strangle constructive change – nothing must happen for the first time. Independent task forces who know their job, and who operate in a climate of healthy competition, are more likely to bring up new and practical ideas.

This necessity for new and free thought is perceived and persuasively argued for in a 2002 book, *The Rise of the Creative Class* by American academic Richard Florida.[1] He says that future economic development will be driven by intellectual elites, groups of creative people who can generate original ideas. According to Florida, the era of supervisory managers is passing, and is already being replaced by new centres of economic growth where universities, social tolerance and high tech industry thrive together. Processes somewhat like this will be a necessary part of the framework of the new society.

Take another look at the two axioms: *Useful change is likely only if it can provide as, equal, obvious and general a benefit as possible. If proposed solutions don't take the lowest common denominators of human nature realistically into account they will not work.*

These axioms need to inform all the areas of proposed change. For instance, plainly, one of the highest priorities must be rapid and massive development of a wide range of alternate energy technologies. Design research for solar, wind, wave and tidal power generators is already well advanced, and indicates that if used in the right places, with the right economies of scale, they can compete economically with power generated by oil or coal, and more cheaply than the real costs of nuclear power. Many wind generators in particular are already very close to being competitive with fossil fuel power stations at about 3.5 to 6 cents per kilowatt hour depending on location, and cheaper than nuclear power at around 7 cents, plus the as yet unknown cost of permanent waste disposal. A modern wind generator can, moreover, replace the energy used to make it in less than six months' operation. Why, then, do the alternatives in total make up barely 2 per cent of world energy supply?

Power is supplied to most people from huge utilities using coal, oil, natural gas, nuclear or hydroelectric generation. These utilities, especially since so many have been 'privatized', have a vested interest in maintaining the maximum use of their investments, and can also 'lean on' governments to determine energy policy. That has been done recently and effectively in the US and Australia. With important exceptions, the policy, almost everywhere, is to pay lip service to a growing popular demand for alternatives by sponsoring pilot plants and research programmes and placing ' we are green' advertising on a large scale, but not going ahead with major projects that would permit a favourable economy of scale. A coal-fired power station, for instance, is estimated to have a useful life of 60 years, during which time its owners want it to go on earning money for them. Their financial interest is served by obstructing competing sustainable infrastructure.

Associated with this is a steady and increasing 'public relations' campaign to revert to fission nuclear power, in spite of its dangers and high cost. I have in my files a syndicated Sunday newspaper article under a full banner headline: NUCLEAR GARDEN OF EDEN, WILDLIFE THRIVES AT CHERNOBYL acclaiming Chernobyl as 'a wildlife paradise of stunning ecological and zoological richness' in which 'safaris are offered to tourists prepared to don nuclear protection suits and open their minds to the baffling outcome of the terrible events of April 26, 1986', and that 'there is now a belief that radiation, while desperately harmful, might not be as uniformly horrendous as previously believed'.

These promotions of fossil and nuclear power, deriving from Axiom Two driven attitudes, need to be rationally taken into account, devising ways to somehow change not in idealistic but in practical ways. The answer comes, of course, from Axiom One. Applying Axiom One would involve offering the big power utilities financial conditions acceptable to them, and not to their disadvantage, to convert to alternatives. This might amount to a determined and well thought through system of guarantees, tax penalties and inducements to make it profitable for them to invest heavily in, such things as hydrogen production for fuel cells.

Concerted action by the governments of the developed world along these lines could be coordinated by a world authority. Its major concerns would logically be standardized economy of scale manufacture and major deployment of the various alternate technologies globally – these would be installed where they are demonstrably appropriate. However, all viable technologies would be deployed on every feasible site as rapidly as possible. Given this, with subsidies no greater than those already given to the nuclear industry, their combined output could meet the 2030 deadline, at least guaranteeing basic energy to the developing as well as a more frugal Western world. However, we need to do this now, not in ten years' time.

Probably the next most important elements are perceptual: the need for the increasingly small minority of the affluent to understand that they can no longer be a self contained island of prosperity in a sea of poverty and misery, and that it is to their ultimate peril to try to be. The connection between inequality and poverty and the destruction of New York's World Trade Center is real and important. It is necessary now for the influential and powerful to understand the justifiable resentment at the rich nations' profligate use of most of the world's depleting resources, and the despair and anger that comes from poverty. It is worth bearing in mind that in the mid 18th century the French aristocracy was absolutely confident of its position, security, and ability to govern and exploit a poor and apparently powerless majority of the people. By the end of that century almost all of these aristocrats had been killed or exiled.

Extremes of wealth and poverty must, therefore, quite quickly become dangerous. Redressing these is necessary, and it is also necessary to accept that a massive diversion of resources and some, but not too much, sacrifice on the part of the affluent, must be involved. It is possible to alleviate poverty and misery in the developing world, but there can be no pretence that this will be either quick or easy. However, if a significant beginning is made, with determination and sincerity, the hatred and envy of the West that drives terrorism, anarchy and religious extremism may be substantially disarmed.

The question of refugees needs to be considered. With our consent, our society is becoming globalized, national boundaries are melting, and societies are becoming dislocated to the extent that millions of people are on the move. Since the majority of the world's people are poor, it should not be surprising that the affluent nations are receiving floods of destitute people. It will go on being that way. Part of the necessary mechanics of change are the means to absorb and use these people in ways encouraging them to be loyal to their new home, self supporting and productive. This will require a very considerable abandonment of prejudice and chauvinism, and comprehensive planning programmes, including re-education, especially in language and social skills, and seed money for new enterprises for incoming migrants.

Since change necessarily involves money, it would be naive to discuss its mechanics without considering how that change might be financed. Chapter 7 looked at the idea that defence and space expenditure are necessary 'balance wheels' within over-productive economies. If we accept the validity of the balance wheel concept – and under present conditions this could be conceded – the necessary large amounts of capital and productive effort are indeed available.

'Balance wheel' spending in the G8 developed nations and the major emerging powers – India and China – is not less than $1.2 trillion a year. Multilateral agreement to reduce these expenditures by 10 per cent would make $120 billion available every year for other purposes, without seriously affecting the capacity of any of those nations to defend itself – provided the agreement were genuinely multilateral and the diversion of funds consistent and equal. Developing countries with relatively large military budgets, such as Pakistan and Indonesia, would share this reduction, on the understanding that they should spend that money productively in their own country.

This would create a 'have your cake and eat it too' situation in which nations would not have to jeopardize their standing as an armed force, but which would permit potent social and economic weapons to be deployed in 'the war against terror'. At the same time, it would mean that there were fewer nuclear bombs, guns and landmines in the world.

The consequences would be very considerable indeed, since the $120 billion would not be a one off amount, but would be available every year. Programmes such as the Billion Artifacts outlined in Chapter 26 would become immediately possible. Guidelines for expenditure would clearly be necessary, strictly limiting the proportion of funds devoted to administration and advisory panels, and guaranteeing maximum funding for actual achievement on the ground. Eligible recipients might be asked to make a case for specific programmes, including evidence of the level of grassroots consultation involved in developing them.

What about change at the lower levels – perhaps the establishment of a 'village' along the lines discussed in Chapter 15? A group of 50 families whose equity in their houses are worth an average of $250,000 dollars – not unusual in most big Western cities – could confidently plan their new habitat, which would engage perhaps half their capital, leaving $6 million to capitalize the sustainable cooperative businesses that would help provide the community with an income. The businesses would be immediately competitive with their urban equivalents because of their freedom from debt, low overheads and absence of the 'top heavy' burden of administrative cost so typical of modern corporations.

Part Three considered the kind of change needed in those areas that impinge particularly on the individual, and which largely control our personal lives. We should now consider the more formal parts of the social machine. How well equipped are they to deal with the processes of trade, government, law and communication, to provide the most satisfying, prosperous and equal benefit to all human beings? After all, the objective should be no less than that.

Influencing reform in these areas is likely to prove difficult, because of a growing tendency for social institutions like government, bureaucracy and industry to become opaque to scrutiny, with an inbuilt resistance to change. The inaccessible bureaucracy, that hides behind a computerized telephone system, and which is becoming increasingly anonymous, sets up barriers between government and citizen. It is driven by powerful Axiom Two considerations. There is a need then, for conscious efforts to make the machinery of government more transparent and accountable. Theory has it that 'democracy' provides all the necessary safeguards. But does it? 'Anti-terror' laws forced through the two government-dominated houses of the Australian Parliament in 2005, and widely opposed in the community, provide for arrest and detention of completely innocent people without being charged and without concrete evidence – just on suspicion by an undercover operative that the detainee might 'know something'. Having gone through the process of secret confinement, the detainee, who legally can be as young as 16, cannot reveal what has happened to them, the media cannot publicize it, on pain of imprisonment for up to 7 years. These laws destroy civil liberties going back as far as the Magna Carta. There has never been a 'terrorist' incident in Australia. Similar repressive legislation in the US and Britain has brought widespread opposition from lawyers, academics and the general public.

At this point it is worth noting that experience in many parts of the world indicates that the social machine works better when power and authority are delegated as much as possible to the individual citizen. Quite apart from the obvious advantages of mass consultation, communities using it have found access to official decision and spending patterns much easier. The machinery for this exists, and is described more fully in Chapter 25.

Governments and public authorities, by the mere fact of their existence, tend to make too much law. They exist to legislate and regulate; they have staff whose function is to dream up and formulate more law. As a result, communities, and especially businesses, can find themselves in a virtual straitjacket – as in the description of planned economies in Chapter 12. People whose main function it is to plan, send out and file forms seem to find it difficult to understand that the people required to fill them in also have other things to do. If this seems oversimplistic, or even unreal, I can only say that during nine years service as an elected representative in a parliament, and on its committees, curbing bureaucratic zeal in such areas plainly emerged as one of my more important responsibilities.

There is a simple safeguard available to protect the community against excessive or outdated law. This is the insertion in bills of a clause limiting the application of the new law or regulation to a definite time span. When that time elapses the law will come before the parliament again. After consideration legislators can either throw it out, if it plainly has no further value, or renew it. Such 'sunset' clauses in legislation are so important they should be used almost universally in the new society. Reviewing existing law in this way might even engage the energies of lawmakers enough to limit the creation of more and more unnecessary legislation.

A second major fault in the social machinery is the tendency to make many judgements in purely economic terms, with so much emphasis on questionable statistical devices like GNP and GDP. Undue emphasis on economic matters is more likely to be harmful than useful, not only because of the unreality of much of the debate, but also because other concerns of greater importance, such as the way people live, whether they are happy, whether they are healthy, whether they feel secure, are forced to yield priority to the strictly economic consideration. It also prejudices long-term values. Manufacturers seek 'productivity', and to keep consumption as high as possible for economic reasons, while the preponderant arguments are for conservation. One valuable early reform would be to discard GDP and replace it with a quality of life index.

A change in attitudes towards travel and transport seems inevitable in the new society. The new decentralized habitat areas we have considered are designed in part to reduce local travel, especially the use of motor transport, as much as possible, in the light of the coming fuel drought. But in a world in which oil powers all aircraft, and almost all shipping, very sharp reductions in world travel and world trade must be envisaged. The implications for globalization are obvious. World travel and trade will of course, remain possible, but they will inevitably be more limited and much more expensive. These issues are discussed in more detail in Chapter 21.

A fundamentally different approach to manufactured commodities would seem to be indicated. Planned obsolescence, which is wasteful, pollutant and expensive, could give place to high quality products designed to stay in use for long periods, and which are readily repairable at a low cost. Standardization of almost everything – measurements, spare parts, language, screws, computers and robots to name but a few items – seems no more than plain commonsense – a necessary part of the mechanics of change. Efficient standardization is, of course, compatible with another concept we shall develop more in this part of the book – the economic and social advantages of leasing, rather than selling, manufactured items. It is also consistent with the future of the almost completely automatic manufacturing discussed in the next chapter.

Chapter 20

Automation and Employment

These two things are very plainly linked – more automatic and robotized manufacturing means fewer jobs. There is the potential for a great deal of trouble in this, hence the new society will need to think carefully about this situation. On the other hand, why should humans labour at boring and repetitive work when robots can do it cheaper and better? Somehow we must balance these two factors – we need to devise a smooth transition that complies with Axiom One – conferring equal benefits to all of the community, rather than the advantages mainly going to a few wealthy corporations. This will not happen by itself, but will require a considerable planning effort, some compulsive legislation, goodwill from big business and sustained pressure from communities. But it must happen if a large and negative Luddite reaction is to be avoided.

It has taken humanity many centuries to design and shape the amenities and machines that are lifting the individual out of a life that was largely brute labour to one of relative ease and independence from the tyranny of physical things. We are now in the midst of the greatest leap forward of all – mechanisms that can make almost anything, which are self controlling, even self repairing, and which may soon even have the power not only to make other automatic machines, but even to replicate themselves.

The implications of this for the new society are profound – we can see this in the presence around us of the first artifacts made by this new manufacturing system: things like pens, watches, lighters, calculators which are elegant and complex, minimal in their use of materials, and yet cheap to produce.

The increasing number and variety of industrial, mining and agricultural robots suggests that humankind could, in the foreseeable future, have almost everything it needs and wants at a very low cost – in fact for almost nothing. Elsewhere, we consider the ill effects of globalization. Now we see a potentially good, even essential, one, in which the economies of scale could operate to the enormous benefit of humankind, mass producing useful commodities at little more than the cost of the raw materials. These economies of scale should permit greater concentration on another important aspect of manufacture – the greatest recycling possible of materials. A number of manufacturers are now planning their products with this in mind.

Meanwhile, 20th century populism had a somewhat different view of robots. Since Czech writer Karel Capek coined the word 'robot' in 1921, much science fiction has featured robot brains wiser than ours, able to solve all our problems. Soon we might have robot housemaids to sweep the house, cook the meals, do the dishes – indeed all of the boring, hard or repetitive work. Achieving this is proving difficult, and while useful devices of limited application are around, there is nothing even remotely approaching the competence of an *au pair* girl. Nor has it been possible to develop a robot with a 'brain' capable of human intelligence, much less an omniscient HAL type. The trouble is that the real thing – living beings – are so complicated, compact and cleverly designed that they are difficult to replicate.

Perhaps the most reliable guide to the state of robotics is the *World Robotics Survey*, the 2004 report of the United Nations Economic Commission for Europe, co-authored by the International Federation of Robotics.[1] This indicates rapid proliferation of robots that can scrub and vacuum floors, mow lawns and control household gadgetry , allowing householders, for instance, to start an oven cooking by calling it from a mobile phone. According to this report 607,000 domestic robots were in use at the end of 2003, two-thirds of them bought in that year. Most – more than half a million – were lawnmowers.

The United Nations report says there are more than three-quarters of a million industrial robots now in use, with close on 1 million projected for 2007. Most are in Japan and Europe, but all the major industrial nations are increasingly using them. The report comments, significantly, that the rapidly falling production costs of robots is making them increasingly competitive with human labour.

These mechanical servants can work 24 hours a day, 7 days a week without getting tired; those designed to do so can work indefinitely under water, in very high temperatures or in a vacuum; they do the task with exactly the same precision every time, much faster than any human. They normally do not risk industrial accidents, and they can make anything from pencils and matches to complex machine parts, mould metals and plastics, paint, rivet, weld, or carry out the most delicate and precise coronary or urological surgery.

Most industrial robots require several days of programming to carry out specific tasks, but early in 2000 a new robot concept was announced, 'an advanced genetic algorithm', able to evolve its own 'brain', determining for itself the best movement sequences for the work required.[2] Similar work is going on in the US to develop a 'polymorphic robot' – that is, one that changes its shape until it evolves the most efficient form for the task in hand.[3] The shaping is carried out by a 3D printer, a device that 'prints' three dimensional objects by adding layer after layer of plastic. These shaping devices, instructed by a computer programme, are now in common use, and can produce anything from gearwheels to delicately painted vases. A team at Bath University in Britain is even developing a self-replicating 3D printer, which would make more and more 3D printers automatically.

The development of agricultural robots is described as a signifi-cant opportunity, because many agricultural field operations are repetitive and carried out in a relatively controlled environment.

One prototype at the testing and trial stages is Demeter, an automated harvester, which has already shown it can cut crops in ways the farmer directs, and remember its instructions for later work. Huge fields almost completely farmed by robot machines are seen as practicable for the near future. Speculation goes even farther to embrace the concept of a harvesting food factory, a one pass machine that harvests crops – perhaps each row of a different kind – and manufactures finished, packaged food products from them.

The search for artificial intelligence is intimately associated with robotics. Its proponents in no way claim to be replicating the human brain, but that is being closely studied. For more than 40 years the Artificial Intelligence Laboratory at the Massachusetts Institute of Technology has been, in the words of its director, Professor Rodney Brooks, 'looking at how the human mind works, where it resides, what is the nature of memory, what sort of representations does the brain use?'[4] Among the project areas being studied by the 200 people who work in this laboratory are active vision systems for mobile robots, image guided surgery, social robots, the intelligent room, bipedal walking, recognition of self and others, and natural tasking of robots based on human inter-action cues. One advanced humanoid robot, Coco, can walk, change posture, approach and avoid objects, and to an extent investigate its environment. As Coco becomes a 'fully functioning creature' future research will look at biologically based models of emotion, and advanced mapping between Coco and other creatures, including humans, as tools for learning, empathy and communication – indeed one objective is to 'acquire an under-standing of how a robot can engage in intelligent and enjoyable social interactions with people'. In 2005, a major conference at M.I.T. saw a decision by US scientists working in this field to cooperate in developing 'dexterous robots' – that is machines that are good with their hands, which can move about and do useful work. Specific programmes are looking at robots that can help with people in nursing homes, and the rehabilitation of stroke victims.

As automatic processes do more work, people will be needed less and less. The workplace – the job – is already showing signs of failing in its traditional role of distributing wealth and status.

Unless these can be provided in other ways, the increasing strains of the future will create dangerous structural weaknesses in society. Radical changes in the nature of work began during the last three decades of Millennium 2. Higher qualifications were required, the demand for 'unskilled' workers dropped, the accent shifted from the youngest and oldest workgroups to the middle aged, and staff numbers were cut in almost every industry in most parts of the world.

'Downsizing' will continue. The volume of repetitive, 'unskilled' work that is now automated is just a beginning. Most of the impact of automation is yet to come. Even in the US and Japan the number of industrial robots was quite small in 2005 – perhaps 2 per cent of the human workforce. However, sales of industrial robots are increasing at about 6 per cent a year.

Industry will eventually need to accept that a major part of its new wealth must be redistributed in some form other than wages to the general community, if only because it will otherwise face steadily decreasing markets for its products. The broader spread of stockholding, at least in some Western communities, could assist the necessary process of redistribution, but it is by no means a complete answer. Work and business opportunities to the advantage of all, including the developing world, could come from huge additional spending on new and better infrastructure, and the provision of better services, free health care, free education, free public transport, and perhaps even free housing. All this lies within the logic of the situation.

Attempting to maintain the 'status quo' and assuming that 'market forces' will solve the problem is likely to lead to unpleasant consequences. If the rich get too rich, they have to live in fortresses. In the Filipino capital, Manila, I visited one such place at Forbes Park, with its high walls topped with broken glass, and armed guards standing at barriers of razor wire. As many as 18 million Americans are living in 'gated communities', and this number is expected to double within 20 years.[5]

Wealth disproportion is increasing almost everywhere. Surveys have put the number of the poverty-stricken in the US as high as 37 million, and increasing. Millions are the 'working poor.' Many have two jobs, but still do not earn enough to survive without charity. What has been called 'the violent trade in Sri Lankan housemaids' represents an extreme edge of the spectrum.[6] Virtual slavery, long working hours, sexual harassment and rape, enforced by impounding the victims' passports, have been reported by young Sri Lankan women working in several Middle Eastern countries. In 2005, there were reports of overworking and underpaying the foreign workers who make up 85 per cent of the population of Dubai. One disquieting trend that has been reported is the use by multinationals of 'bonded labour' in poor countries – virtual slaves who have been sold by desperately poor parents into years of unpaid work. 'The logic of using the cheapest raw materials worked by the cheapest labour now drives corporations across borders.'[7] All these things indicate that a critical area of human activity is going 'off the rails'.

American sociologist Richard Sennett believes the modern workplace is destroying valuable social patterns, stability, mutual commitment, and the pursuit of long-term goals.[8] These social effects were confirmed in England by a study by the University of Manchester's School of Management indicating that downsizing caused guilt feelings, shock and anger not unlike those following bereavements, with serious risks to relationships.[9] The Japanese media have carried stories about men who have lost their jobs continuing to dress and catch their trains every morning, rather than admit to their families that they were unemployed. A high suicide rate has been reported among the recently laid off.

OPTIMAL FUTURE HISTORY

- Continued major use of robotized and automated manufacture, accompanied by legislative safeguards to distribute benefits broadly across communities.
- Redistribution of money through high taxation of industry, the proceeds going to new public infrastructure.
- Increasingly, services and facilities to be provided free of cost – this involves abandonment of the 'user pays' principle.
- Inception of minimum guaranteed income.
- 'Job-sharing' plus progressively shorter working hours.
- Competitive 'task force' type work environment, rather than pyramidal management systems.
- Co-operative businesses, owned by those who work in them.

CHAPTER 21

TRAVELLING LESS?

Petrol and diesel vehicles can kill if there is an accident, as we all
know. Less well known is recent research indicating that the small
particle pollution they emit is probably killing more people
worldwide from heart and lung disease than die in accidents. Two-
thirds of a billion cars are major polluters and consumers of oil
fuel. Research over the last decade or so has confirmed that
burning fossil fuel contributes massively to small particle
pollution in the air. Regardless of remedial technology, like
catalytic converters and low sulphur diesel fuel, this is still dangerous. Research in several countries shows a major effect on heart as
well as lung function, causing deadly arrhythmia. People with
pacemakers or a history of arrhythmia are especially vulnerable. In
2004, Professor Nino Kuenzli, of the University of Southern
California, announced the findings of research involving 800
people living in Los Angeles showing that significant hardening
and restriction of arteries – often a precursor to strokes and heart
attacks – correlates with the extent of exposure to vehicle
pollution. The effect was said to be most severe in people over 60,
especially women, and those taking cholesterol-lowering drugs.

Transport – so vital to Western lifestyles – is increasingly
turning up factors like this that demand change. The most
challenging is the fast-approaching exhaustion of economically

recoverable oil. Not the least consequence must be a severe restriction of world trade, transport and tourism which will be an inevitable knock-on effect of the 2030 drivers. Changes will need to be made urgently if widespread hardship is to be avoided. Ships will need to be powered by sail, fuel cells or coal, and nuclear propulsion is certain to be advanced as an option. Cars will have to be smaller, and use new technologies. Magnetic levitation trains run by solar arrays beside the track could link the new energy conserving habitat forms outlined in Chapter 15, and are likely to replace internal air services. Quite innovative new devices such as unmanned solar powered airships could be useful freight carriers in some parts of the world where high winds are unusual.

As cheap and abundant oil dwindles, most existing transport forms will become at best uneconomic, at worst impracticable – the airliner operating on short intercity routes, the petrol or diesel motor vehicle and oil fuelled shipping, which means almost all ships. Around 30,000 major ships in the world now consume almost 2 billion barrels of oil a year. Oil produced from shale or similar costly and energy hungry sources could keep some aircraft flying – probably military aircraft – but would be too expensive for air cargo and personal transport.

However, the world's first hydrogen/fuel cell electric aircraft flew in June 2005. Essentially a large unmanned glider, AeroVironment's aircraft is likely to be developed for military surveillance. The picture where large airliners are concerned is much less clear. Naturally, the technology is being vigorously pursued in several parts of the world – NASA spent $7 million on it in 2003. But there still seem insuperable obstacles unless new technology emerges. These include the high cost of the platinum catalyst in the fuel cell, a high weight to power ratio, and problems over how the hydrogen fuel could be economically stored. Because it is difficult to foresee how fuel-cell aircraft could be as cost effective as kerosene-powered jetliners, commercial interest in the technology seems limited.

Should we have nuclear ships? At the present rates of shipping accidents, nuclear propulsion could result in severe, virtually permanent ocean pollution and grave risks to port cities. Considering merchant ship loss rates in World Wars I and II, a fleet of nuclear freighters in wartime would be catastrophic. Cruise ship passengers might not feel particularly carefree travelling with a nuclear reactor. Three nuclear powered merchant ships, the US *Savannah*, German *Otto Hahn* and Japanese *Mutsu* were built, but all were considered uneconomic. However, the technology could be revived at any time. Florida corporation Adams Atomic Engines, which describes itself as 'an independent power system designer', is offering fission powered motors not only for merchant ships but even pleasure craft.[1] Nuclear power is used for over 100 naval vessels, mostly submarines. Russia has 8 nuclear icebreakers, one of which, *Lenin*, has been in operation for more than 30 years. By 2005 several web sites were advocating a return to nuclear power for shipping.

Several billion dollars were expended by the US government in an effort to build nuclear powered aircraft – the Nuclear Energy for the Propulsion of Aircraft (NEPA) programme and its successors, before the programme was cancelled in 1961, 15 years after its inception.[2] NEPA's director in 1954, B C Briant, said 'manned nuclear aircraft pose the most difficult engineering job yet attempted this century'. Cancelling the programme, the then US President Kennedy observed that 'the possibility of nuclear aircraft is still very remote'. In 1950 the Soviet Union proposed a nuclear flying boat to weigh 1000 tons, carry 1000 passengers and fly at 1000 kilometres an hour. This project was never realized. There appeared to be no overt programme for nuclear aircraft in 2005, although there is internet conjecture that there may be unmanned nuclear drones. Nuclear rocket engines are being considered for space vehicles.

If we are to continue our love affair with the car it will not be the sort we are used to. The car needs to become cheaper, quieter, less polluting, easier and safer to drive, and independent of oil fuel – and that is basically the trend in some sections of the automotive industry. Severe pollution around the north Italian industrial city of Milan resulted in plans by the Lombardy regional government to ban the sale of all new petrol or diesel cars from 2005.[3] However, by that date no ban appeared to have materialized, although a series of car-free Sundays was planned.

Fuel cells don't store electricity in batteries, they produce it on demand. General Motors released its HydroGen 1 wagon in 2000, the result of more than $150 million spent on research and development. The company says it is aware of the need for fuel cell cars to be cost competitive, one of its executives remarking that company research indicated 'that consumers will not pay one extra cent for the sake of the environment'.[4] Even if this is so, higher oil prices are likely to drive the new technology.

Ballard Fuel Systems, one of the technology leaders, is already marketing fuel cell bus engines and is building a factory with a productive capacity of 300,000 fuel cells a year – Ballard fuel cell buses have been operating on regular services in Vancouver and Chicago since 1998.[5] DaimlerChrysler is making fuel cell electric cars – its first production vehicle, the A class Fcell, was introduced to several markets in small numbers in 2003. It uses compressed hydrogen gas, has a range of 150 kilometres, and a top speed of 140 kph.[6] Honda's FCX project, a fuel cell car, was scheduled for limited release to the market in 2003. The prototype of this car and a similar one developed by Toyota were publicly shown in 2002. Shell opened its first hydrogen retail outlet for cars in Hamburg early in 1999, and three were planned for Tokyo in 2003. By 2005 most car makers were researching fuel-cell vehicles. The most advanced appeared to be the Mercedes F600 Hygenius, claimed to have a range of 400 kilometres and a top speed of 170kph, due for production about 2012. Meanwhile, Mitsubishi are developing a completely electric car, using lithium ion batteries, which they say will have a range of 250km and a top speed of 180kph.

However, regardless of these developments, conventional means of travel – cars, wheeled trains and aircraft – continue to present increasing problems. According to one commentator in this area the cost of transportation delays in the US alone was predicted to rise from $15 billion in 1985 to $61 billion in 2005[7] – to say nothing of the resultant overall frustration and higher accident risk. Traffic congestion, urban chemical and noise pollution, and the high cost of building or improving roads have induced many countries to introduce faster and faster conventional trains – the earliest and classic example is the Japanese bullet train linking Tokyo with other Kansai cities. While these trains can average well over 100 miles an hour there are physical limitations for any tracked vehicle, so they are unable to compete with commercial air services, nor have they had any serious impact on the volume of urban motor traffic.

Meanwhile, air traffic itself, especially short flights, has reached a stage of serious, seemingly intractable problems. Air services are still, to an extent, dependent on weather conditions. They require large and expensive stretches of land on which to arrive and depart, they inflict noise and chemical pollution on the communities they serve, and are notoriously vulnerable to hijacking and terrorist attacks. Because they can only pick up and discharge at airports, there is always a further traffic and cost factor in getting to and from them. Airliners are fundamentally inefficient, using huge quantities of fuel simply taking off and reaching cruising altitudes. They are also relatively slow, and likely to become more so, because speed eats fuel.

'Winglock' – severe air traffic congestion in and around airports – is reducing safety standards, and resulting in major delays to services and higher costs. 'Near misses' of aircraft on the ground have increased alarmingly. And these can be dangerous. When two 747s collided on a runway in Tenerife in 1977, 583 people were killed. The apparent answer to these problems – more and more new airports – causes further problems. No residential area wants a new airport in or near it. Noise levels from existing airports are bringing massive and often well organized opposition from residents.

The conventional aeroplane is, then, overdue for a rethink. A substitute might be a train/aircraft hybrid, which is under research and showing promising results. This vehicle has wings, but these lift it only a short distance off the ground, and it is confined to its 'track' by walls on either side engaging with rudder-like vertical extensions to the wings. It is planned to power these Japanese 'aerotrains' sustainably with solar panels installed along the track.[8] One bold area of research is into long range HyperSoar passenger aircraft designed to fly in space at up to 6700 miles per hour. The technology for aircraft of this type, which skip in and out of the atmosphere during their flight and re-enter near the destination, is being developed. Visualized as dart-shaped, rather like a folded paper plane, it is claimed this aircraft could reach any destination on Earth from the US in about two hours, with greatly improved fuel economy.[9] Some downsides are high G rate acceleration and cosmic radiation exposure to passengers, and huge vapour trails that could affect climate, since these aircraft would be powered by hydrogen rocket motors and emit large quantities of water.

Airships were the first successful powered flying machines, and now have important defence values for such things as artillery spotting and coastal surveillance. In the new society their inherent buoyancy might well give them advantages for long distance, non-urgent carriage of goods in areas where high winds are unusual, such as in the interiors of some continents. Because their power requirement is so low, it is possible to envisage cargo blimps with electric motors powered by arrays of solar cells on top of the envelope, or clad in one of the solar cloths now being produced. Such aerial 'tramps' could even be totally crewless, operated by remote control, and so almost costless to operate, in terms of both energy and money. In the absence of a crew they could be inflated with hydrogen rather than rare and expensive helium. The European Space Agency has put together a consortium to build solar powered HALE (high-altitude long-endurance) airships to replace satellites as telecommunications relays.[10]

Maglev, short for magnetic levitation, describes trains which 'fly' a short distance above or below their single line track without physically touching it. The first such train in service links the Shanghai industrial suburb of Pudong with the airport – a distance of 30km, which the train covers in 8 minutes. It is, however, capable of 430kmh. Intensive research into maglev is being carried out in Dalian, China, in the US, Britain and the Philippines. In 2005, the first Japanese maglev train, driverless and automatic, began operating over a 10km track in the suburbs of Nagoya. Germany is planning a maglev train system to travel at over 600 kilometres an hour between Berlin and Hamburg. Switzerland plans to link all its major cities with tunnels under its mountains. Evacuated of air, these would permit maglev trains to operate at 650 kilometres an hour. This ambitious project, which will cost more than $20 billion, is expected to be complete by 2030, linking 10 major cities and cutting travel time from Zurich to Geneva from 3 hours to 57 minutes. Because maglev trains operating in tunnel vacuums would be completely frictionless, there is no theoretical limit to the speeds that can be achieved. Planners are hence looking with some seriousness at the science fiction vision of undersea tunnels linking continents. One such proposal envisages tunnels under the North Atlantic linking the northern tip of Scotland with the northern coast of Labrador.

Early experiments, especially in Germany, have relied on conventional electromagnets, but these trains have proved very expensive. Japan, the nation that has made the most advances in this technology, has been researching it for almost 40 years. Powerful magnets using chilled superconductors are now being employed to gain greater efficiency. The magnets on board the train provide the levitation effect. The train is propelled by linear electric motors outside the vehicle itself, giving precise control over both speed and regenerative braking, which returns power to the supplying grid. The cost of the controlling track, which could be suspended above existing highways, is regarded as more than competitive with roads and conventional railways. This is because maglev trains can climb grades of up to 10°, eliminating the need for tunnels in most cases. In 1999, a Japanese train of this kind set a new speed record for a train at 552 kilometres an hour.[11] This was highly significant, because it means a maglev train can compete effectively with airliners in terms of journey times.

Sailing ships became impracticable and uneconomic for three principal reasons: the availability of cheap hydrocarbon fuels, coal and later oil, the lack of strong, long lasting materials for sailcloth, and unreliable weather forecasting. Now weather forecasting is much more reliable, there are durable synthetic materials for sails, and oil fuels are about to become scarcer and much more expensive. A few modern vessels around the world are already using sail as a supplement. Any hull type can gain fuel savings from sails when the wind is astern, and there are a number of vessels doing this. Specialized passenger sailing ships could operate on suitable routes, substantially crewed by their passengers – there are already tour ships carrying sail. They could also operate as cargo tramps – ships not bound to definite trade routes and time schedules.

The traditional windjammer is most unlikely to reappear in large numbers, nor will crews be required to clamber aloft along yards high above deck to wrestle with huge square sails. A distinguished marine architect, Norman L Skene, forecast more than 50 years ago that sailing ships would be used again: 'The wind is an unfailing source of power, whereas the supply and cost of fuel for mechanically propelled ships in the years to come are a matter for great uncertainty.'[12] He remarked that a study of long voyages by sailing ships had shown that low average speed was due to calms or head winds over a small part of the journey. The answer is to provide auxiliary power, which Skene believed should be diesel electric, but seems now more likely to be fuel cell electric, powered by methane.

Writing long before the advent of computers, Skene foresaw ships in which all sail movements and other ship management would be controlled by one deck officer 'from a central instrument board'. His drawing is of a staysail schooner rigged ship with four equal sized masts, each bearing identical fore and aft rig, and fitted with two retractable centreboards. Japanese designers have experimented with folding plastic sails rather than fabric, and these have been found to be more efficient. These contemporary designs include sensors to detect favourable winds, slow the ship's engines and set and trim the sails automatically, reducing the fuel consumption of a conventional ship by as much as half. The Danish government financed naval architects Knud E Hanson to develop a six-masted windship in 1995. At that stage it could not compete with oil-fuelled freighters, but could well do so as oil prices advance.

The new sailing ships will almost certainly be 'hybrids', with auxiliary engines to propel them in times of danger or through 'doldrums' – largely windless zones which lengthened passage times in the last era of sail and made reliable timetables virtually impossible. At least partly solar powered electric auxiliaries are a feasible prospect. One Australian ferry, which can carry 100 passengers at up to 12 knots, uses solar panels which double as sails as its basic power source.

The Scandinavian designers Wallenius Wilhelmsen are working seriously on a hybrid ship of the future, which will use wind, solar power, wave energy and hydrogen fuel cells to propel it on a completely sustainable basis. The huge trimaran, planned to be almost 800 feet long, is designed for cargo carrying, and could cruise at 15 knots. Twelve fins on the hull harness wave energy, while the three large sails are covered with solar energy collectors. One of the more elegant – and difficult – sports is kite-driven windsurfing. There are now experiments with this technology for ships, which can be pulled along as fast as 13 knots by huge kites as much as 500 metres overhead, where winds are stronger and steadier than near the surface of the sea.

All these developments, when considered together, indicate an urgent need for greater and more practical recognition of imminent transport problems and the rapid development of new forms adapted to 2030 conditions. The modern world is so dependent on its forms of transport that serious problems like mass starvation, and regional hotspots of terrorism and war, could develop if they fail. Major transport systems have very long lead times – the two or three decades available are barely enough. Serious development of the alternatives needs to be advanced as fast as possible.

OPTIMAL FUTURE HISTORY

- Phasing out of fossil fuel vehicles and their replacement with fuel cell/electric propulsion.
- Finding an economic alternative to kerosene-powered airliners.
- Major development of high-speed trains, either railed or maglev, preferably powered sustainably, to replace short-distance air services.
- Development of cars in which automatic systems replace drivers.
- Conversion of shipping away from fossil fuels, using fuel cells with solar power and sail assistance where appropriate.

CHAPTER 22

WORKING ONLINE

There are strong indications that the cheap world computer, powered by the sun or a simple crankhandle power generator, is on its way in large numbers – and not before time. It is beyond doubt that modern information technology could contribute, perhaps decisively, to better health, happiness and prosperity in the developing world. And since by 2030 the developing world will make up 85 per cent of global population, this may well be one of the more significant developments in the history of the future. Regrettably, the current tendency toward unnecessarily expensive, complex and non-standardized personal computers has limited this potential – in the words of Yale University computer science professor, David Gelernter, modern computers, laden with incomprehensible user manuals and unneeded features are 'more a source of irritation, dissatisfaction and angst than a positive benefit'.[1]

This unrealized potential suggests development and global distribution of a simple, standardized, inexpensive computer, powered by batteries backed up with solar or hand powered – even spring wound – chargers. This machine would need to be competent for little more than word processing and internet access. However, although internet penetration in Asia and Africa has grown from about half of 1 per cent in 1995 to more than

10 per cent, most of this has been in developed countries and urban areas. Singapore, for instance has 68 per cent penetration, Bangladesh 0.2 per cent. Hence an important aspect of aid efforts will need to be the provision of technology for internet access in under-developed areas.

An initial output could be located in village schools, not only for children, but also to convey useful information on health, agriculture and appropriate technology for adults. Happily, a number of researchers are now looking at this possibility. The Massachussets Institute of Technology Media Lab is considering production of a $100 computer in millions, and has already interested the governments of Brazil, China, Thailand, Egypt and South Africa in the project. Electricity for this computer may be provided by a hand crank mechanism. The former head of the lab, Nicholas Negroponte, proposes 'stripped-down' laptops, in which 'obese memory and processing capacity are cut down.' Professor Raj Reddy of Carnegie Mellon University is working on a wirelessly networked computer that could double as a TV, telephone and videophone to cost less than $350. The Indian Simputer, based on the Linux system, came on the market in 2005 for about 9000 rupees – $200. The village computer is an item of the Billion Artifacts programme discussed in Chapter 26. At present, internet access is unavailable to the great majority of humanity – in 2005 about 15 per cent of world population, almost a billion people, had online access.[2]

Nevertheless, computers and the internet now influence almost all aspects of life in the developed world – and that influence will increase enormously over the next few decades. They drive industries which reduce demand on the material resources of the Earth, and construct complex 'models' of future plans and events. Among the world's most powerful computers is the half billion dollar Earth Simulator, built in Japan to assess and predict global changes in weather and climate trends, and even to give prior warning of earthquakes and financial market movements. Capable of making 35 trillion calculations a second, the Earth Simulator can complete in six seconds a computation that would have taken the fastest 1980s computer a full year. Its makers, NEC, claim it can 'create a virtual planet Earth'.[3] IBM has under construction an even more powerful computer, Blue Gene/L.

Information technologies have minimal raw material requirements, and are taking forms that will reduce such demand in other areas. A striking example is eBook programs, which offer readers downloads of a huge variety of books, many for free. However, eBook can also refer to a hand-held computer which feels, looks and reads like a book, but can store as many as 200 volumes in its memory, and can access thousands more, plus the newspapers and magazines of the day, through the internet. Thousands of books from libraries everywhere in the world, are now available in one or both of these forms. The potential of these to take literacy and education quickly, easily, and at low cost, to the developing world, could be epoch making, and is a further argument for cheap computers and useful amounts of internet access there.

But as with much modern technology, computers, along with their advantages, come with considerable risks. Major infrastructure almost everywhere is controlled by computers – power and water supply systems, food distribution, traffic flow, major transport areas such as railways and airlines, social and financial networks. And these computer systems are fragile, subject to sudden breakdowns and, even riskier, sabotage through 'hacking' – deliberate electronic intrusion into computer systems by outsiders. Electric power grids for large areas of modern nations are normally dependent on perhaps two or three computers, and breakdowns in these have caused chaos and hardship, especially in large cities in winter.

A computer network defence task force attached to the US Space Command in Colorado Springs was established in June 1999, when an exercise called Eligible Receiver showed that foreign hackers could disrupt US war operation plans coordinated in the Pentagon, and disable associated telephone, power facilities and fuel distribution systems. Nevertheless, regular attacks on the computer systems of five key US defence systems were subsequently reported – more than one a day on the navy's Space and Naval Warfare Weapons Command Center in San Diego. In 2001 the Defense Department revealed that its more than 1 million computers had been attacked in 23,662 incidents in 2000.[4] A major underground computer network has been assembled as both a defensive and offensive 'cyber war' facility in the US, and without doubt has its equivalent in almost every other country. It is claimed that the American system has the power to disrupt major services anywhere in the world – even to influence records of individual bank accounts. The existence and proliferation of these systems has added another dimension of risk and expense to the already huge armaments burden the world carries.

However, while the threat of war remains, vital networks need to be more dependable, able to continue working if any of their constituent computers malfunction or are destroyed. The internet provides a model for this. It was originally designed to operate even if almost all of its many nodes were destroyed. The same approach seems reasonable for computer controls of vital infrastructure, since 'cyber war' is now an established military weapon, and that infrastructure is an obvious target. In 1999, East Timor activist Jose Ramos Horta threatened to rally hackers all over the world to wreck Indonesia's computer systems unless a vote for self determination in East Timor were allowed to proceed. Taiwan has developed an arsenal of around 1000 computer viruses designed to attack China's computer systems if it ever launches an attack on its island neighbour.[5]

How have ordinary people, at a touch of a computer keyboard, at no cost to themselves or the recipients, provided 300 million meals to the starving people of the world? The answer is an internet site, www.thehungersite.com, which organizes enough of a basic foodstuff, perhaps rice, for a meal for someone somewhere in a developing country. When the site is called up a button appears – 'Donate free food'. A click on the mouse, and that someone gets the meal. The food is paid for by advertisers on the display, 1.1 cups of the local staple for every 'hit' on the site. The money goes to Mercy Corps and America's Second Harvest, who carry out the food distribution. Do this first every time you go on the internet, it will take you about 30 seconds.

Intelligently organized, computers can help to ease the shock of the coming reductions in fossil fuel use for travel. Already small, but increasing effects on traffic peaks are resulting from 'telecommuting' – the opportunity to work via computer at home, rather than having to travel to a central office. It has even been suggested that businesses should pay a tax for every worker they require to travel into a central business district office to compensate for the social and environmental problems caused by commuting. The American Telecommuting Association claims many advantages beyond the savings in travel time and cost.[6] According to this source the employer benefits from greater productivity – regularly clocked at 10 to 15 per cent over the last 2 decades. Distance becomes of no importance – a manager in Seattle can access an employee in Tel Aviv as easily as one in the same building. Working time on a task is reduced by the ease with which resources can be accessed immediately anywhere in the world – much of the research behind this book is an example.

The ability to work away from a central office greatly increases the feasibility of the decentralized habitat areas described in Chapter 15. And there are other advantages. When both parents are away at work for most of the day there is a considerable increase in the rates of burglaries and family breakdown. Suburbs are largely silent and empty during the day, community interaction is reduced. The fewer employees who have to be located in central offices, usually at high floor space rentals, the lower business overheads become. One estimate predicts that the internet could make an eighth of all retail premises superfluous, resulting in a worldwide saving of about $5 billion.[7] Further huge energy savings would come from fewer shopping trips in cars.

Shopping online for books, music, electronic equipment – and even wives and husbands – is an established reality with the success of cyberstores like Amazon.com, and dating services like Match.com, which claims over a million members. As online expertise increases, most areas of shopping will become easier, quicker, more convenient, and less energy hungry. Even shopping for clothing will become feasible. Virtual models have been foreshadowed which, after your measurements and colour choices have been typed in, will walk across the screen, sit in chairs, and move in any other way that would assist a decision on what sort of clothing would be convenient and attractive. Software exists now that would allow you to get a three dimensional scan of your feet, email the result to a shoemaker, and get a pair of shoes delivered to your home that fit perfectly.

'Power buys' represent bad news for the retail trade, but good news for consumers, who can use them to buy goods a lot cheaper than in a store. Two innovative American group buying sites, Accompany and Mercata, negotiate with manufacturers for the best price on bulk delivery of an item – say 100 computers. They then seek, through the internet, 100 people who are prepared to pay their money in advance for that computer at a price well below recommended retail – 'a fundamentally new way of doing business on the internet'.[8] Once the 100 buyers are enrolled, the deal is completed and the computers are delivered to the homes of the buyers. The larger the group sale, the lower the price that can be negotiated. Buying goods from stores, which humans have been doing for at least 3000 years, is a fundamentally inefficient way of distributing goods, due to high overhead costs and frequently excessive markups, in many cases well above the return to the producer.

The need for global democratic consultation of individual humans has already been raised in this book. The internet, accessed by computers in homes and at polling stations, could become the vehicle for future voting, greatly reducing the cost of elections and referenda. The issue is one which is hotly debated, occupying scores of websites. Several public interest groups which are concerned at low American voter turnout and lack of civic involvement in the electoral process see internet voting as a solution, noting that voters would have access to candidates' records and objectives before they cast their votes.

The states of California and Washington, in America, have had task forces investigating internet voting, with largely favourable recommendations, Arizona allowed it for some presidential primaries. When electronic voting was introduced by Riverside County, California, 99 per cent of voters approved of it. However, several polls have indicated that the majority of the US public do not want it, basically because they are concerned at the lack of security on the internet. Almost daily there are reports of successful hacking into computer systems, and estimates place credit card fraud on the internet at around $5 billion annually. 'Cookie' files can be planted in individual computers using the internet. These 'spies' could identify the voting intentions of their victims. Particular voting groups might then be attacked, either by blocking their vote altogether or diverting it to a bogus site where the vote would not be counted.

These are some examples of possible fraudulent activities quoted in the literature. Their net effect has been to deter people from the idea of electronic voting. However, recent developments offer better prospects for maximum security in voting systems. PINs and voter identification cards similar to credit card systems, combined with a system of biometrics – using fingerprints as encryption keys – should provide security at least as good as that of personal written voting. That system also is far from immune from fraudulent voting.

Japan and most European Union nations have rejected the idea of electronic voting at this stage, ostensibly because of security difficulties. There has been a major campaign against electronic voting machines in the US, because problems with these are considered by many to be responsible for the reelection of George W Bush in 2004. However, an important Axiom Two consideration should be noted – major political parties and their backers feel it is all 'less trouble' if individual participation in decision making can be restricted. Hence citizens of the world will need to apply considerable pressure on politicians if they want to be consulted regularly on major public issues – whether or not, for instance, a nation should go to war.

OPTIMAL FUTURE HISTORY

- Development and distribution of a standardized low-cost computer capable of word processing and internet access independent of reticulated electric power, and internet access technology for conveyance of education and information in the developing world.
- Inception of reliable and secure systems of electronic voting, capable of enabling regular individual decision making on major political and social issues.
- Internet marketing systems that provide reliable barriers to credit card fraud, so enabling extensive development of internet shopping, especially power or group buying.

CHAPTER 23

THE INFORMATION OVERLOAD

Finding the truth about things is getting more and more difficult, not only because of the enormous volume of available information, but also because so much of it is inaccurate or misleading. Comment and news, once clearly defined, are now becoming increasingly blurred at the edges. Media content, especially in privately owned areas, is often strongly selective, giving, in its appeal to lowest common denominator instincts, considerable credence to the idea that readers and audiences are being 'dumbed down'.

Putting forward a challenge like this induces a response that 'dumb' media are giving people what they want – basically, what will sell – and so in turn prompts a further question, do they fall short – dangerously short – of fulfilling the need for reliable and broad ranging information? There is considerable evidence that media run by trusts, or independent corporations financed by governments, and not beholden to advertisers, give a fairer and more reliable service, and that it is more necessary than ever to maintain them in a healthy state to balance the output of commercial media.

Search engine Google in 2005 identified 8.2 billion pages available on the internet, on every conceivable subject. Television, newspapers, books, CD-ROMs with staggering areas of content, all add to the cacophony of facts battering the individual human.

We seem likely to 'contend with levels of information that will be of such volume that it will be little more than noise'.[1] Out of this chaos, what the media emphasizes becomes highly influential. This has not escaped the attention of government and very large business. Influence the media, and you are halfway towards achieving control of your population.

Spin doctoring, public relations – call it what you will – is now a huge industry which neither government nor business can afford to ignore. Public gurus – columnists and commentators – do not hesitate to use collective pejoratives – critics of 'free market' business become 'the loony left', people who discuss issues 'the chattering classes'. But one looks in vain for 'the rapacious – or perhaps, rip off? – right'. 'The silent majority' are virtuous and, although silent, miraculously seem to go along with whatever barrow the pundit is pushing at the time.

Beyond influence comes government action to censor the media, forcing it not to mention criticism of officialdom, or matters which it considers disadvantageous to itself. Talk of war and terror helps this process along enormously. There is a distinctly Orwellian flavour, for instance, even to the name of the US Defense Department's Office of Strategic Influence, designed to plant news items, allegedly sometimes not necessarily true, in the media of America's allies, who, in the words of a Pentagon spokesman 'sometimes needed to be helped to see the light'.[2] Commenting on this allegation, Defense Secretary Rumsfeld said the Pentagon might engage in 'strategic or tactical deception … but would not deliberately spread falsehoods'.[3] However, there was a considerable scandal in 2005 when it was revealed that journalists in Iraq were being paid to run pro-American material.

The temptation to bias information comes most easily in times of war and internal social strife, when governments see it not only as a security matter, but also as a legitimate weapon. Wartime censorship of a famine in Bengal in 1943 and 1944, which killed as many as 4 million people, is a painful example. Britain, at that time governing India as a colony under martial law, did not take the necessary actions to get relief supplies of rice into Bengal, even worse, they withdrew necessary shipping from the area.

Wartime censorship suppressed all but a few fragments of news about this huge tragedy, and even since then many histories and other reference sources have ignored or understated it.

It is a short step from this type of influence to the propagation of actual disinformation – the politically correct term for deliberately manufactured lies. Such tendencies to rewrite history have become common. There was a determined attempt in Germany in recent years to claim that the holocaust never happened – that very few Jews were killed or, alternatively, that the whole matter had been greatly overstated. In Japan, the facts of World War II, and indeed of the atrocious Japanese massacre of the people of Nanjing in 1936, are avoided. Instead, a Japanese film was produced in 1998 which idealized the wartime Prime Minister, General Tojo, rewriting history in a number of other significant ways.[4] It played to capacity audiences. School history books released in 2001 and 2005 caused an angry reaction from Japan's neighbours for similar reasons.

A 'fringe' area of disinformation, but also one of fundamental importance, is the increasing tendency to 'shut up' academics who take individual viewpoints, especially those who speak out in opposition to the conventional wisdom of business and politics. This is frequently considered to be a consequence of the 'corporatization' of universities and their increasing dependence on funding from business. Courses in the humanities are dwindling, while those in commercial areas such as marketing – even shelf stacking in supermarkets – are on the increase. Once the ill effects of this trend begin to be felt, and that will be soon, we will need to consider reestablishing universities with adequate inalienable funding. These could offer room to work to the free-thinking, expert and exceptional minds whose output will be so much needed.

The enormous amount of talk on radio and the circulation of knowledge and opinion in almost every conceivable field on the internet must broadly emerge as good influences. They not only satisfy increasing public curiosity about public affairs, but also focus a remorseless and intense enquiry on to politics, business, medicine – every avenue of public, and often private, life.

Nevertheless, a significant point has been made by a social psychologist that because the violent and extraordinary are seen as having high news value, news presentations mislead the public by indicating that the extreme and bizarre are more prevalent than they actually are.[5]

Controversy over censorship has been given a fresh impetus by the extensive availability of erotic and pornographic material on the internet. Those two words are useful because they make some distinction possible between different kinds of sex material. 'Erotic' has come to mean, in the censorship debate, sexual material that deals with 'normal' behaviour between consenting adults. 'Pornography', in this context, can be taken to mean material that involves violence, sadism, dominance, gross perversity and the exploitation of children and animals.

The controversy is unlikely to cease in the new society, which must decide whether pornographic material should be controlled, and at what level. Evidence of 'copycat' crimes, inspired by a film or a TV programme, indicates that such material can and does have harmful effects, extending as far as sadistic torture and murder. There is evidence that sex material is the largest single area sought on the net, with some pages scoring millions of hits. It is also among the most profitable, with the annual earnings of many websites in the millions of dollars. The internet is a reflection of humanity itself, with all its extremism, hang-ups and hatreds – this should not be surprising. The real issue is whether such subject areas as making nuclear and terrorist weapons, sexual exploitation of children and sadistic and violent abuse of women, should be generally accessible – and they are available, often without the need for money or a credit card, in 'sample' offerings.

Consider the following sentence: 'If, for a while, the ruse of desire is calculable for the uses of discipline soon the repetition of guilt, justification, pseudoscientific theories, superstition, spurious authorities and classifications can be seen as the desperate effort to "normalize" formally the disturbance of a discourse of splitting that violates the rational, enlightened claims of its enunciatory modality.'

This extract, from an academic book written by a professor of English, was runner up for the *Journal of Philosophy and Literature*'s Bad Writing Contest in 1998.[6] The use of jargon and jaw cracking, obscure synonyms in scholarly works is the target of the organizers of the contest, themselves academics. In 1996, the packaging of vague ideas in impenetrable prose so annoyed New York University physics professor, Alan Sokal, that he put together a paper on a quite preposterous premise – that the laws of physics were subject to political influences, and might apply differently to different people. Apparently carefully researched and bristling with footnotes the paper, called *Transgressing the Boundaries: Toward a Transformative Hermeneutics of Quantum Gravity*, was submitted to an academic journal, which duly published it as a serious contribution. So opaque was its prose that the article was not questioned until the author revealed it was a hoax.[7] Such happenings invite speculation as to whether opaque prose really hides dubious scholarship – a kind of smokescreen designed to obscure meaning rather than to elucidate. Its association with the 'shutting up' of academics, mentioned above, is obvious – extremes of obscurity can hardly be controversial.

Jargon, the development of a language which only the 'in' group can understand, and which implies a specialized superiority to the rest of the world, is used extensively by almost all the professions. Words which mean one thing to the general populace are invested with special meanings – a kind of code. Doctors, lawyers, many other professional groups and, as we have seen, academics, play this game. Distantly related to jargon is 'political correctness', which uses complex euphemisms for essentially simple things, so that 'rubbish dump' becomes 'recycling centre', the blind become 'visually impaired', and so on. There is nothing new about this. What were plain, commonly used Anglo Saxon four letter words became and are still regarded as vulgar or obscene as a result of the Norman conquest of Britain 1000 years ago.

Take a moment to look at this book – look at it just as an object. It may be among the last artifacts of its kind – the printed codex – that have had an honoured and influential life for a millennium since the Chinese invention of printing. Books have become electronic – millions are available online now for downloading. Beyond this is an actual electronic page, a computer that looks like a sheet of paper and is not much thicker, on which it will be possible to replace the text millions of times, as desired. So, instead of a bookcase full of volumes you will need only a single one. While early versions of this proved to be hard on the eyes, Sony's Reader, launched in the US in 2006, promises high resolution electronic paper said to be virtually indistinguishable from the real thing. On it you can call up almost any book you want to read from Sony's library. Classics and other books out of copyright can be accessed free. A newspaper that fits in your pocket, updates itself continually and has moving pictures is not available yet, but it is likely to be about 2008. An electronic replacement for sheet music is also being developed.[8] A thin, flat screen that can be placed on a music stand will not only display musical scores stored in a built-in computer, but will follow the performer and 'turn the pages' at the right time.

Without doubt, then, the means exist, or are not far away, for quicker, easier and potentially cheaper transmission of information than the world has ever seen. But this is very much a double edged weapon, with which it will be just as easy to distribute vast quantities of nebulous misinformation to billions of people as to inform them about what is actually true. Bear this in mind and be guarded – Straussian ideas for beguiling myth that doesn't have to be true will always attract politicians who are sure they know best. Granted this, it seems a necessary priority for the new society that this readily accessible information should be comprehensive, clear and accurate, and that legal sanctions are introduced to guarantee this. This way we would have a fair chance of a coherent history of the future, rather than the current confusion of misinformation and selectivity.

OPTIMAL FUTURE HISTORY:

- Truth in public utterances, resulting from realization by governments and businesses that a significant proportion of their public statements are now generally considered to have so much 'spin' as to lack credibility.
- Establishment and maintenance of public information media free from commercial or government influence, run by independent trusts.
- Penal sanctions for biased, inaccurate or deceptively selective 'news'.
- An academic discipline to formulate standards of clear language.
- Abandonment of unnecessary jargon, such as dead language use, in the professions, and the writing of law, as much as possible, in plain vernacular.
- Availability of bodies of internet information validated and endorsed by independent panels expert in their field.

Chapter 24

The Toxic Culture

The world has quite enough evil, so when it seems to be increasing there is good reason for concern. Such is the case with slavery, which has reappeared on a major scale, and now involves millions of people. Kevin Bales, from the University of Surrey, who is considered a world expert on contemporary slavery, puts the number of slaves in the world at 27 million.[1] Most of these are not legally owned by other people – they are 'bonded labour'. Driven by desperate poverty, the people of many developing countries sell themselves, or too often their sons and daughters, into effective slavery for an indefinite period. Children as young as nine are taken away to brothels, where they are raped and beaten until they are stupefied and compliant, or are forced to work long hours, often in appalling conditions.

Bales quotes an eyewitness to an incident in one of the gold mining towns on the Amazon River, describing what happened to an 11 year old girl when she refused to have sex with a miner: 'After decapitating her with a machete, the miner drove around in his speedboat, showing off her head to the other miners, who clapped and shouted their approval.' According to Bales, bonded prostitutes are often killed when they are no longer serviceable. When they are ill, generally with AIDS, they are left to die.

Just how many people are slaves is difficult to determine. The British organization Anti-slavery International says that there are more than 200 million people in 'bondage'. What this means is something like this: You were sold by your impoverished parents into a work contract to say, make carpets in Pakistan, at the age of four. You are held in place by force – there is evidence of such things as cutting the Achilles tendons so the child can only hobble, to prevent escape – you are paid nothing, given minimal food and shelter, beaten regularly and compelled to work 12 hours or more a day. The debt can never be repaid, in fact it gets larger because of ruinous interest rates and money penalties added if you make any work mistake. Such cases, and there are millions of them, are part of the price of world poverty. It is estimated that there are more than a million children enslaved like this to make Oriental carpets. If you want to buy these make sure they carry the tag 'Rugmark', which should guarantee that child labour was not used.

Anti-slavery International estimates that there are 43,000 slaves in the very poor and backward African state of Niger, although other estimates run as high as three quarters of a million. Slavery here is on the medieval model, with generation after generation born into servitude. These people, known as the *bellah*, have been an underclass for centuries, subject to regular beatings, rape and hard work without pay.

According to estimates made early in 2000, sex slavery is probably the most serious aspect of the return of slavery.[2] While the numbers trapped in enforced prostitution were considered difficult to establish, they were estimated to approach 2 million, most of them women and children from west and southeast Asia, South America, and some of the states of the former Soviet Union. Young women promised legitimate work in other countries, perhaps domestic work or waitressing, are regularly forced into prostitution.

Among these victims, as among many other humans, the toxic culture has already bitten deep. The casualties in recent decades among young people of the Western world run into tens of thousands dead from drug overdoses – 10,000 a year in the US alone. Anorexia, suicide and violent murder, often 'copycat' killings, take an additional toll. The phrase 'toxic culture', coined by film director Peter Weir, defines the dark side of human technology and culture which is now increasingly in evidence, and which tends to condition societies towards acceptance of the extreme abuse of large numbers of people. Weir asserted that movie violence and media overload could make children capable of such acts.[3] 'When they wander about with guns shooting, it's as if they're actors in a movie, with no understanding of the reality of what they're doing.' His message to parents was: 'Switch off the television, switch the computer off, pull the plug out of the Walkman. Let them be bored. Let their own imaginations take over.'

Veteran futurist Arthur C Clarke became so deeply concerned about 'the annihilative theme' of modern science fiction films he remarked that he no longer had the heart to write stories about spaceships leaving Earth, since the Earth had barely a 50 per cent chance of surviving Millennium 3.[4] 'What would an intelligent alien think of a culture that incessantly depicts horrible ways of destroying life, but censors the act of actually creating it?' Clarke said. 'He would surely decide such a culture must be mortally sick.'

According to a 1999 American report, among people aged 15 to 24 the major cause of death after accidents was murder, 85 per cent of it committed with a gun.[5] A Michigan University study reported an increase in school age drinking every year since 1993, almost a third of final-year high school students (age 17–18) saying they had consumed 5 drinks or more at least once in the previous fortnight. Tobacco, alcohol and gun lobbies contributed $18.8 million dollars to the US political parties in the 1998 elections, 70 per cent of it to Republicans.[6] The use of alcohol directly kills three quarters of a million people a year, making it one of the world's major causes of death and serious injury.[7] Although road deaths have decreased in countries with random breath testing, in Britain alcohol is a factor in 12 per cent of road deaths. In the US the figure is more than twice that – as high as 65 per cent in single vehicle crashes.

.Do unnaturally thin female dolls, pencil slim models and actresses, and fashion writers in women's magazines contribute to the death of hundreds of thousands of young women? Does the introduction of such 'ideal' models precondition many girls in such a way that they go on to develop anorexia nervosa, the condition in which sufferers literally starve themselves to death? How widespread is this condition? An accurate worldwide estimate is not feasible, since anorexia is generally not a notifiable disease, but over 5 million American men and women are said to be affected by eating disorders, according to the American Anorexia Bulimia Association.[8] Of these, many thousands will die. The association's description of America as 'a society where thinness is equated with success and happiness' can apply to most of the developed nations of the world. According to one American clinical psychologist, 'We are living in a culture that promotes a monolithic, relentless ideal of beauty that is quite literally just short of starvation for most women.'[9] Anorexics usually refuse to concede that their weight loss is a problem, even though it may have severe medical consequences. It is true that in many cases their condition has underlying psychological reasons, which might have led to some form of disabling illness in any case. However, there is research evidence that social and peer pressures, and especially media influence, can be a direct cause of anorexia.

At best, 'thinness' fashion propaganda seems likely to trigger anorexia in otherwise disturbed people. At worst, it can affect whole communities of young people. A study in Fiji by Professor Anne Becker, of Harvard Medical School showed a marked increase in anorexic tendencies among Fijian girls after a TV model of thinness was presented to them.[10] Professor Becker observes that, until 1995, Fijian women were normally robust and large, and saw the establishment of a large social network as the most satisfying element of life. However, after 1995, Western TV 'sitcoms' became popular in the islands. Amanda Woodward, the slim heroine of 'Melrose Place' suddenly became a model for most Fijian girls, and the yearning for thinness became widespread. Professor Becker calls this 'the Melrose effect'.

Is the depiction of violent hitting and kicking, casual killings, torture, and 'zappings' of hordes of aliens, likely to influence the behaviour of children who watch them? Will it condition them to accept violence, even commit it, unrestrained by conscience, in real life? The answer, attested to by most of the examples in the literature, is yes. F S Anderson collected together 67 studies, made over a 20 year period, on the correlation between violent TV and aggression in children. He discovered that three quarters of the studies found a connection.[11] Young people who are well adjusted in other respects might not be affected, but a definite proportion who are not well adjusted will be influenced, often to the extent of replicating the visual violence in real life. Elliott Aronson quotes a University of Nebraska survey which asked 15,000 children which they would prefer to lose, their TV or their father.[12] Around half said they would keep their TV. Even if one assumes that many of the respondents were simply calling the bluff of such a grotesque proposition, there are presumably some who meant exactly what they said.

The health risks of exposing young children to television, always suspected, were more closely defined by 1999, when paediatricians in the US and Australia identified TV viewing as a factor in illness, especially behavioural and personality disorders. The American Academy of Pediatrics recommended that children under two should not look at television at all, and that older children should not have sets in their bedrooms. A 17 year study of 700 Americans from adolescence to adulthood indicated that watching more than one hour of TV a day made adults more aggressive.[13] There is a view that watching violence on the media has a 'cathartic' effect – that it satisfies the need for violence and makes it less likely in real life. Here again Aronson quotes experiments that appear to contradict this, even indicating that seeing violence on TV or film increases aggression.[14] In these experiments children or young people from similar backgrounds showed a marked increase in aggression directed at other children compared with control groups who watched non-violent movies.

The Columbine High School child murderers 'were avid players of *Doom* – a video game that teaches killing skills so effectively that the US military uses a modified version to train its soldiers'.[15] Two controlled studies in America in 2000 showed a marked increase in aggressive behaviour and delinquency in those who played violent video games. According to one expert on driver psychology and road rage, car racing video games induce more reckless and aggressive driving in the mostly youthful users.[16]

A few hours of research into the pornography offered on the internet must identify this medium as a potent element in the toxic culture. Point one is that a great deal of hard pornography is easily accessible, even to those, like children, who might not have a credit card, in 'sample' pictures and text offered by the operators. Point two is that even this 'sample' material goes beyond normal eroticism into bondage, violence, sadism, exploitation of women, especially very young women, and animals. Point three is that this extreme material is so extreme because of competition between the websites offering pornography to attract the voyeur's credit card. A study in the US of 9000 internet users indicated that 15 per cent were 'addicted' to sexual sites, and spent an average of 11 hours a week online for sexual purposes.[17] This survey also found that 20 per cent of male workers and 12 per cent of women used computers at their workplace to 'engage in virtual sex'.

Civil libertarians say there should be no censorship, that it is a basic human right to see, read or hear anything one wishes. Others point to the apparent ill effects of violent and perverse material and say that there is a duty to protect the impressionable, especially children, from it. However, it is relevant to our context that the ill effects of the toxic culture must aggravate the other social and economic pressures endangering the future. The world will need well balanced, tolerant and compassionate people more than ever, and most of them will have to come from those now at school and college – the young and impressionable. If the disturbed, violent and uncaring become typical, the consequences during the difficult decades to 2030 could be grave indeed.

OPTIMAL FUTURE HISTORY

- A Oneworld agency, with enforcement powers, to investigate and eliminate slavery in all its forms.
- World funding to financially assist families in areas so impoverished they sell their children into bonded labour or prostitution.
- Controls to prevent easy access by children to violent and pornographic internet sites and video games.
- Additional taxing on drugs, including tobacco and alcohol, equal to the costs of the damage by these products to the community and to individuals.

CHAPTER 25

RUNNING THE SHOW

In the world's pioneering democracy, ancient Athens, all citizens dropped either a white or a black pebble into a jar to decide on issues. That worked in a small city-state, but as national populations grew direct democracy was seen as too complicated, and representative government was eventually introduced, in which we elect delegates to theoretically do as we want. But this system is failing. Why? Three things seem basically wrong with representative government. One, populations tend to elect their average, rather than their best; two, elected representatives are usually members of political parties, which tend to look to their own interests and those of their supporters, and increasingly, and impudently, ignore the clear view of voters except at election time. The disproportionate reaction to 'terrorism' in at least three nations is a typical consequence of these factors. The third, and perhaps most important failure of the system is that large numbers of people in the 'democracies' feel alienated from the political process.

Do they? Only 60 per cent voted in the 2004 US presidential election – and that was the highest turnout since 1968. Surveys in several 'democracies' place politicians at the bottom of trust ranking. The BBC carried out a survey to find out why only 60 per cent of those eligible voted in a general election in 2001. 'They weren't apathetic,' Martin Vogel of the BBC was quoted as saying (*New Scientist*, 29 November, 2003) 'They just felt alienated from the established political process.'

So what do we do? The time has come when individual citizens must be given more political power. In those places where this already happens, people become much more involved in the issues and make greater efforts to inform themselves. Accordingly, why not go back to real democracy? Modern technology like the internet does indeed make it possible for us to drop the pebbles into the jar again, decide collectively what is best for us. iCan, a BBC site (www.bbc.co.uk/dna/ican) provides a virtual meeting hall, in which people interested in almost any cause can find common ground. MoveOn.org in the US is another multi-role lobbying force which claims to be in touch with two million activists worldwide.

Good government, so necessary to the new society, is notoriously difficult, and on the whole, as a global community, we are failing at it. In many nations the warlord phase is back. These quasi or overtly military dictatorships are, on the whole, self seeking and conservative, with little concern for the future, or for individuals. They tolerate such things as uncontrolled slavery and dangerous buildings – even connive at them – and do not hesitate to torture or kill those who dare to dissent. The 'war against terror' is causing even the 'democracies' to become more secretive, authoritarian and restrictive, to give financial priorities to military and security purposes, and abandon hard won legal and human rights.

Is anything better possible? Yes, but it won't be easy, and again it can only come from community insistence, community initiatives, and more direct participation by individuals in the political process. Many parliaments accept petitions, but usually they are merely noted, rarely even influencing policy, much less making it. There is even a positive resistance to greater public participation in politics. Bob Geldof, in his autobiography *Is That It?* remarks: 'One of England's most respected political commentators' called Geldof's massive aid effort, Bandaid, 'a subversive phenomenon in that it wrested the political initiative from the parliamentary process into the hands of ordinary people'.

Some optimism can be found in the relatively small number of states where major decisions are made by the citizens, who have the right to initiate proposals for new laws, and then have the total electorate decide whether or not to accept them by referendum. In places like Switzerland and over half the American states this sort of political process happens regularly, and the results frequently run directly counter to what the political and business establishment want. Basically, if a large enough group of citizens sign a petition for a law to be introduced or changed (the initiative), it must then be put to popular vote (the referendum). If approved by a majority, the decision becomes final, overriding any parliament or congress, although, in the US, it can still be challenged in court and struck down if it is found to be unconstitutional. The citizen's initiative process can generally be used to change a constitution, but a greater number of signatures on the petition and a two thirds vote at the ballot are usually required.

This procedure works particularly well to decide issues that are emotive or difficult, like euthanasia, abortion, the control of drugs, which politicians frequently avoid as being difficult – 'the too hard drawer' is the phrase. In a 1997 referendum, 71 per cent of Swiss voters reaffirmed measures to control drug abuse, including a heroin trial, injecting rooms, and much more money spent on treating addicts and a resolute campaign against criminals working the trade. As a result of these measures, Switzerland was able to halve the number of drug overdose deaths between 1992 and 1997, and substantially control drug associated crime and HIV infection rates.[1]

Perhaps the best remembered American state citizen's initiated ballot measure was Proposition 15 in California, which successfully curbed government tax levels that had swollen because of inflation. In a similar way, Maine refused industry backed proposals for clear felling of forests, and rejected a grant of voting rights to guardians of mentally ill people. Oregon established, and a few years later decisively rejected repealing, America's only law permitting assisted suicide for the terminally ill. Arizona is one of four American states, so far, to have used the citizen's initiative to bring in public funding of elections, and one of two where it has been implemented. In each of these states, candidates can choose to take donations or public funding, but not both. In 2002, the 'Clean Elections Law' in Arizona led to the Democratic gubernatorial candidate who opted to take public funding defeating the incumbent Republican who took large donations from corporations. This happened against the trend of an election which generally favoured Republicans. Similar public funding initiatives are underway in many other American states. Why are they needed? Simply because without public funding only very rich people, or those beholden to them, can afford the huge costs, such as extensive media advertising, involved in a successful campaign. One of the more curious twists of politics is the tendency of voters to favour candidates who can afford lots of advertising. The voter might well ask where the money came from to pay for that advertising, and what favours might be required for it later on

When the citizen's initiative was introduced in the US early in the 20th century it quickly became apparent that it could be manipulated by powerful pressure groups, especially if they had access to publicity, or could spend extensively on advertising. Political systems, no matter how apparently enlightened, depend on the will and intelligence of large numbers of people to work well. Granted that, this system, applied generally and with enthusiasm, could not only make the new society possible but would also allow whole communities to consider and decide on how it should be organized. It has been shown that difficult decisions made by referendum, like universal military training in Switzerland, have been better accepted when made by the peer group than when handed down from above.

Voters might also like to consider whether they can find independent candidates for elections – preferably good people who don't particularly want to be politicians, and who are not members of parties – in the interests of genuine democracy, rather than continue to tolerate party machines.

Representative government, after all, evolved in conditions where consultation of the mass electorate on issues was impracticable, where the majority were not well educated, and where there was much less public interest in politics than is now the case. And party politics springs from a powerful Axiom Two consideration – the human tendency to aggregate in clans or gangs allied by common interests. Whatever their protestations, most political parties are like this. In the words of Alexis de Tocqueville, behind the facade of great political parties 'private interest, which always plays the greatest part in political passions, is there more skillfully concealed beneath the veil of public interest'.[2]

It is naive, and probably offensive, to assert that Western representative government should extend to all parts of the world, and that other forms of government are 'undemocratic' and therefore inadequate. This is especially so considering that the 'legalized bribery' of campaign contributions gives corporations and the rich far more influence and control than average citizens in many so-called 'democracies'. There are forms of government which have existed for thousands of years that are virtually unknown in the West. One is consensus, evolved in village communities which depend economically on their ability to cooperate. Rice growing societies in Asia are typical. It is quite possible to visualize effective political systems that work this way. One, indeed, exists, in Japan. Ostensibly a parliamentary democracy, the real decisions are made in consensus discussions which involve senior bureaucrats and business leaders as well as elected members of parliament. The Liberal Democratic Party, which has governed Japan for most of the last half century, consists of a number of *ha*, factions which negotiate common policies by consensus. Successive Japanese prime ministers are usually faction leaders who achieve that position in turn.[3]

Government by a controlled and trained elite has been the other major Asian form, and at least a third of humankind is still administered this way. Whatever the rhetoric, the Communist government in China seems to be strongly informed by the imperial mandarinate, which was probably the longest lived administration over the greatest number of people in human history. There are similarly influenced state systems in Korea and

Vietnam, and 'controlled democracies', where the forms of representative government exist, but are generally over-ruled by elites, in Singapore, Malaysia, Thailand and Indonesia. While in these countries government has almost always been authoritarian, elites have not been exclusive, and there has always been an elaborate system of checks and balances to attempt control of nepotism and corruption. Corrective measures in imperial China included the shifting of mandarins to new posts every few years, their oversight by independent inspectors, and severe punishment for offences such as bribe taking and manifest injustice.

A basic measure of the success of government might not be so much how systems are organized, as the extent to which they serve the general community interest, rather than that of the pressure groups which finance them, and the extent to which they will allow the community to decide on public policy and public issues through some effective means of consultation. It has been said that people get the government they deserve, and this is true to an extent. People who interest themselves in public issues only at election time, and complain that 'they' are not doing what 'they' should do, are not really in a position to complain if matters don't work out the way they like.

In Samuel Butler's classic novel *Erewhon* the sick in his fictional mountain state are confined to institutions and severely punished; the criminals are treated kindly and re-educated. While none of this is likely to be acceptable in public policy, there is a certain logic in these ideas.

It is, or should be, a basic responsibility of governments to make laws of overall benefit to the community, with particular regard to rehabilitation of criminals, and they can fairly be judged on their success or otherwise in this area. However, systems of law , while being modified in detail, have fundamentally changed very little over many centuries, and are still basically punitive. Their deficiencies are an obvious economic and social handicap to the new society. More than half of the world's nations use torture as a routine part of their legal systems, 86 retain capital punishment,[4] and in almost all countries the law routinely punishes the mentally handicapped, uneducated and socially disadvantaged. Keeping large numbers of people in prison is unproductive and expensive, yet most countries do it. Making the law easy to understand, of equal application and cheap to access seems a desirable ideal, yet few legal systems achieve it. In most countries, including most 'advanced' Western societies, high legal costs unfairly advantage the wealthy.

There are possible solutions – the new society could, for instance, take legal proceedings out of the hands of private operators offering their services for money, and instead institute legal corps operated and financed by the community, in which a body of trained practitioners on fixed salaries could act either as counsel or as magistrate according to their experience and expertise. Compliance with Axiom One would require reasonably large salaries to people who had put many years and much money into acquiring their expertise, but much lower than the extravagantly high fees barristers now typically charge.

It is tempting to associate this money factor with another well known deficiency of legal systems – the delays, often as much as years, to complete matters. After all, the longer a matter is protracted to adjourned hearings and mentions, the more numerous the fees the lawyer can charge. I have felt obliged to intervene (through the use of parliamentary privilege, when I was a senator) in several public interest cases where very wealthy defendants such as large corporations used legal machinery to force up plaintiffs' costs until they had to withdraw from socially useful and altruistic actions to avoid bankruptcy.

A second, less than reassuring commentary on the success or otherwise of legal systems is the large and increasing numbers of people in prisons. In the US the figure rose in 2004 to more than 2.2 million, almost one-quarter of the world's incarcerated people, the world's highest per capita incarceration rate, and a doubling for each of the last two decades. The number of black males in prison per 100,000 population was 12 times that of white men.[5] China has the next largest number in prison, 1.5 million, but this is on a population base four times larger. Statistics and commentary from many parts of the world indicate that the majority of those in prison are not violent habitual criminals, but the underprivileged, the mentally disturbed, the victims of broken homes and childhood abuse, or members of racial minorities.

One of the more experienced observers of British prisons, Stephen Tumim, a former barrister, county court judge and Chief Inspector of Prisons from 1987 to 1995,[6] remarked that dangerous criminals were perhaps 2 to 3 per cent of the total – less in the case of women. The majority, he adds, 'are inadequates, who have not, in modern parlance, got their act together ... male and under 30. Their offences are mainly concerned with drink, drugs and motorcars, and stealing money to acquire more. They come from impoverished city areas. If they are violent, it is not planned, but part of their social inadequacy.' He notes an ominous rate of recidivism among juvenile offenders at 80 per cent reconvicted within 2 years of discharge from prison – a trend also apparent in other Western countries.

About half of the world's nations retain the death penalty, but of those 86, 35 actually implement it regularly. There were at least 3797 executions in 2004 in 27 countries.[7] Eighty per cent, an estimated 3400, were in China, most of the rest in Iran, Vietnam, Singapore, Indonesia, Saudi Arabia and the US. Does capital punishment deter crime? In 1974, the year before the abolition of the death penalty in Canada, the murder rate was 3.09 per 100,000. In 1980 the figure was 2.41, in 1999 1.76. One basic objection to the death penalty – the possibility that people might be found innocent because of evidence turning up after their execution – came into prominence in the US in 2000. One researcher concluded after a study of more than 4000 capital punishment cases appealed between 1973 and 1995 that serious problems, including unreliable evidence, poor legal represent-ation and racism, were evident in almost 70 per cent of the cases.[8]

It is characteristic of almost all legal systems that, by and large, adult individuals are regarded as equally responsible for their actions, whether good or ill, and should be rewarded or punished on that basis. Behavioural psychologist B F Skinner asserted 'unsuspected controlling relations between behaviour and environment' as a major influence overruling or even overriding 'free will'.[9] He did not accept the view that 'a person is responsible for his behaviour, not only in the sense that he may be justly blamed or punished when he behaves badly, but also in the sense that he is given credit and admired for his achievements', contending 'a scientific analysis shifts the credit as well as the blame to the environment'.

Whether or not one accepts the Skinnerian view that human conduct is substantially due to 'conditioned reflexes', or indeed the Dawkins view that we are driven by our genes, there is sufficient good sense in this idea to warrant a closer look.[10] Is the law unfair if it fails to take environmental, health and genetic influences on the plaintiff into account? There is evidence that it usually does so fail, with positive correlations in most countries between major sanctions such as capital punishment and imprisonment with poverty, mental disability, abuse as children, lack of education, and low social status.

There is a further point: to what extent should society hold individuals responsible for the deficient environmental influences on them, and hence their high 'crime' rate? Often they are not responsible for these influences, which have been forced on them by economic, social and health factors beyond their control. For instance, a New South Wales government committee in 1999 found that while the intellectually impaired are around 2.5 per cent of the population of that state, they make up 20 per cent of those in prison.

There is informed opinion that brain deficiencies can contribute to violent, criminal behaviour. University of Southern California psychologist Adrian Raine, who has worked in high security prisons, identifies brain damage resulting from birth complications and poor frontal lobe functioning as likely factors.[11] Are there 'genes for crime'? According to University College London Professor Steve Jones, 'there is plenty of evidence that genes are involved in crime. A man who has an identical twin with a criminal record is himself at a 50 per cent increased chance of being imprisoned.'[12] These facts and statistics suggest an important point that may seem obvious after it has been stated:

that the mentally deficient and ill educated are overrepresented in prisons because they are just that – not as smart as the criminals who get away with it – and hence are easier to apprehend and convict.

New prisons, and the cost of supporting them, are now a major public expense. They often turn out to be virtual schools for crime, and first offenders frequently go on to commit more crimes when they are released, due to the associations made and ideas learned in prison, and their inability to find work when released. Mandatory sentencing laws, introduced in America and in parts of Australia during the 1990s, showed signs of falling into disrepute after brief periods in operation. The principle is that after three offences of any kind, a person automatically goes to prison, in some US states for life, with penal sanctions in some cases following the second offence. One result has been a large increase in prison populations. In California in 1999 more than 160,000 prisoners were in prisons designed to hold only 80,000.[13] Each prisoner serving a 25-year to life imprisonment was costing the taxpayer half a million dollars; the annual cost of housing 29,000 non-violent second and third strikers was $632 million.

Experience showed that a relatively small proportion of dangerous criminals were involved, 78 per cent of second strikers and 50 per cent of third strikers in prison having been convicted for non-violent crimes. One man in California was sentenced to life in prison because he stole a pizza from some children while drunk, after two previous convictions for vandalism when he set fire to garbage cans. One study found that African Americans, making up 12 per cent of the population, accounted for half of all three strike sentencing.[14]

In the tiny west Pacific nation of Palau things are different. Palau inherited an American type justice system when it became independent in 1992, but since then it has tried to return to its precolonial traditions of tolerance and community support for the errant. Criminals – even murderers – are allowed out of prison during the day, and lead ordinary lives with their families, have jobs, meet with relatives and friends. In the evening they must report back and are locked up for the night. According to Palau's

Justice Minister, Elias Chin, locking up prisoners permanently 'created more bad men than good ones'.[15] Palau, a group of islands inside a coral reef, has only 18,000 people, and close family and social networks. Hence there is a climate of opinion that favours helping offenders rather than punishing them. The experience of this small island republic tends to support the view that this area of crime and punishment, like so many others, can best be managed within relatively small, mutually supportive communities, and is a further argument for them.

There is a fairly general public perception that the law is unduly complex, and is couched in a special jargon and mystique designed to feather the nests of a specialized and highly expensive legal profession. Lawyers would, however, argue that effective laws have to be complex, that specialized legal terminology is necessary, and that these things take years of training and a certain expertise to understand. Because they have this training and expertise, they are entitled to be paid well.

Appeal procedures, allowing a dissatisfied litigant to take his case to successively higher courts, are obviously designed to promote fairness – but this intention is often subverted by the high costs involved. The expenses of law must suggest that the system as it stands is not satisfactory, and the fact that organized and wealthy crime rings are among the lawyers' best customers serves to underline the point. Much greater access to legal aid – inadequate in many places and non-existent in most – would seem to be a possible early answer to these problems.

OPTIMAL FUTURE HISTORY

- Extensive use of the internet to allow all citizens input to lawmaking using initiative petitions and referenda.
- Political groups to abandon the idea of party 'solidarity' and allow their parliamentarians free votes on legislation.
- All members of congresses and parliaments to publicly declare their assets, and contributions or donations to them, their party, relatives and associates.
- Systems of public funding developed to cover candidates' election costs.
- Abolition of the death penalty and legal torture as a matter of world law.
- Evolution of sentencing codes which take into account social, mental or educational disadvantages the defendant might have.
- Strict segregation of violent or habitual offenders from others.
- Conversion of prisons as much as possible to rehabilitating criminals – perhaps by 'graduating' them to facilities offering work and leisure comparable with those in the normal world during the second half of their sentences.
- Generous funding for community groups offering support to released prisoners.

CHAPTER 26

GETTING THE WORLD WE WANT

On present showing we are writing a stormy and somewhat catastrophic history for the next five or six decades. And all this is totally unnecessary – we could avoid trouble if we made the right choices, but we will fail the 2030 deadline on most counts if we make the wrong ones. In that case those who have organized their lives towards a degree of self-sufficiency will come off best. The big urban areas must fare worst. On the available evidence about the rate of advance of the drivers, it seems reasonable to predict at best worsening recession from about 2015 for perhaps 50 years. The severity of this phase, and the success of the eventual recovery from it, will depend on the extent to which the world recognizes the danger of the drivers and does things about them. Doing nothing, just going on living, consuming and polluting as we do now, must prove disastrous.

The facts and arguments in this book are intended to signpost new directions of thought and action for a better rather than a worse future – ways to cope with the drivers and to plan for sustainable improvement beyond them. But are the goals they point to achievable? Certainly they will involve change, and pretty radical change at that, and as past experience shows, it will not happen without strict observance of the axioms. The youth of the world – the 2030 generation – are the ones with the most to gain or lose, and hence the strongest motivation to act. This chapter is especially addressed to them and to the adults of today who have concern for their children and grandchildren.

Before considering how our optimal future history might come together; it might be useful to look again at the base point – what sort of world is likely if we simply go on as we are now:

- If we continue to squander our hydrocarbons without major and immediate development of clean and sustainable energy alternatives our industries, our cities, our transport and especially our food supply, will be at severe risk.

- If disease rates from the mass killers continue to rise, so also will the preventable death rate, while the risk of cross infection of pandemics like H5N1 from the developing world to the West must also increase.

- If we continue the present rates of damage to the environment, its natural systems will deteriorate, perhaps beyond 'tipping point', with dangerous, unpleasant and very long-lasting consequences.

- If the West reacts to world poverty preponderantly with armed force, regional wars and terrorism, driven by anger and despair, must increase. As the financial and moral costs of 'fighting terror' grow, Western economies and freedoms will continue to deteriorate.

- If nuclear armaments increase and acceptance continues of a dangerous idea – that the use of atomic weapons can be limited – nuclear war on an unpredictable scale is only a matter of time, probably before 2030.

- If problems of water shortage and soil degradation are not addressed, they will add their effect to already diminishing world food production and rising populations, causing extensive and long-lasting famine.

- If the gap between rich and poor widens, millions of painful, undignified and unnecessary deaths among the poor, the helpless and children will become permanent and regular events.

What shape, then, might the new society take to avoid these things? The future is, of course, difficult to predict, but not totally inscrutable – we can now perhaps outline two strategies, one for the developed world, the other for the developing world. Although the models necessarily differ, especially in the early stages, the first priority is to cope adequately with the 2030 drivers. Beyond this the broad objectives would be a reasonable equality of wealth, health and quality of life for all humans in a world free from war and able to guarantee sensible levels of personal freedom and human rights. Sustainability, based on renewable energy, intelligent recycling and the frugal use of resources, will be essential, since it must be the only possible basis for a future history of prosperity and happiness. Granted this, what priorities for action logically emerge?

A massive development of alternative energy sources must be at the top – not just so that we can run around in cars and aircraft, not even just to sustain our trade and industries. Consider the provision of fresh water to a country that needs it desperately. Almost 98 per cent of the world's water is in the sea. Given access to that, the problem disappears – but desalination of seawater is energy hungry, and we can scarcely squander huge amounts of non-renewable resources on it. However, put a solar tower or a solar-thermal system with a desalination plant beside the sea, and the picture changes immediately. And there are other examples. If large improvements can be made in pollution and greenhouse gas emissions, oil can be obtained almost indefinitely from shale and similar resources, given a large supply of renewable energy. The oil would still be expensive in monetary terms, and would need to be used frugally, but it would be there for necessary non-energy purposes such as lubrication and as a feedstock for plastics. Large scale availability of renewable energy will also be essential to the second priority.

Lifting the developing world from its poverty, and thus controlling population growth and 'terrorism', must therefore be that second priority, for all the reasons outlined earlier in this book. Anyone who cannot see this has no heart, no soul and no brains. It should be totally unacceptable to modern humanity that

10 million of our children die every year from starvation and preventable illness, that at least as many more are illiterate and that poverty continues to drive runaway population growth.

The third priority must be to stop the dangerous and stupid devotion of so much of our resources to weapons of war, and use those resources in a better way. Somehow this must happen, and the sooner the better. Since some form of world government would plainly be needed to make this possible, so that must also rank as a high priority.

Associated priorities must be to limit and repair the effects of environmental damage and climate change, institute at least the beginnings of effective world law, with a priority to limiting war, and provide international policing to prevent gross exploitation and abuse of people – such things as torture, military dictatorship, slavery, child prostitution and arduous and dangerous working conditions.

To meet these objectives, certain practical steps seem necessary, and must be taken soon. The cities could evolve into places of largely automated manufacture, entertainment and vacation, but permanent living must increasingly be in energy saving new towns, offering high standards of culture, sport and congeniality, and a considerable variety of low cost habitat. They, and all other communities, must eventually be part of a world-wide electorate of individual consultation, empowered by regular electronic referenda to decide on key areas of world law and policing.

These towns would be of varying population size to suit individual preferences, but never above 50,000. Even one of that size would preferably be made up of perhaps a dozen largely independent and self sufficient 'villages'. There is abundant evidence that small communities like this find it easier to use democratic procedures, and that consensus decisions made by their councils could be the basis for systems of worldwide consultative decision making. It seems almost self-evident that properly planned, such towns would offer far safer, simpler and better living conditions, as well as coping more effectively with the drivers than big cities could.

The 'villages' could be linked together and to the city residues by high speed trains, powered by electricity from sustainable sources, quite possibly from banks of solar panels along the track. They would be planned so pedestrian or bicycle traffic, or at most, small electric 'pedicabs', served almost all purposes, and designed so that most amenities, including schools, could be reached on foot from the housing. Shops could be supplied through freight pipes linking the habitat areas with manufacturing centres.[1] In Japan the Sumitomo Capsule Liner system has been transporting two million tons of limestone a year over 3.2 kilometres for 20 years using wheeled capsules propelled through pipes by compressed air. By 2005 similar technology was being actively developed in several countries. Fuel cell cars for longer journeys would normally be pooled rather than owned to reduce the energy cost of large production runs. These cars would need to be designed for long life and easy maintenance, with a high rate of standardization and minimal model changes.

The new urban centres must become virtually self sufficient for energy through the use of high efficiency solar generators. For many decades, energy will be scarce and expensive, especially initially, until renewable energy resources, and perhaps methane hydrate and fusion, can be developed. The use of hydrocarbons as fuel must in any case become minimal, partly because of cost, partly because of greenhouse considerations, but also because they are a non-replaceable raw material vital to future generations for such things as essential plastics and chemicals. The central renewable power source for a community of 'villages' – perhaps a solar chimney – would supply a basic electricity grid, supplemented and augmented by wind generators or solar panels on all buildings. Power surpluses to households when they occur – probably through much of the day – would be fed back into the grid. On this basis the overall demand from the grid would be modest.

Because they would have access to more arable land than the cities, the 'villages' could become virtually self sufficient for their food from cooperative gardens and orchards. This is likely to become essential anyway, since the huge energy cost of processing, packaging and transporting food can scarcely continue. Clean rainwater held in tanks would provide for cooking and drinking and expensive sewerage infrastructure avoided through the use of low water and energy use composting toilets. 'Grey' water at a controlled standard would be reused for gardens and other outdoor purposes. Housing would use a minimum of wood and metals, relying on modern plastics highly resistant to fire, decay and insect attack, and designed to withstand the more violent weather conditions which now seem inevitable. Since most suitable plastics rely on petroleum as a feedstock, this is a further argument for ending the squandering of dwindling oil reserves. Property ownership and conveyancing laws, now generally complicated and expensive to use, would need radical streamlining.

Systems of local law could deal with most criminal and civil issues. The law advisers, who could act in either advisory or judicial capacities would, like other 'professionals' such as doctors, dentists and architects, be stipended by the community. Community issues would be decided democratically, preferably using established consensus techniques. Appeal to higher courts would continue, as a right, at no cost to the appellant provided a reasonable *prima facie* cause could be established.

The economic base of these communities would best be perhaps one or at most two, automated industries, so providing an acceptable economy of scale and the basis of trade with the outside world. Their relative affluence would allow them to employ sportspeople, artists, musicians, sculptors on a major scale, with people like this touring regional theatres and sports venues regularly. Their contribution to the community would rate as 'work', the value of their 'stipends' set by popular opinion polling. They could act as instructors in their accomplishments to the local community, particularly to the school.

Community businesses would best be owned by the people working in them and linked into a regional network designed to expedite trade. Normal business competitive practices would operate within these networks, recognizing the basic motivation of self-interest, and work credits would vary according to the productivity and skills of the worker. This would maintain a lively competition within the community. However, all citizens would be guaranteed an adequate minimum income – the additional proceeds of work would be used for luxuries, perhaps a larger house, private ownership of a car, art items, outside travel. 'Money' could depreciate in value from its day of issue, thereby ensuring its ready circulation and the elimination of its immobilization in 'investments'. Consider the longstanding problems of Japan, where fears of an insecure future have induced people to save so much and spend so little that the economy, potentially very productive, is crippled. Even with interest rates at zero levels, people still save, and refuse to spend. What would happen if the government removed that insecurity with a guaranteed minimum income and introduced a slight 'negative' interest rate? People would start to spend their money, the economy would boom, and it would probably be back on its feet in months.

Cities would have to be profoundly modified because it seems unlikely that there would be enough available energy to maintain them in their present form, and because their transport demands and capacity for pollution would become unacceptable. Struggles with city infrastructure would cease once it was generally understood that high urban land values are artificial – apparent rather than real. Even now, only 3 per cent of the land in the US is built on – in most places there is plenty of land outside major cities and its value is intrinsically the same as that of urban land. But even in crowded places like The Netherlands, the village concept could be adopted in some cases through reorganizing existing infrastructure, converting some streets into open space, some buildings into 'neighbourhood' centres, blocks of apartments to communal living by people who want to live together, carparks into real parks. But if present urban conditions continue, the losing battle with infrastructure must make large cities shabbier and less attractive places to live in – this is already happening in many places. This tends to make them magnets for terrorists and other criminals, and to promote more extreme social divisions. 'Urban renewal', already proving highly expensive, would become so much more so as to be impracticable in most cases.

The reform of education and social support systems, as well as the lifting of anxieties about money from most people, should create healthier, happier and more relaxed new generations. As suggested in Chapter 13, the pursuit of individual happiness should become a major and specific public concern, if only for economic and health maintenance reasons. Think back to the expert assessments of the reasons for happiness described in Chapter 13. The people of the new society would feel they were working for a better world, not a deteriorating one. The work that would come to their hands would, on the whole, be creative and absorbing, presenting a challenge, but not an overwhelming one. There would be a lively and very personal sporting and artistic life, a much stronger sense of community, and an easier environment in which to offer or find social support. Indeed, many of the problems of relationships sketched in Chapter 13 should have been greatly minimized. Adjustment to life for children, in particular, should become easier and more successful, due to less family stress, more constructive interplay with peer groups, and more flexible methods of education, especially for younger children.

On the whole, people in the new society would tend to stay at home more, because home would be a good place to be. Those who wished to travel could do so in hybrid sailing ships, which would dominate what remained of the world tourist trade. Eventually some undersea tunnels might play a part in travel, using linear accelerating trains operating at high speeds in a vacuum. However, these would prove so expensive that their development would be slow. Very high speed rocket or nuclear driven aircraft operating in the stratosphere may not prove appealing to travellers.

The concepts outlined above would ideally apply worldwide in time, but different pathways seem necessary at first for the developing countries. Some radical 'pump priming' will be needed here. Acute poverty, due to lack of work, and disastrous urbanization, suggest a planned bypassing of the megapolis stage, building instead on the millions of existing villages in ways that would not only improve quality of life, but also allow development of a stage of labour intensive intermediate technology and added value manufacture for export. And there would be other advantages – more even and economical use of land, planned sustainable development of industries, and retention of existing village values and social structures to the extent that better educated generations wanted them.

Money, expertise and manufacturing capacity will be needed in large quantities, and it can only come from the wealthy industrial nations. If this is to happen, a programme of needs and priorities will have to be established, and it has to be big enough and selective enough to achieve the desired breakthrough. What needs to come first is what gives the best results for the money spent. This is the reasoning behind the following proposal for the making and distribution of no less than a billion artifacts in the developing world every year, designed to have a maximum beneficial effect.

Four things, created by the Billion Artifacts programme, could introduce this first phase of development. They are: a standard word processing and internet access capable computer, independent of reticulated power, and associated internet penetration technology; easily installed, impervious roofing, simple filtration systems and tanks to provide safe drinking water; small electric motors with solar panels for pumps and other small machinery; and fuel conserving cooking stoves to replace open hearths.

These would all need to be provided in very large numbers, at least in the tens of millions, and provided they were standardized and made as much as possible by automatic processes, economy of scale should keep the unit costs quite low, probably at an average of no more than $40. Plainly, the stoves would be cheapest, the computers the most expensive. On this basis, a billion items would cost around the minimal estimated cost of putting a man on Mars for a couple of days. Add $10 billion to cover such things as internet penetration, distribution, installation and training in use, and it is still only half the $100 billion estimated final cost of the uncompleted international space station, the value of which is very much in doubt, and only 5 per cent of what the world spends on arms.

Why have these four items in particular been picked out from an almost endless list of needs? The computer internet programme would bring education and the means of technical know-how and interchange that might double village prosperity, health and living standards within a generation and permit modest industrial growth. Not every family would need a computer – two to five in a village depending on its size would be enough. It is probable that much of the new appropriate technology needed will evolve within the developing world – some of it is already doing so. The internet link would allow fast, efficient communication of new ideas and techniques throughout the areas of need, with values that can scarcely be overestimated.

It is probably difficult for people who have access to the conveniences of modern life to understand how disabling it is not to have them – most developed world households would have at least four devices powered by electric motors. One motor can do the work of scores of people, and do it better and faster. Hence the motors – powered by a renewable energy source – would permit a huge release of effort from repetitive and laborious work like lifting and carrying water. They would also make possible many areas of necessary manufacture and maintenance – they can run lathes and other machinery. With this artifact, a huge input of new developing world labour saving devices could be made, or at least maintained, locally.

The means to ensure safe drinking water is perhaps the most important factor in limiting disease, and it could best be provided as rainwater runoff from impervious roofs, associated with simple and established purification technology. Groundwater is usually infected with a variety of diseases – when people are forced to use it they are trapped in a permanent cycle of re-infection. Sadly enough, this is often fatal, especially for children, on a scale not generally understood. The most conservative estimates of deaths caused by infected water are in the millions every year. Even this figure is horrifying, placing this cause of death on a par with the other major killers like malaria, tuberculosis and AIDS. The World Health Organization puts infant deaths from diarrhoea as high as 5 million a year, and this is usually caused by infected water. But even if people don't die from water borne infections – others, such as liver fluke, make them permanently debilitated and listless. That, combined with the mindless everyday tasks that consume so much time and effort, like fetching water and finding firewood, makes it difficult for people to raise themselves from their poverty. They will not be able to do so without outside help.

Is it really necessary for the poor to have a nice convenient stove? This issue, too, takes us into an area of mass avoidable death. Smoke filled houses kill as many as 2.8 million a year, with research evidence from China that people using traditional fuels in inefficient fireplaces have a sevenfold higher risk of stomach and liver cancer.[2] It is possible to make, quite cheaply, stoves which are fuel efficient. This would avoid millions of deaths from cancer, and greatly reduce the destruction of trees for firewood and the unproductive labour involved in finding and carrying it.

The last two items would preferably be designed so they could be carried into village areas on men's backs or by oxcart, and installed without special knowledge or tools. The impervious roofing could be rolls of lightweight aluminium with attachments that hook around roof purlins – usually bamboo – and fasten on top with a sealing washer and a wing nut. The weight – and hence transportability – of the stoves could be reduced by providing a chimney tube, and steel cooking top and front door module only that could fit into a fireplace made on the spot of stone or clay.

Other important needs of developing societies – broadly those described in Chapter 3 – could be met in subsequent annual programmes. Control of diseases like AIDS and malaria and care of their victims should take a high priority here.

The new society will need to address world poverty and health problems by means such as these as a matter of urgency, with the objective of a demonstrable lift in world standards of nutrition, health and affluence by 2010. 'Balance wheel' military budgets could be progressively transferred to these areas and they should take an absolute priority over very expensive research areas such as particle accelerators and space travel. The solutions to the worst problems, like the world's appalling rate of avoidable blindness, are already known and require nothing more than money and organization.

The reader at this stage may well be thinking that the hundred or so 'optimal future history' strategies proposed in this text, no matter how justifiable they seem, represent an enormous and even impossible burden of change, if only because of an important Axiom Two consideration – a considerable resistance of human nature to innovation. But the key point is that these are not suggestions – they are logical projections from the facts. We will either adapt to something like them, or we will eventually and painfully be compelled to do so by the drivers.

Accept the fact that for every person who wants to do something, there will be five around saying it can't be done. This is something that has to be overcome – people who want to do things overcome it regularly, and can do so again. A certain ruthlessness may be necessary here – for instance, how much influence should we allow people who don't want wind generators because they don't like the way they look and sound? Such subjective judgements must be weighed against the actual need for, and value of, new technologies.

Also, the proposals are progressive, in the sense that any one of them, implemented to any degree, represents a move towards the greater good. There are already many small organizations, for instance, providing efficient fuel stoves to developing countries. Every stove they can get to a deprived household is of value. If they could combine their efforts, attract support, and supply stoves in the tens of thousands, so much the better. More than half of the proposals are amenable to this sort of organized citizen approach.

Now we turn to the really big issues, getting rid of war and poverty, establishing a decent world order. This also becomes a matter of organization, and an appreciation that the common cause is to the benefit of every individual in the long run. It is the mass of individual humans who own the world, and they must decide how to run it. If enough people use their combined buying and voting power and moral influence, and insist on real democracy, the necessary changes will become possible. They will happen. Politicians and responsible businesses respond to well organized public opinion when it becomes large enough and insistent enough to outweigh the influence of special interests.

And what lies beyond 2030? If, indeed, there is a successful adaptation to the 2030 drivers, the world may well emerge from those difficult four or five decades a better place in almost every respect. Concentration on a more equal and humane world order, automated manufacture and the stability that would come from sustainability would, towards 2100, promise a bright future. The age old dream of Utopia? Almost certainly not, if only because of Axiom Two considerations. But if Utopia cannot be achieved, it can at least be approached. That is a worthy ambition for Millennium 3.

NOTES

CHAPTER 1

1   In the BBC's Dimbleby Memorial Lecture presented at the Institute of Education, London, 14 December 2001, available at www.bbc.co.uk/arts/news_comment/dimbleby/clinton.shtml.

2   Quoted in 'Sunrise for Renewable Energy?' *The Economist*, 10 December 2005.

3   International Water Management Institute estimates; UNEP, *Global Environment Outlook 3*, United Nations Environment Programme/ Earthscan, London, 2002.

4   *Science*, 19 November 1999.

5   DH Meadows, DL Meadows, J Randers and WW Behrens, *The Limits to Growth: A Report for the Club of Rome's Project on the Predicament of Mankind*, Universe Books, New York, 1972.

6   H Kahn, W Brown and L Martel, *The Next 200 Years: A Scenario for America and the World*, William Morrow, New York, 1976.

7   EF Schumacher, *Small is Beautiful: Economics as if People Mattered*, Harper & Row, New York, 1973 (25th anniversary edition published by Hartley & Marks, Vancouver, BC, 1999).

8   *The Wealth of Nations*, first published 1776.

CHAPTER 2

1   P and M Pimentel (eds), *Food, Energy and Society*, University Press of Colorado, Niwot, CO, 1996; W Youngquist, 'The Post Petroleum

Paradigm – and Population', *Population and Environment*, Vol 20, No 4, 1999.

2   B Fleay, *The Decline of the Age of Oil*, Pluto, Sydney, 1995.

3   J Pilger, *The New Rulers of the World 2002*; EL Morse and A Myers Jaffe, *Strategic Energy Policy Challenges for the 21st Century*, Council on Foreign Relations and James A Baker III Institute for Public Policy, New York; J Record, 'A Note on Interests, Values and the Use of Force', US Army War College Quarterly *Parameters*, Spring 2001, pp15–21.

4   International Energy Agency, US Geological Survey, CJ Campbell, Petroconsultants of Geneva. Some sources place the reserve as high as 1.2 trillion barrels, while conceding that world consumption is likely to rise as high as 40 billion barrels a year, representing an exhaustion time of 30 years. CJ Campbell and JH Laherrer, in a 1998 article in *Scientific American* remark: 'Companies and countries are often deliberately vague about the likelihood of the reserves they report, preferring to publicize whichever figure suits them.'

5   International Energy Agency, www.iea.org, 2003.

6   *Washington Post*, 16 May 2000.

7   Both quoted in BBC News *Money Programme*, 8 November 2000.

8   United Nations statistic.

9   The means to do this are discussed in Chapter 26.

10 Xinhua News Agency, 3 January 2002.

11 ITER originally stood for International Thermonuclear Experimental Reactor, www.iter.org.

12 ITER, www.iter.org, 2002.

13 *Fire in the Ice*, The National Energy Technology Laboratory Methane Hydrate Newsletter, 18 April 2002. See also www.netl.doe.gov.

14 B Lomborg, *The Skeptical Environmentalist: Measuring the Real State of the World*, Cambridge University Press, Cambridge, 2001.

15 The target date set by Mr B Skulason, general manager, Icelandic New Energy Ltd, www.newenergy.is.

16 Professor Bragi Amason, University of Iceland, in *Environmental News Network*, 26 December 2000.

17 They are Canadian fuel cell pioneer Ballard Power Systems, the Shell Oil Company, the Norwegian power utility Norsk Hydro, and DaimlerChrysler Automotive.

18 In its issue of 16 July 2002, the magazine claims to have got this information from leaked government policy documents.

19 Schlaich Bergermann und Partner, 'The Solar Chimney', www.sbp.de/de/html/projects/solar/aufwind/pages_auf/principl. htm.

20   China Three Gorges Project Corporation newsletters.
21   Global Wind Energy Council figure, www.ewea.org.
22   *New Scientist*, 8 January 2000.

CHAPTER 3

1   Joan Holmes, president of The Hunger Project, www.thp.org, 2002.
2   Catherine Bertini, executive director (1992–2002) of the World Food
     Programme, in a 2002 statement.
3   Speaking at the World Food Summit: Five Years Later, Rome, June 2002.
4   International Labour Organization, www.ilo.org.
5   UNFPA, *State of World Population 2001: Footprints and Milestones –
     Population and Environmental Change*, United Nations Population Fund,
     2001, available at www.unfpa.org/swp/2001/english/
     index.html.
6   LR Brown, M Renner and B Halweil, *Vital Signs 1999–2000*, Earthscan,
     London, 1999.
7   WaterAid and Tearfund, *The Human Waste: A Report by WaterAid and
     Tearfund*, WaterAid and Tearfund, London, 2002, available at
     www.wateraid.org.uk/site/in_depth/in_depth_publications/.
8   Amrit Dhillon in *The Guardian*, 26 February 2002.
9   Seedlings planted when smaller, flooding *padis* much later in
     the growing period, use of natural compost rather than artificial
     fertilizers.
10   Professor Jules Pretty, University of Essex, Colchester, 2001.
11   *New Scientist*, 26 January 2002.
12   By Marco Goldschmied, president of the British Royal Institute of
     Architects.

CHAPTER 4

1   Released at a conference in Shanghai early in 2001.
2   *Science*, 19 November 1999.
3   By Carl Sagan and colleagues, published in *Science*, December 1975.
4   United Nations statistics.
5   According to Munich RE, the world's largest reinsurer, 1999.
6   According to the Inuit Circumpolar Conference.
7   By the British Meteorological Office.
8   T Radford, *The Crisis of Life on Earth*, Thorsons, London, 1990.
9   Jenny McIlwain, University of Sheffield.
10   As from oceanographer Ian Jones and Tokyo University, Tokyo.

11   'Discrediting Ocean Fertilizing', *Science*, 2 October 2001.
12   By an international study group at the Rowett Research Institute, Scotland.
13   Montreal Protocol Conference, Beijing, November 1999.
14   UNEP's *Global Environment Outlook 2000* report (United Nations Environment Programme/Earthscan, London, 1999) forecast a beginning to repair of the ozone layer by 2032.
15   University of Bergen's Nansen Centre.
16   By the Lamont-Doherty Geological Laboratory.
17   Professor of Geography at the University of Oxford, AS Goudie, *The Future of Climate: Predictions*, Weidenfeld & Nicolson, London, 1999.
18   Conducted by the American National Science Foundation.
19   The National Research Council, Washington, DC.
20   N Calder, *The Weather Machine*, BBC Publications, London, 1974.

CHAPTER 5

1   UNFPA, *State of World Population 2001: Footprints and Milestones – Population and Environmental Change*, United Nations Population Fund, 2001, available at www.unfpa.org/swp/2001/english/index.html.
2   Catherine Bertini, executive director (1992–2002) of the World Food Programme, speaking in Kansas City, 10 April 2001.
3   According to a 'Declaration on Global Change' released after some 1700 scientists from 70 countries and representing 4 major programmes met at the Global Change Open Science Conference in Amsterdam in July 2001.
4   UNEP, *Global Environment Outlook 3*, United Nations Environment Programme/Earthscan, London, 2002.
5   Klaus Töpfer, executive director of United Nations Environment Programme.
6   Worldwatch Institute, *State of the World 2002: Progress Towards a Sustainable Society*, Earthscan, London.
7   J Bennett and S George, *The Hunger Machine*, CBC Enterprises, Ontario, 1987.
8   Devinder Sharma, in *New Scientist*, 8 July 2000.
9   According to Rainer Horn, Kiel University, Germany.
10   UNEP estimate.
11   FAO statement.
12   E McLeish, *The Spread of Deserts*, Wayland Publishers, Hove, UK, 1989.
13   By the State Forest Administration.

14 S Postel, *Pillar of Sand: Can the Irrigation Miracle Last?* WW Norton, New York, 1999.

15 LR Brown and B Halweil, Worldwatch Institute, www.worldwatch.org.

16 Second World Water Forum, The Hague, March 2000.

17 International Water Management Institute estimates.

18 International Water Management Institute estimates.

19 *Agenda 21* was adopted by more than 178 governments at the United Nations Conference on Environment and Development (commonly known as the Earth Summit) held in Rio de Janerio, Brazil, in June 1992. The full text is available at www.un.org/esa/sustdev/ documents/agenda21/index.htm.

20 On its website. (In 1998 the Ministry of Forestry became the State Forestry Administration, www.forestry.gov.cn). See also Ministry of Forestry, *China's Agenda 21 – Forestry Action Plan*, China Forestry Press, Beijing, 1995.

21 By Lisa Curran, University of Michigan.

22 According to the Coastal Research Institute, Cambridge University.

CHAPTER 6

1 'Atomic War or Peace?', *Atlantic Monthly*, November 1945.

2 A Jolly, *Lucy's Legacy: Sex and Intelligence in Human Evolution*, Harvard University Press, Cambridge, MA, 1999.

3 A Giddens and C Pierson, *Conversations with Anthony Giddens: Making Sense of Modernity*, Polity Press, Cambridge, 1998.

4 World Commission on Environment and Development, *Our Common Future*, Oxford University Press, Oxford, 1987, p317.

5 World Trade Organization, www.wto.org, 2002.

6 G Robertson, *Crimes Against Humanity: The Struggle for Global Justice*, The New Press, New York, 1999.

7 Amnesty International statistic, www.amnesty.org.

8 Comments made at a 1999 meeting of the Joint Economic Committee of the US Congress.

9 Free University of Brussels.

10 Devised in 1887 by LL Zamenhof.

CHAPTER 7

1 J Bronowski, *The Commonsense of Science*, Heinemann, Oxford, 1951.

2 *Time's* Vision 21 series, June 2000.

3 The Nuclear Posture Review.

4   MV Ramana, Princeton University.
5   H Caldicott, *The New Nuclear Danger: George W Bush's Military–Industrial Complex*, The New Press, New York, 2002.
6   Sponsored by the International Atomic Energy Agency and Interpol.
7   Dr Anil Kakodhar in *The Hindu*, 9 December 2000.
8   *Sydney Morning Herald*, 28 January 1999.
9   BMA, *Biotechnology, Weapons and Humanity*, British Medical Association, London, 1999.
10   K Alibek, *Biohazard: The Chilling True Story of the Largest Covert Biological Weapons Program in the World*, Random House, New York, 1999. (Since defecting to the US, Alibekov has adopted the name Ken Alibek.)
11   *Sydney Morning Herald*, 22 June 2000.
12   Medical Educational Trust, London.
13   Future Combat Systems programme.
14   Molly Ivins, *Eugene Register-Guard*, 25 July 2001.
15   Congressional Research Service.
16   J Bourke, *An Intimate History of Killing: Face-to-Face Killing in 20th Century Warfare*, Granta, London, 1999.
17   DW Black, *Bad Boys, Bad Men: Confronting Antisocial Personality Disorder*, Oxford University Press, New York, 1999.
18   K Lorenz, *On Aggression*, Methuen and Co, London, 1963.

CHAPTER 8

1   By the International Peace Institute, Stockholm.
2   D Suzuki and P Knudtson, *Genethics: The Ethics of Engineering Life*, Allen & Unwin, Sydney, 1988.
3   For example, P Davies and J Gribbin, *The Matter Myth:Dramatic Discoveries That Challenge Our Understanding of Physical Reality*, Pocket Books, London, 1991.
4   SJ Goerner, *After the Clockwork Universe: The Emerging Science and Culture of Integral Society*, Floris Books, Edinburgh, 1999.
5   R Dawkins, *The Blind Watchmaker*, Penguin, London, 1986.
6   Such as the Learning and Research Development Center at Pittsburgh University, among others.
7   Such as that for the NEUROLAB shuttle mission in 1998.
8   At the US National Space Biomedical Research Institute, Houston.
9   PD Ward and D Brownlee, *Rare Earth: Why Complex Life is Uncommon in the Universe*, Springer-Verlag New York, 2000. (Peter Ward is professor of geology at the University of Washington. Don Brownlee is principal investigator of NASA's Stardust mission.)

10   By IBM researchers in 1990.

CHAPTER 9

1   F Dyson, *The World, the Flesh and the Devil*, JD Bernal Lecture, 1972.
2   B Katz Rothman, *Genetic Maps and Human Imaginations: The Limits of Science in Understanding Who We Are*, WW Norton, New York, 1999.
3   C Linnaeus, *The Systems of Nature*, first published 1735.
4   A Hitler, *Mein Kampf*, first published 1924.
5   S Jones, *The Language of the Genes*, HarperCollins, London, 1993.
6   As in RJ Herrnstein and C Murray, *The Bell Curve: Intelligence and Class Structure in American Life*, The Free Press, New York, 1994.
7   By Andrew Sims in *The Guardian*.
8   J Rifkin, *The Biotech Century: Harnessing the Gene and Remaking the World*, Weidenfeld & Nicolson, London, 1998.
9   A/F Protein.
10   Director of the International Centre of Insect Physiology and Ecology, Nairobi.
11   *Science*, May 1999.
12   At the 11th World Congress on IVF, May 1999.
13   R Winston, *The Future of Genetic Manipulation*, Phoenix Orion, London, 1997.
14   By Professor T Brouchard, University of Minnesota.
15   Emory University, Atlanta, 1999.
16   Mark Westhusin, Texas A&M University, in *Time*, 19 February 2001.
17   *The Future of Genetic Manipulation*, p43.
18   Dr Martin Pera, Monash University, Melbourne.

CHAPTER 10

1   JL Mero, *The Mineral Resources of the Sea*, Elsevier Science, Amsterdam, 1965.
2   D Dekker, mining/science coordinator CSIRO, Australia.
3   Formerly Celebes.
4   International Seabed Authority background paper, www.isa.org.jm.
5   Smithsonian Institution, Ocean Planet, http://seawifs.gsfc.nasa.gov/ocean_planet.html.
6   Mangrove Action Project, www.earthisland.org/map/, 2002.
7   World Wildlife Fund, www.wwf.org, and US Natural Resources Defense Council, www.nrdc.org.
8   *New Scientist*, 17 May 2003.

9   Ransom Myers and Boris Worm, Dalhousie University, Halifax, Nova Scotia.

10   Greenpeace quoted by CNN Interactive Earth Story Page, www.cnn.com/EARTH/9805/07/depleted.fish/,7 May 1998.

11   Sydney, Columbia, Conception in Chile.

12   Carl Seubert, Sydney University.

13   M Markels, *Fishing for Markets*, 1995, available at www.cato.org/pubs/regulation/reg18n3h.html.

14   SW Chisholm et al, 'Oceans: Discrediting Ocean Fertilization', *Science*, 2 October 2001.

CHAPTER 11

1   Quoted in the *Sydney Morning Herald*, 27 February 2001.

2   *The Guardian*, 4 March 2000.

3   World Bank and *Fortune* magazine.

4   Ministry for Economy, Trade and Industry.

5   In a 2001 TV documentary *The New Masters of the World*.

6   JG Fuller, *The Poison that Fell from the Sky: The Story of a Chemical Plague that Destroyed a Town and Threatens Us All*, Random House, New York, 1977.

7   Bhopal People's Health and Documentation Clinic.

8   Australian Broadcasting Corporation (ABC), *Earthbeat*, 5 June 1999; Interface Sustainability, www.interfacesustainability.com.

9   D Kidd, vice-president for corporate responsibility, *Wall Street Journal*, 22 February 2001.

CHAPTER 12

1   M Yunus with A Jolis, *Banker to the Poor: The Autobiography of Muhammad Yunus of the Grameen Bank*, Aurum Press, London, 1998.

2   *The Role of Microcredit in the Eradication of Poverty*

3   *Time*, 28 January 2002.

4   M Hardt and A Negri, *New York Times*, 20 July 2001.

5   'Beyond Chaos and Dogma', *New Statesman*, 31 October 1997.

6   George Soros on Globalization.

7   *New York Times*, 15 January 2002.

8   US Census Bureau figure.

9   *Fortune*, March 2002.

10   AC Nielsen reported by Dow Jones.

11   Reported in *The Guardian*.

12 US Agriculture Department statement, October 1999.
13 US Treasury Secretary Lawrence Summers.
14 R Lekachman and B Van Loon, *Capitalism for Beginners*, HarperCollins, London, 1986. (Robert Lekachman is economics professor at City University of New York.)
15 C Cobb, T Halstead and J Rowe, *Atlantic Monthly*, October 1995.
16 H Schacht, *Confessions of an Old Wizard*, first published 1953.

CHAPTER 13

1   CA Reich, *The Greening of America*, Random House, New York, 1970.
2   BF Skinner, *Beyond Freedom and Dignity*, Jonathan Cape, London, 1971.
3   DW Clark, *The Life of Bertrand Russell*, Jonathan Cape, London, 1974.
4   Speaking in Melbourne, May 2002.
5   Dr K Sheldon, University of Missouri-Columbia.
6   Professor R Williams, Duke University, North Carolina.
7   Dr D Marazziti, University of Pisa.
8   By the Mayo Clinic, Minnesota.
9   *Journal of Personality and Social Psychology*, Vol 74, No 6.
10 DG Myers, *The Pursuit of Happiness: Discovering the Pathway to Fulfillment, Well-being and Enduring Personal Joy*, Avon Books, New York, 1993.
11 B Russell, *The Conquest of Happiness*, first published 1930.
12 R Franks, *Luxury Fever: Why Money Fails to Satisfy in an Era of Excess*, Free Press, New York, 1998.
13 O James, *Britain on the Couch: Treating a Low Serotonin Society*, Arrow Books, London, 1999.
14 David Lykken, University of Minnesota.

CHAPTER 14

1   A Giddens, 'Runaway World', Reith Lecture, 1999, available at http://news.bbc.co.uk/hi/english/static/events/reith_99/default.htm. For a summary, see www.lse.ac.uk/html/2000/10/06/20001006t1521z005.htm.
2   Economic and Social Research Council, www.esrc.ac.uk.
3   H Glitzer, Australian Institute of Family Studies.
4   Calgary and Australian National Universities.
5   J Pryor and B Rogers, *Children in Changing Families: Life After Parental Separation*, Blackwell, Oxford, 2001.
6   R Whelan for the Family Education Trust.

7   NSW Child Protection Council.

8   *Time's* Vision 21, June 2000.

9   M Jordan, *Witches: An Encyclopedia of Paganism and Witchcraft*, Kyle Cathie, London, 1996.

10   R Ardrey, *The Social Contract*, Collins, London, 1970.

Chapter 15

1   UNCHS (Habitat), *The State of the World's Cities 2001*, United Nations Centre for Human Settlements, Nairobi, 2001.

2   Formerly Calcutta.

3   National Science Foundation report of reconnaissance team, www.nsf.gov.

4   K Kobayashi, 'Dangerous Concrete', 1999.

5   Environment USAID, www.usaid.gov/environment.

6   Such as Dutch group MURDV.

7   Awawaroa Bay.

8   *Tomorrow, a Peaceful Path to Reform*, 1898.

9   Barbara Ehrenreich, *Time*, 26 January 2000.

Chapter 16

1   4th century BC.

2   *The Politics*, Book 8.

3   J Dewey, *Democracy and Education*, first published 1916.

4   I Illich, *Deschooling Society*, Calder and Boyars, London, 1971 (republished by Marion Boyars Publishers, London, 2000).

5   H McRae, *The World in 2020: Power, Culture and Prosperity*, Harvard Business School Press, Watertown, MA, 1998.

6   P Clifford and S Friesen, 'Hard Fun: Teaching and Learning for the 21st Century', *Focus on Learning*, Vol II, No 1, 1998.

7   A Toffler, *Future Shock*, The Bodley Head, 1972.

8   J Piaget, *The Growth of Logical Thinking*, first published 1958.

9   By delegates to the Professional Association of Teachers conference, Cheltenham, 1998.

10   Formed in 1999 to oppose Early Learning Goals.

11   Professor Anne Locke, University of Sheffield, quoted in the *Sheffield Telegraph*, 22 October 1999.

12   *The Guardian*, 29 March 2001.

13   A Giddens, *Sociology*, Polity Press, Cambridge, 1989.

CHAPTER 17

1 International Red Cross estimate.
2 Joint United Nations Programme on HIV/AIDS (UNAIDS) figure, www.unaids.org.
3 World Health Organization figure, www.who.int.
4 KC Gautam, UNICEF Asia/Pacific.
5 World Health Organization figure, www.who.int.
6 A Lopez, senior epidemiologist, World Health Organization.
7 WHO Fact Sheet, World Health Organization, Geneva, April 2002.
8 D Broderick, *The Last Mortal Generation*, New Holland Publishers, Sydney, 1999.
9 R Kursweil, *The Age of Spiritual Machines: When Computers Exceed Human Intelligence*, Penguin, New York, 1999.
10 Harvard Medical School statistics, www.hms.harvard.edu.
11 World Bank statistics, www.worldbank.org.
12 Study by Kirsten Myhr, Oslo, Norway, 2000.
13 S Muziki, regional officer, World Health Organization.
14 Karen Davis, former professor of economics, Johns Hopkins University.
15 Christian Blind Mission statistics, www.cbmi.org.
16 World Health Organization figure, 2001, www.who.int.
17 P Davies, *Catching Cold*, Michael Joseph, London, 1999.
18 TL Ogren, *Allergy-free Gardening*, Ten Speed Press, Berkeley, CA, 2000. See also www.allergyfree-gardening.com/index.php.
19 From the Royal College of Physicians, www.rcplondon.ac.uk.
20 Clive Bates, director of anti-smoking organization ASH.
21 Chinese Smoking and Health Association statistics.
22 Nils Daulaire, president and CEO of Global Health Council.

CHAPTER 18

1 *Time*/CNN poll, 2002.
2 M Mason, *In Search of the Loving God*, Dwapara Press, Eugene, OR, 1997, pp141–151.
3 July 1999.
4 Capetown, December 1999.
5 W Golding, *The Lord of the Flies*, first published 1954.
6 435,000 Australians of 19 denominations in 2001.
7 *Time*, 3 July 2000.
8 A Einstein, *Science and Religion*, first published 1939.
9 H Morris *The Genesis Flood*, first published 1961.
10 Such as R Dawkins, *The Blind Watchmaker*, Penguin, London, 1990.

11   LC Thurow, *The Future of Capitalism*, William Morrow, New York, 1996.
12   Quoted in P Davies, *The Mind of God*, Simon & Schuster, London, 1992.
13   At the United Nations University, Tokyo.
14   Dimethyl sulphide.
15   C Birch, *Biology and the Riddle of Life*, UNSW Press, Sydney, 1999.

CHAPTER 19

1   Professor of Public Policy and Management, Carnegie Mellon
     University, Pittsburgh.

CHAPTER 20

1   K Karlsson, *World Robotics 2001*, United Nations Economic Commission
     for Europe/International Federation of Robotics, Paris, 2001.
2   By carmaker Daimler/Chrysler.
3   At Brandeis University, Massachusetts.
4   Massachusetts Institute of Technology, www.mit.edu.
5   LC Thurow, *The Future of Capitalism*, William Morrow, New York, 1996,
     p264.
6   Oxfam CAA, *Horizons*, Vol 8, No 1, 1999.
7   K Bales, *Disposable People: New Slavery in the Global Economy*, University
     of California Press, Berkeley, CA, 1999.
8   R Sennett, *The Corrosion of Character: The Personal Consequences of Work in
     the New Capitalism*, WW Norton, New York, 1998.
9   By Professor Gary Cooper, 2000.
10 J Siddons, *Spanner in the Works*, Macmillan, Melbourne, 1990.
11 International Co-operative Alliance, www.coop.org.
12 Shanghai Ximen Cooperative Economy Consultancy Service Agency,
     'Introduction to "All Masters" Printing Factory',
     www.cic.sfu.ca/ximeng/masters.html.
13 WF Whyte and KK Whyte, *Making Mondragon*, ILR Press, New York,
     1988.

CHAPTER 21

1   Adams Atomic Engines, www.atomicengines.com.
2   Federation of American Scientists, 'Nuclear powered aircraft',
     www.fas.org/nuke/space/c03anp.htm.
3   *The Guardian*, 2 February 2002.
4   Dr E Schubert, GM/Opel.

5   Ballard vice president Paul Lancaster, Australian Broadcasting
    Corporation (ABC), *Earthbeat*, 24 May 2000; Ballard Fuel Systems,
    www.ballard.com.
6   DaimlerChrysler, www.daimlerchrysler.com.
7   W Kitchens, 'Maglev Trains: An Attractive (and Repulsive) Option for
    Future Travel', *The Harvard Science Review*, Spring 1998.
8   Environmental News Network, 'Flying Trains', 16 July 2000.
9   A Parker, 'Space Hopping Hyperplane', www.firstscience.com/site/
    articles/hypersoar.asp. See also NASA's Langley Research Center
    website, www.larc.nasa.gov.
10 European Space Agency, www.esa.int, 1 July 2002.
11 MLX01 Project; Japan Economic Foundation, www.jef.or.jp/en/.
12 NL Skene, *Elements of Yacht Design*, 1947 edition (first published 1904).

Chapter 22

1   *New York Times*, 7 September 2001.
2   www.internetworldstats.com.
3   NEC Global Gateway, www.nec.com, 8 March 2002.
4   Major D Bryan speaking to a house armed services subcommittee.
5   Lin Ching-ching, Taiwan Defence Ministry, in a 2000 statement.
6   American Telecommuting Association, *What's So Good About
    Telecommuting*, www.knowledgetree.com/ata-adv.html.
7   OECD estimate.
8   Tom van Horn, CEO of Mercata.

Chapter 23

1   Senator N Stott-Despoya at the Global Forum for Women Political
    Leaders, Manila, 17 January 2000.
2   *New York Times*, 19 February 2002.
3   Reuters.com, 21 February 2002.
4   *Pride – Unmei no Toki* (Pride – The Fatal Moment), director Shunya Ito,
    1998.
5   E Aronson, *The Social Animal*, WH Freeman, New York, 6th edition
    1992.
6   Professor D Dutton, University of Canterbury, Christchurch, New
    Zealand.
7   J Baggini, 'The Abuse of Science: An Interview with Alan Sokal',
    available at www.philosophers.co.uk/noframes/articles/sokalnf.htm.
8   Xerox Corporation's Palo Alto Research Center, www.parc.xerox.com.

CHAPTER 24

1   K Bales, *Disposable People: New Slavery in the Global Economy*, University of California Press, Berkeley, CA, 1999.
2   From the UN and US Department of State.
3   Speaking to the Singapore Film Commission, April 1999.
4   Interviewed by Uli Schmetzer, 1999.
5   R Brownstein, *Los Angeles Times*, 9 August 2001.
6   According to the Center for Responsive Politics.
7   WHO, *The World Burden of Disease*, World Health Organization, Geneva, 1996.
8   National Eating Disorders Association (formerly the American Anorexia/Bulimia Association), New York, NY, www.nationaleatingdisorders.org.
9   M Pipher, *Eating Disorders: What Every Woman Needs to Know About Food, Dieting and Self-concept (Positive Health)*, Vermillion, London, 1997.
10 A Becker, *Body, Self and Society: The View from Fiji*, University of Pennsylvania Press, Philadelphia, 1995.
11 Quoted by A Giddens, *Sociology*, Polity Press, Cambridge, 1989.
12 E Aronson, *The Social Animal*, WH Freeman, New York, 6th edition 1992.
13 By Columbia University and the New York Psychiatric Institute.
14 E Aronson, *The Social Animal*, WH Freeman, New York, 6th edition 1992, p256.
15 *Time*, 8 May 2000.
16 Leon James, University of Hawaii.
17 By Dr A Cooper, Stanford University.

CHAPTER 25

1   C Collin, *Switzerland's Drug Policy*, report prepared for Canadian Senate Special Committee on Illegal Drugs, 14 January 2002, available at www.parl.gc.ca/37/1/parlbus/commbus/senate/com-e/ille-e/library-e/collin1-e.htm.
2   A de Tocqueville, *Democracy in America*, first published 1935.
3   Nobutaka Ike, *Japanese Politics: Patron–Client Democracy*, Alfred A Knopf, New York, 2nd edition 1972.
4   Amnesty International's Campaign to Stamp out Torture, http://stoptorture.amnesty.org/info.html; Amnesty International, 'Take a Step to Stamp Out Torture', 2000, available at http://web.amnesty.org/library/index/ENGACT400132000.
5   US Department of Justice prison statistics.

6   S Tumim, *Crime and Punishment*, Phoenix, London, 1997.

7   Amnesty International figure, www.amnesty.org.

8   Columbia University Professor of Law JS Liebman.

9   BF Skinner, *Beyond Freedom and Dignity*, Jonathan Cape, London, 1971.

10   R Dawkins, *The Blind Watchmaker*, Penguin, London, 1986.

11   Interviewed in *New Scientist*, 13 May 2000.

12   S Jones, *In the Blood: God, Genes and Destiny*, Flamingo, London, 1996.

13   Joe Klass in *The Los Angeles Times*, 5 August 1999.

14   Professor of Law F Zimring, Berkeley University.

15   Australian Broadcasting Corporation, *Asia Pacific*, 1 January 2000.

CHAPTER 26

1   Considerable research is going on into freight transport systems which are automatic and unmanned. Large diameter pipe networks accommodate drum shaped containers driven by air pressure introduced into the system by pumps outside. Such a system could be driven completely by electricity provided by solar panels adjacent to the pumps. Distribution 'point changing' would be computerized.

2   *Indoor Air Pollution Newsletter*, World Bank and World Health Organization. See also D Schwela, 'Cooking Smoke: A Silent Killer', *People & the Planet*, Vol 6, No 3, 1997, available at www.one world.org/patp/pap_6_3/Cooking.htm.

INDEX

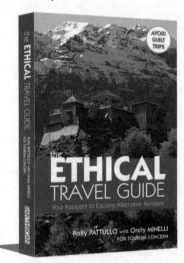

Join our
online community
and help us save paper and postage!

www.earthscan.co.uk

By joining the Earthscan website, our readers can benefit from a range of exciting new services and exclusive offers. You can also receive e-alerts and e-newsletters packed with information about our new books, forthcoming events, special offers, invitations to book launches, discussion forums and membership news. Help us to reduce our environmental impact by joining the Earthscan online community!

How? – Become a member in seconds!

>> Simply visit **www.earthscan.co.uk** and add your name and email address to the sign-up box in the top left of the screen – You're now a member!

>> With your new member's page, you can subscribe to our monthly **e-newsletter** and/or choose **e-alerts** in your chosen subjects of interest – you control the amount of mail you receive and can unsubscribe yourself

Why? – Membership benefits

✔ Membership is free!
✔ 10% discount on all books online
✔ Receive invitations to high-profile book launch events at the BT Tower, London Review of Books Bookshop, the Africa Centre and other exciting venues
✔ Receive e-newsletters and e-alerts delivered directly to your inbox, keeping you informed but not costing the Earth – you can also forward to friends and colleagues
✔ Create your own discussion topics and get engaged in online debates taking place in our new online Forum
✔ Receive special offers on our books as well as on products and services from our partners such as *The Ecologist*, *The Civic Trust* and more
✔ Academics – request inspection copies
✔ Journalists – subscribe to advance information e-alerts on upcoming titles and reply to receive a press copy upon publication – write to info@earthscan.co.uk for more information about this service
✔ Authors – keep up to date with the latest publications in your field
✔ NGOs – open an NGO Account with us and qualify for special discounts

Join now?
Join Earthscan now!

name

surname

email address

Earthscan Member
[Your name]

Click to Change

My profile
My forum
My bookmarks
All my pages

www.earthscan.co.uk